Wonders

FLORIDA

McGraw Hill

ABOUT THE COVER

Monuments

Take a look at the Castillo de San Marcos National Monument in St. Augustine. It is the oldest fort in the United States! The Spanish built the fort over 350 years ago, in the shape of a star to help protect it from attacks. It has thick walls, battlements, towers, and a moat. Its first resident was the governor of St. Augustine.

This monument has become a symbol of the endurance and determination of the people of Florida and the United States. All monuments serve as reminders of important moments in history.

mheducation.com/prek-12

Mc Graw Hill

Send all inquiries to:
McGraw Hill
1325 Avenue of the Americas
New York, NY 10019

ISBN: 978-1-26-418355-5
MHID: 1-26-418355-0

Printed in the United States of America.

2 3 4 5 6 7 8 9 LWI 25 24 23 22 21 B

Welcome to an Amazing Year of Reading!

This book is like an awesome library, right in your hand—or on your device. Just like a library, it's filled with many different types of wonderful texts you will want to read and reread. You will discover new places and new ideas. In the next few pages, we'll tell you more about what you will explore throughout the year and how this book will help you.

Reading and Writing Through *Florida Wonders*

Using what you already know and what you learn every day gives you the power to read more. Working with your peers, you will spend time talking and writing about the texts, bringing them to life, and exploring how they connect to you and your world.

Building Knowledge

Reading these texts will help you build knowledge about different topics and themes. Each text starts off with an **Essential Question.** This question helps you set a purpose for what you will learn from the text you will read.

Genre • Expository Text

Spiders

by Nic Bishop

Some spiders are as small as a grain of sand. The biggest, the Goliath birdeater tarantula from South America, is as big as a page in this book. Yet all spiders share similar features. They have eight legs, fangs, spin silk, and eat other animals. At first you might confuse them with insects. But it is easy to tell the difference. Insects have six legs; spiders have eight. And spiders never have wings.

The Goliath birdeater tarantula likes to stay near its burrow on the rain forest floor. It waits for prey to come close enough to grab.

Essential Question

What helps an animal survive?

Read how spiders have adapted to survive.

Go Digital!

90

91

Essential Question

Your New Learning Partners

This book and your **Reading/Writing Companion** are connected. They work together as your partners in reading, writing, and thinking. The work you do in the Reading/Writing Companion will prepare you to read the texts in this book. You will learn to think more deeply about each text you read.

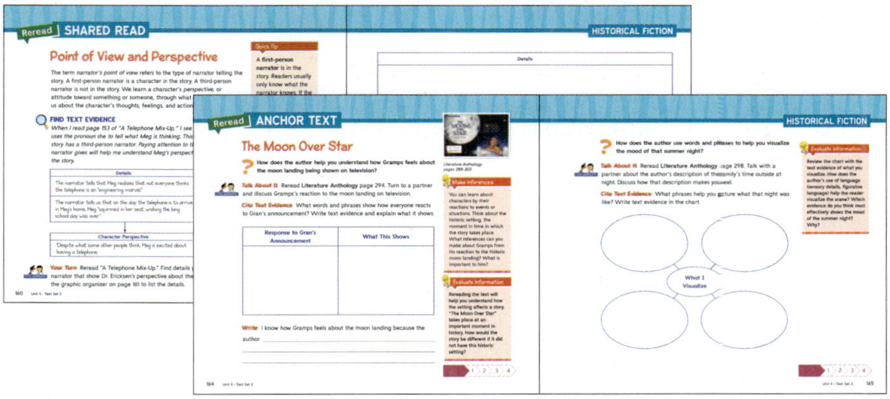

Reading/Writing Companion

Literature Anthology

Ready to Read More?

You will find additional texts called Independent Reads. These texts help you explore other Essential Questions that you might be interested in. You can choose your own texts to read from this book or from your classroom library.

What You'll Read

You will find many different types of texts, or genres, in this book. You will use what you learn about the features of each genre in the **Reading/Writing Companion** to read the texts in this book.

Amazing Stories

There are wonderful fiction stories that were created in the imagination of each author. The stories include realistic fiction, fantasies, historical fiction, myths, and tall tales.

As you read, you will think about how an author develops the characters, describes the events, and uses the setting through the plot of the story. You might enjoy reading these stories because they invite you to use your imagination!

Powerful Poetry

You will find a diverse collection of poems, such as rhyming poems, free verse poems, and narrative poems. The special form and structure of each poem and the words the author chooses will help you understand the meaning of each poem. As you read poetry, think about how it is different from the other texts you read.

Interesting Informational Texts

There are many different types of informational texts, but they all give facts about a topic. Thinking about how the author organizes the ideas in the text helps you build more knowledge from what you read. It also gives you a good model for your own writing. Paying close attention to how the text features provide information will help you learn even more.

Sneak Peek at the Stories and Poems

Reading great stories and poems invites you to imagine yourself in other places and times. Take a look at a few of the texts in *Florida Wonders* that will transport you!

In the story ***Aguinaldo*** by **Lulu Delacre,** you will learn about a girl named Marilia who lives in Puerto Rico. You will read about how Marilia overcomes her fears and makes a big difference through a simple act of kindness.

This book is filled with wonderful poetry by well-known poets, such as **Nikki Grimes** and **Carl Sandburg.** The poets share their feelings about different topics, from animals to finding your place in the world. As you read, you might find that you share the same feelings with the poets!

You will read stories from long ago that have been told for generations. In **"Pecos Bill and the Bear Lake Monster,"** you will learn about a fictional American folk hero who wrestles a monster. You will also read tales from other places, such as **Carmen Agra Deedy's** retelling of ***Ranita, The Frog Princess,*** a folktale from Cuba, and **"Anansi and the Birds,"** an African trickster tale. You will discover that the themes in all these stories are still meaningful today.

In ***The Game of Silence*** by **Louise Erdrich,** you will learn about a young girl from the Ojibwe Nation in the 1850s. Nine-year-old Omakayas tells how she and her family played a game to help them cope with serious life changes.

Sneak Peek at the Informational Texts

Florida Wonders is filled with texts that will help you build knowledge about science and social studies. These texts are just a few examples of the ideas and information you'll discover.

Earthquakes by **Sneed B. Collard III** explains how science is helping people prepare for natural disasters and how you can protect yourself if an earthquake strikes near you.

In ***A Drop of Water,*** author **Walter Wick** describes what water looks like up close. His photographs show how heat and cold affect molecules of water and how clouds and snow form.

SOE THAN WIN Stringer/AFP/Getty Images

You will discover important figures in our history, such as W.W. Law, a mailman who became a civil rights leader in Savannah, Georgia, in ***Delivering Justice: W.W. Law and the Fight for Civil Rights*** by **Jim Haskins,** and the Davis family, who together fought peacefully for civil rights in **"Keeping Freedom in the Family: Coming of Age in the Civil Rights Movement"** by **Nora Davis Day.**

Reading the texts in this book will help you to learn more about a wide range of important issues in our world today, such as bullying in "**Speaking Out to Stop Bullying,**" and farming products to feed the world while protecting our environment in ***A New Kind of Corn.*** As you come to understand the authors' perspectives and claims about a topic, you can form your own opinions.

David Frazier/Corbis

"Let's get reading!"

UNIT 1

Think It Through

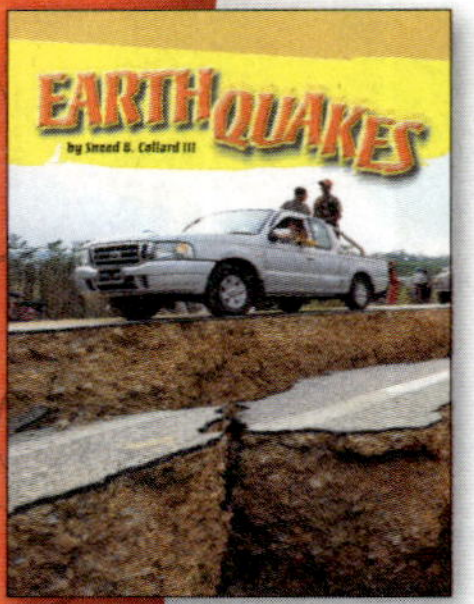

Text Set 1 • Expository Text

WEEKS 1 AND 2 TAKE ACTION

Text Set 2 • Realistic Fiction

WEEKS 3 AND 4 THINK OF OTHERS

Text Set 3 • Argumentative Text

WEEK 5 TIME FOR KIDS

INDEPENDENT READING

NONFICTION IDEAS IN MOTION

FICTION CLEVER IDEAS

my.mheducation.com

UNIT 2

Amazing Animals

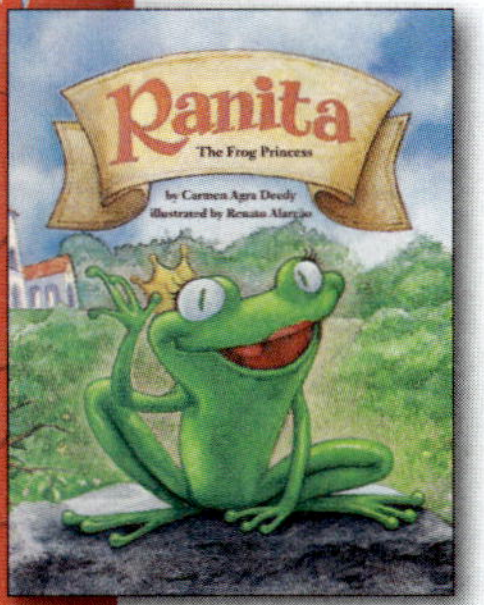

INDEPENDENT READING

my.mheducation.com

UNIT 3

That's the Spirit!

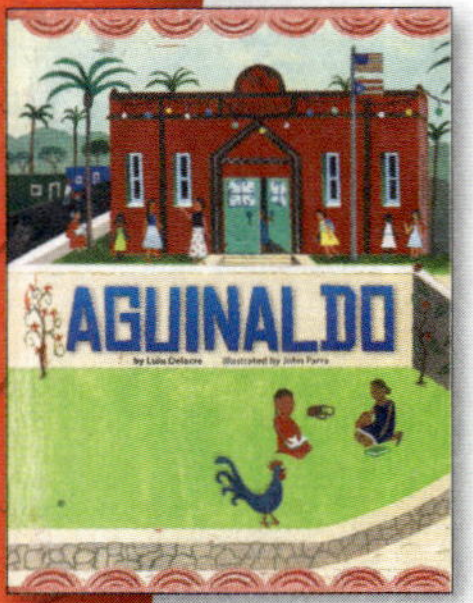

Text Set 1 • Realistic Fiction

WEEKS 1 AND 2 HELPING THE COMMUNITY

Text Set 2 • Biography

WEEKS 3 AND 4 LIBERTY AND JUSTICE

Text Set 3 • Argumentative Text

WEEK 5 TIME FOR KIDS

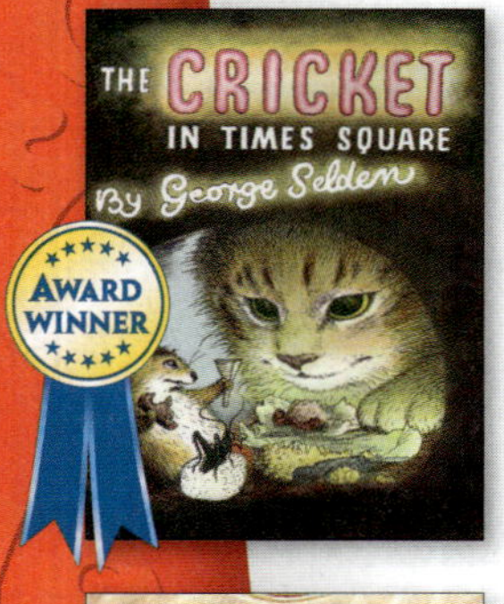

INDEPENDENT READING

FICTION FRIENDSHIP

NONFICTION POWERFUL WORDS

David Frazier/Corbis

my.mheducation.com

UNIT 4

Fact or Fiction?

Text Set 1 • Narrative Nonfiction

WEEKS 1 AND 2 OUR GOVERNMENT

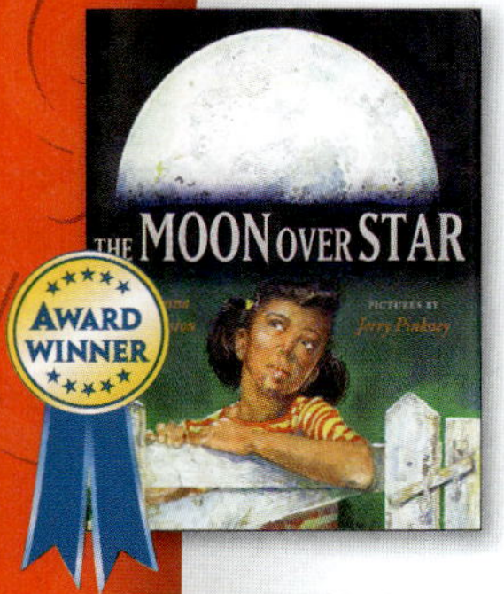

Text Set 2 • Historical Fiction

WEEKS 3 AND 4 BREAKTHROUGHS

Text Set 3 • Poetry

WEEK 5 ACHIEVEMENTS

INDEPENDENT READING

NONFICTION WONDERS IN THE SKY

FICTION LEADERSHIP

my.mheducation.com

UNIT 5

Figure It Out

James Quine/Alamy

my.mheducation.com

UNIT 6

Past, Present, and Future

Text Set 1 • Narrative Nonfiction

WEEKS 1 AND 2 RESOURCES

Text Set 2 • Historical Fiction

WEEKS 3 AND 4 OLD AND NEW

Text Set 3 • Poetry

WEEK 5 FINDING MY PLACE

INDEPENDENT READING

NONFICTION MONEY MATTERS

FICTION NOTES FROM THE PAST

Genre • Expository Text

EARTHQUAKES

by Sneed B. Collard III

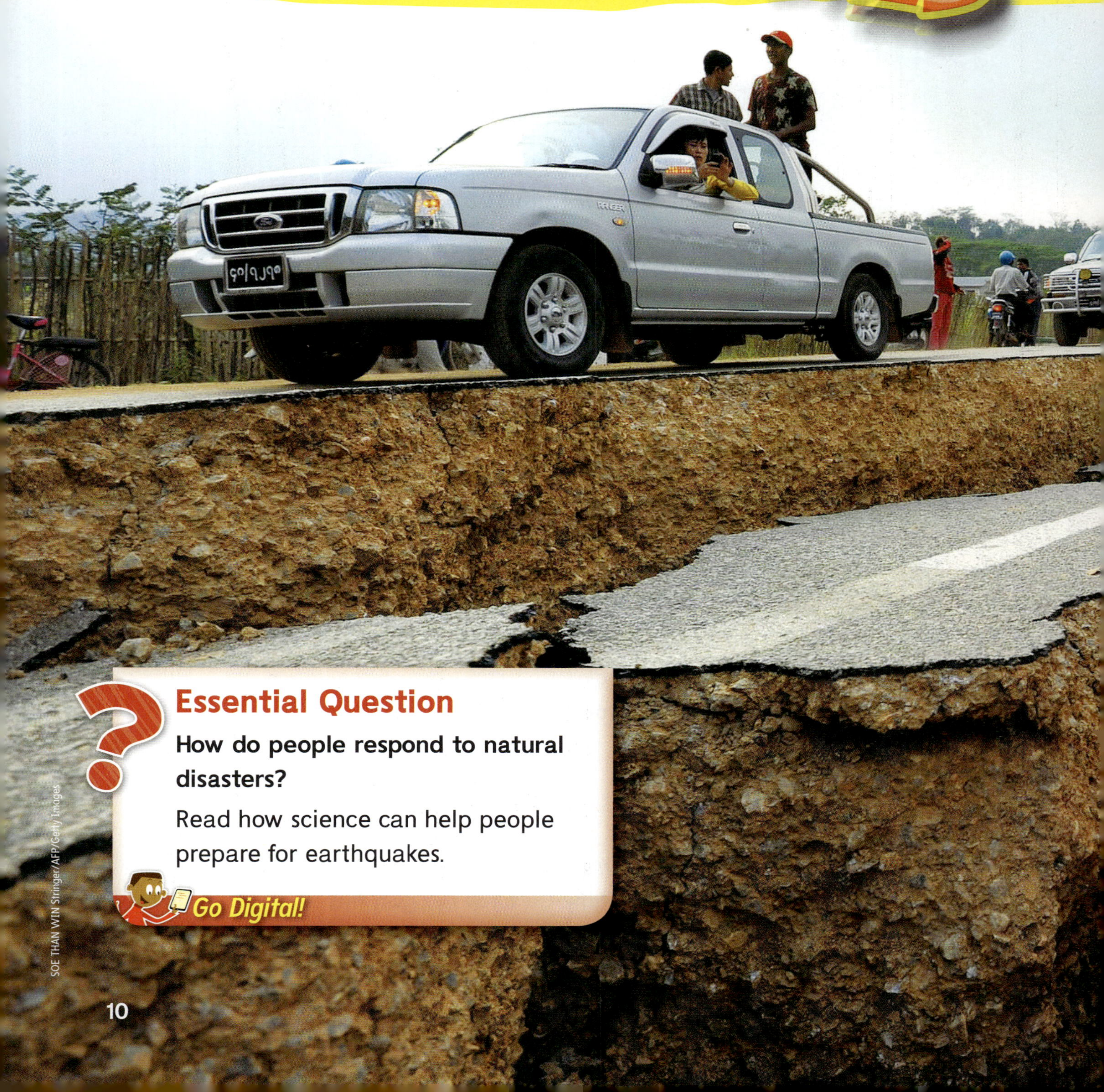

Essential Question

How do people respond to natural disasters?

Read how science can help people prepare for earthquakes.

Go Digital!

A Shifting Planet

We like to believe that the ground under our feet is solid and secure. People who have felt the ground shake know differently. They have lived through an earthquake.

Earth's crust resembles a jigsaw puzzle more than a solid sphere. Like a puzzle, the crust is divided into different pieces that fit together. These pieces are called plates. Earth's plates float on top of a layer just below the crust called the upper mantle. The upper mantle is solid rock, but it behaves like a thick gel. Heat from deep inside the earth moves through the rock and causes it to slowly swirl and flow.

Myanmar residents inspect large cracks on a road after an earthquake struck the area.

Dr. Inés Cifuentes is a seismologist—someone who studies earthquakes. She likes to compare the movement of Earth's plates to boiling milk. "When you boil milk," she says, "you get that little surface layer of cream on top that moves and dances around. That's what's going on in the earth, except that Earth's crust is much harder than the layer of cream."

As the mantle "boils," it pushes and pulls the plates above it. "It's at the edges of these plates," Dr. Cifuentes explains, "where we have most earthquakes."

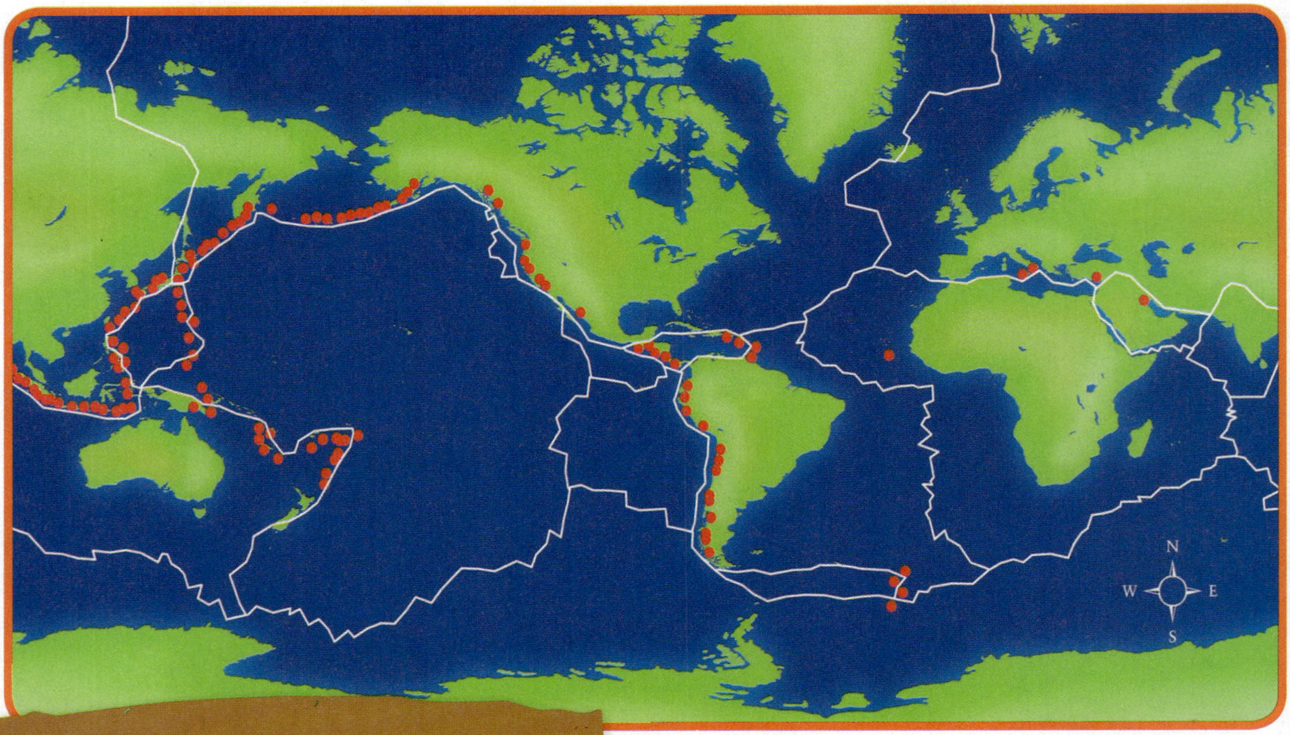

The white lines on the map above show plates on Earth's surface. The red dots show where earthquakes have occurred.

Neil Stewart

People stare at a gigantic crack on a street in Valdivia caused by the 1960 Chilean earthquake.

Earth's Largest Quake: A Firsthand Account

Dr. Inés Cifuentes became a seismologist for a very good reason—she and her family lived through the largest recorded earthquake in history. This was the 1960 earthquake that struck Chile. As Dr. Cifuentes explains: "In April, 1960, my family moved to Santiago, Chile. Just a few weeks later, on May 21st, we were woken up by strong shaking. Then, thirty-three hours later a gigantic earthquake hit the southern part of Chile, and with it, an enormous tsunami. About a year later, we took a trip to the northern end of the earthquake zone. And that's where I saw that the land had actually been raised up a meter or so. I saw these huge changes, and that impressed me—that the earth could actually do that! Later, as a graduate student I wanted to know how big that earthquake was, how long it lasted, and whether it was preceded by a 'slow' earthquake. I worked on this problem for four years. I was able to calculate that Earth's largest recorded earthquake had a magnitude of 9.5. I also confirmed that a slow precursor [forerunner] had occurred 15 minutes before the main earthquake. I am very proud of this work."

Whose Fault Is It?

Earth's plates crash together, spread apart, and slide against each other. Wherever they do this, they cause breaks in Earth's crust. Seismologists call these breaks faults. Usually, the blocks of rock on each side of a fault just sit there stuck together. But when enough pressure builds, the two sides of the fault can suddenly shift, or slip. This sudden movement releases waves of energy. These waves travel through the earth. We feel them as earthquakes.

Most faults do not slip and cause earthquakes. Around the globe, however, active faults cause hundreds of earthquakes every day. Most are too small for us to notice. Once in a while, Earth unleashes a whopper.

The diagram below shows a normal fault, which is a crack or fracture in the Earth's surface. Movement along the fault can sometimes cause earthquakes.

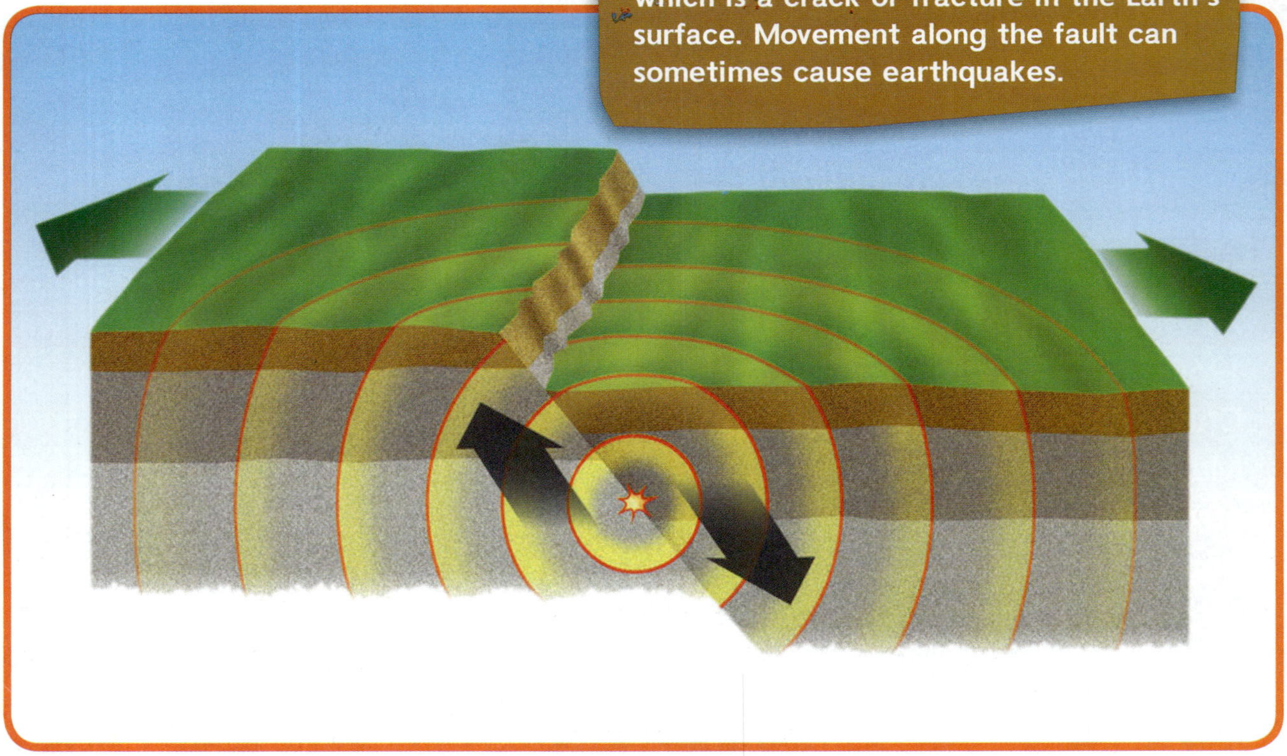

Neil Stewart

Measuring Earthquakes

Seismologists record earthquakes using machines called seismographs. These measure shaking, or ground motion. After an earthquake, scientists read their seismographs. They use their readings to calculate the earthquake's size, or magnitude. Magnitude scales are set up so that each whole number is ten times larger than the number before it. A magnitude 7.0 earthquake, for instance, is ten times larger than a magnitude 6.0 quake.

Truly giant earthquakes happen about once a year. These are quakes with a magnitude of 8.0 or greater. They occur only on very large faults and can cause **severe destruction**.

Dr. Cifuentes explains, "The only way you can get an earthquake like the 2011 Japan earthquake is where one of Earth's plates is sliding under another one. This is the only kind of place where you have a fault long enough and wide enough to release that kind of energy."

Seismologists gave the 2011 Japan earthquake a 9.0 magnitude. It was the fourth largest earthquake ever recorded. They believe that the earthquake occurred on a fault more than 150 miles (250 kilometers) long. It shook Japan for three to five minutes. It was so powerful that it **altered** the geography of the country. Surprisingly, it wasn't the shaking of the ground that did the most damage. A massive wave proved much more destructive.

Seismographs he p scientists determine the magnitude, or size, of an earthquake.

kickers/Getty Images

The disaster zone in Kesennuma, Japan, 2011, 100 days after the massive earthquake and tsunami

KAZUHIRO NOGI Staff/AFP/Getty Images

Tsunami Terror

When an earthquake occurs under the ocean, it often moves a **substantial** amount of water above it. This creates a fast-moving wave called a tsunami (soo-NAH-mee). Out at sea, the wave may be only a few feet high. As it reaches shore, however, the wave can tower into a monster. It can hurl water for miles inland.

Tsunamis can travel thousands of miles. In 1960, Earth's largest recorded earthquake struck the country of Chile. It produced tsunami waves up to 82 feet (25 meters) high along the coast. The tsunami also raced across the Pacific Ocean at a speed of more than 150 miles per hour. It struck the shorelines of Hawaii, Japan, Alaska, and other places. Hundreds of people drowned.

The 2011 Japan earthquake produced tsunami waves more than 30 feet (10 meters) high. The 2004 Indian Ocean earthquake in southern Asia produced 50-foot (15-meter) tsunamis. These tsunamis engulfed entire cities and shorelines. The waves swept away buildings, cars, and people.

Japan, southern Asia, and Chile had experienced many powerful earthquakes and tsunamis before. Why were so many people unprepared?

Predicting Earthquakes

Seismologists are very good at measuring earthquakes. However, they still can't predict when earthquakes will happen.

"There was a time," Dr. Cifuentes explains, "when I think scientists felt that predicting earthquakes was just around the corner—that we were going to be able to predict earthquakes very soon. But it's clear now that it's not around the corner. In fact, some have given up entirely on predicting earthquakes."

One reason that earthquakes are **unpredictable** is that scientists cannot collect enough information to understand where and when an earthquake might happen next. Although scientists have placed special instruments in many earthquake zones, earthquakes still surprise us. Scientists, for example, had believed the next big earthquake in Japan would happen farther to the south, closer to Tokyo. Instead, it struck farther north.

A powerful tsunami forced people to flee to the roof of a control tower in a flooded airport.

AFP PHOTO/HO/NHK/Getty Images

Planning for Earthquakes

Even though we can't predict earthquakes, we can prepare for them. Many seismologists help make information **available** to people so they can plan for and respond to earthquakes. This is especially important near coastal areas.

"Once the shaking goes on for more than thirty seconds," Dr. Cifuentes says, "it's pretty simple. You have to run away from the ocean and run up hill. You have maybe fifteen or twenty minutes to reach higher ground."

How cities are built also affects how many people survive an earthquake. Cities in many countries have special building laws. Buildings must be strong and flexible. That way, they won't **collapse** during an earthquake. In some countries, however, buildings are often poorly built. The 2010 Haiti earthquake, for example, killed between 46,000 and 316,000 people. Unlike the earthquake in Japan, many of these people were killed by collapsing buildings and falling debris.

However, earthquakes don't just destroy. They also create. "They help make the mountains, coasts, and other landscapes we see around us," Dr. Cifuentes explains. This is worth remembering as we learn how to predict and survive earthquakes in the future.

Utility ducts like this one are being constructed to protect underground wires, cables, and pipes in the event of an earthquake.

(t) Heath Korvola/Aurora/Getty Images; (b) Koichi Kamoshida Staff/Getty Images News/Getty Images

What to Do During an Earthquake

If you are indoors

- Drop to the ground and crawl under a sturdy piece of furniture until the shaking stops.
- Stay away from glass, windows, outside doors and walls, and anything that could fall, such as a hanging light or fan.
- Stay in bed if you are there when the earthquake strikes. Protect your head with a pillow. Only move from the bed if there is a heavy light or fan above you.
- Use a doorway for shelter only if you know it is strongly supported.
- Stay inside until the shaking stops and it is safe to go outside.
- Do not use elevators.

If you are outdoors

- Move away from buildings, streetlights, and utility wires.
- Avoid any space where there is falling debris, such as glass.
- Once in the open, stay there until the shaking stops.

Students raise awareness about earthquakes by participating in a nation-wide earthquake drill.

David McNew/Getty Images News/Getty Images

About the Author

Sneed B. Collard III believes that people can find science anywhere they look. His mother and father were both biologists, so Sneed grew up with exposure to science every day. He has written more than 40 science books for kids, many of them inspired by his own life and interests—including his Frisbee-catching dog! Today he lives in Montana and enjoys writing about the American West and its natural beauty.

Author's Purpose

Sneed B. Collard III uses interviews with scientists to inform readers. How did reading about Dr. Inés Cifuentes's work help you to better understand earthquakes?

Sneed Collard III

Respond to the Text

Summarize

Summarize what you learned about earthquakes. Information from your Venn Diagram may help you.

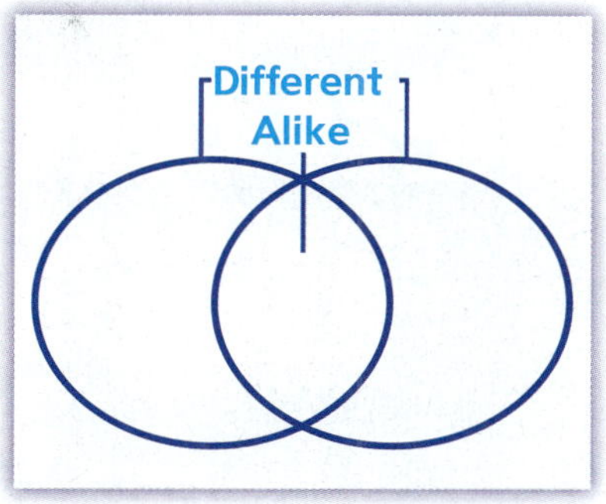

Write

Why is it important to understand how earthquakes affect people? Use these sentence starters to organize your text evidence.

One effect of an earthquake is . . .
Understanding this effect helps . . .
Another effect is . . .
If you understand . . .

Make Connections

How can science help people prepare for earthquakes? ESSENTIAL QUESTION

Why should people take warnings about tsunamis seriously? TEXT TO WORLD

Genre • Personal Narrative

Compare Texts

Read a personal narrative about being caught in a flood.

Weathering the Storm

by Anna Whittemore

The **severe** floods came on the same weekend that the Girl Scouts of Tennessee had scheduled a "camporee." This is an event where troops come together at a Girl Scout camp.

There had been forecasts of thunderstorms all week. That hadn't discouraged me, my mom (our group leader), and two of the other Girl Scouts in my troop. We were going, no matter what. On Friday afternoon, we loaded our bags and food into my mother's tiny red car and set off on the two-hour journey.

Our cabin had running water, a full kitchen, a bathroom, and four bedrooms. We were sharing it with another troop. After setting up our beds and telling stories, we went to sleep.

That night, it started raining.

I woke up at 5:00 AM to thunder and lightning. All morning it was pouring. All programs were canceled, which meant no horseback riding or tree climbing. Some of the troops had left that morning in case of flooding.

After lunch, I was walking to the bridge over the river. I looked at the field I had to cross and saw another river! Twenty-four hours earlier, the field had been dry. Our road was submerged, too. One thing was for sure: nobody was leaving our "island" any time soon.

That night, a Brownie troop moved in with us. Their original cabin had been flooded through the chimney. There were tornado warnings that night, so to avoid more **hazards**, all of us kids piled into the bathroom to sleep.

When morning came, we were a little sore and tired, but we were all fine. The same could not be said for the road out! The water level was even higher than before. We hesitated to call the EMS because they were busy taking care of real emergencies. We had plenty of food, water, and board games, so we were not in **crisis**.

Some local troops left that day, taking the "emergency exit," an extremely muddy dirt road. But the problem of getting ourselves out remained. The main road was underwater, and the bridge would likely be ripped off by raging water. My mother's tiny car would never make it out on the muddy emergency exit road. We couldn't go on foot. We had to accept that we would have to stay another night and miss school and work.

The next day brought great news. The water had completely receded, leaving the bridge crossable. We waited till 11:00, packed the car, and with only a slight delay—getting stuck in the muddy driveway—we made our way out.

Even though some parts of the trip were less than amazing, I had fun. I got to see flash floods, play in puddles for the first time in years, and get a tiny taste of what it was like to be in a natural disaster—without ever really being in danger. I'm grateful that no one got hurt. Next time I go camping, though, I am going to cancel at the slightest hint of rain!

Make Connections

What steps did the narrator take to protect herself during the flood? ESSENTIAL QUESTION

In what ways are floods similar to and different from earthquakes? TEXT TO TEXT

Genre • Realistic Fiction

EXPERTS, Incorporated

by Sarah Weeks • illustrated by Chuck Gonzales

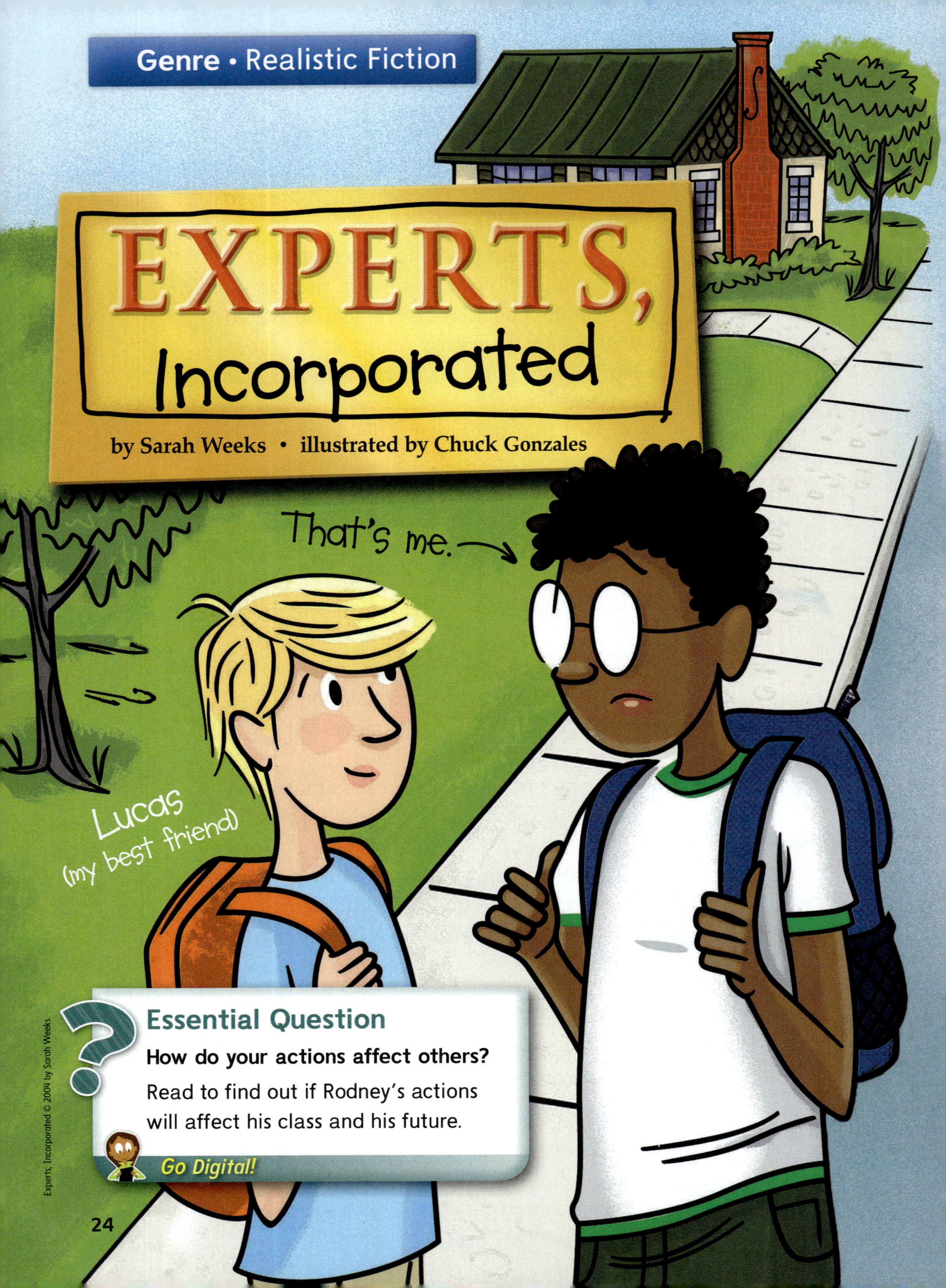

Essential Question

How do your actions affect others?

Read to find out if Rodney's actions will affect his class and his future.

Go Digital!

Things I can't stand

There are three things in this world I can't stand—cucumber salad, wool sweaters, and creative writing. Cucumbers make me burp and wool makes me itch, but if you gave me a choice, I would rather burp and itch at the same time than have to write something creative.

"You finished your essay, right, Rodd-o?" my friend Lucas asked me as we walked toward school together early one morning.

I **hesitated**. Lucas is my best friend and we always shoot straight with each other.

"Yeah, I finished it," I said.

"Phew, that's a relief," he said. "If you hadn't, I would never forgive you, you know."

"Yeah, I know," I said.

The problem began on the first day of the school year when our humanities teacher, Mrs. Greenberg, promised that if nobody got an F in her class all semester she would give us a pizza party.

"Just remember," she'd laughed, "there are no F's in *pizza*."

Here it was, the last week of the semester and I was about to earn not just an F, but the F that would ruin everything. Because, you see, I hadn't done the assignment. Not one word of it.

As we rounded the corner and headed up the block toward school, Jeremy and Russell, two friends from our class, caught up with us.

"You guys did the assignment, right?" Russell asked us.

"Yep," Lucas answered for us both. "How about you?"

"Of course," said Jeremy. "What do we look like, idiots? I can taste that pepperoni already. Last year's class got the party and somebody told me she let them have all the soda they wanted too."

When I get nervous, I sometimes get hives on my neck, and I could feel one beginning to prickle up under my collar.

"What profession did you pick?" Lucas asked.

"Doctor," Jeremy said. "'Cause they get to save people and stuff."

"I picked truck driver," said Russell. "They get to travel and eat at diners. I love diners, but my mom says they're too greasy, so we never get to go. What about you, Lucas?"

"Star pitcher for the New York Yankees," he said. "Man, can you imagine getting paid to play baseball?"

The assignment had been to write an essay about what you want to be when you grow up. Sounds easy enough, unless you're like me and have no idea what you want to be, and no matter how hard you try, you can't think of even one thing that feels the least bit right.

"I bet all the girls are going to say they want to be teachers 'cause they know Mrs. Greenberg will eat that up with a spoon," Russell said with disgust.

"Yeah, probably," Lucas agreed. "So, what did you pick, Rodd-o?" he asked, turning to me.

We were just starting up the steps of the school, when a familiar cry went up from the playground.

"Hey look, everybody! There goes Mucus! Hey, Mucus!"

Lucas blushed and hung his head as we walked up the steps and into the building. It happens to him all the time, poor guy. He has one of the worst names. Not only does *Lucas* rhyme with *mucus*, but even if you shorten it to *Luke*, you're still in trouble because then it rhymes with *puke*. He's been tortured his whole life on account of that name.

Having a bad name is something Lucas and I have in common and probably part of the reason we became friends all the way back on the first day of kindergarten. My name is Rodney Curtain. My parents and my teachers call me Rod, my friends call me Rodd-o, and my sister, who's only two, calls me Rah-rah. Rodney Curtain may not be the greatest name in the world, but front-ward like that it's not so bad. The thing is, at school when they call out your name for attendance they say it backward. Lucas Bromberg becomes Bromberg, Lucas. Samantha Smith becomes Smith, Samantha.

Unfortunately, I become Curtain, Rod. That's bad.

As we made our way down the hall to homeroom, I felt sorry for Lucas on account of the teasing, but secretly I was relieved that he'd forgotten about the question he'd asked me. How was he going to take it when he found out I hadn't done the assignment?

After she took attendance, Mrs. Greenberg—we have her for homeroom as well as humanities—announced that she would be collecting our papers after lunch. There was still hope left. All I had to do was come up with an idea between now and then, scribble it down in time to hand it in with the others, and maybe I wouldn't have to ruin the party after all. The problem was, I still didn't have any ideas.

"What do I want to be?" I asked myself. "Come on, Curtain, think."

I thought about it during math, history, and science lab, but with lunchtime only minutes away, my mind was still a complete blank. The only thing I could think of that I wanted to be was someone else. Someone who had written the stupid essay already.

As I looked around the room **desperately** hoping to find some **inspiration** somewhere, I asked myself, "Do I want to be a scientist? Do I want to fix clocks? Write books? Build desks? Make pencils?" No, no, no. And then suddenly without warning, everything shifted into slow motion as my eyes came to rest on the face of the girl sitting in the second seat in the third row from the left. That's when it hit me. I knew what I wanted to be. What the world needed me to be.

When the bell for lunch rang, I didn't join the others in the cafeteria.

Instead I took out my notebook and began to write. When the fifth-period bell rang, I was already in my seat in Mrs. Greenberg's room with a stack of four handwritten sheets of paper in front of me and a huge grin on my face.

"Why are you sitting there smiling like a dork?" Lucas asked as he slid into the seat next to me. "And where were you at lunch anyway? And another thing, you never answered my question from before, what did you choose as your profession?"

"Name expert," I told him happily. "That's definitely what I want to be, a name expert."

"A name expert? Whoever heard of that?" he said.

"Nobody. It hasn't been invented yet. But I'm going to be the first one," I told him.

"Oh, yeah? And what exactly are you going to do?" he asked me.

"I'm going to **advise** people about what not to name their kids."

"No offense, but that is so dumb. Why would anybody pay you to tell them what not to name their kid?" he asked.

"Because I'm an expert," I said.

"Says who?" he said.

"What's your name?"

"What do you mean, what's my name? You know my name, fish-for-brains." Lucas snorted.

"Come on, just answer the question. What's your name?"

"Lucas," he said.

"And what do all the kids call you?"

He hesitated **uncomfortably** for a second before answering.

"Mucus," he said quietly.

"Exactly," I said. "See? If I had been around when your parents were deciding what to name you, I could have warned them that every name needs to be checked for bad rhymes. A kid named Leo is gonna end up getting called B.O., anybody named Gabby is gonna get called Flabby, it doesn't take a rocket scientist to figure that out. Your name is particularly bad, because it's a double whammy."

"Tell me about it," said Lucas, shaking his head sadly.

"The way I see it, a name expert should be hired every time a baby gets born, to protect it from being saddled with a name that could ruin its life," I went on.

"How much do you think you'll get paid?" he asked.

"A lot. Parents pay a bundle for braces to straighten their kids' teeth. Don't you think they'd shell out even more to save their kids from being **humiliated** at school?"

"Here's a question for you—do you think there's any way a name expert could figure out whether a name is going to fit when the kid gets older?" Lucas asked me.

"What do you mean?" I said.

"Well, for instance, you know how Melody Adams is tone-deaf?"

"Yeah, she sings like a moose," I said.

"If her parents had known she was going to be unmusical, maybe they wouldn't have given her a musical name like Melody."

"Maybe they would have named her Moose," I said.

We both laughed.

"I suppose a name expert could be trained to look carefully at the parents for signs of what's to come," I said. "Like for instance, if there's a history of baldness in a family, it's probably not a very good idea to use the name Harry."

"Yeah, or like if the parents have big noses they shouldn't name their kid Honker," said Lucas.

"Who names their kid Honker?" I said. "That's not even a real name."

"Oh, and Curtain Rod is?"

I punched him in the arm, but not too hard because like I said, we're best friends.

"Hyphenated names would have to be looked at very carefully too, don't you think?" Lucas said. "Like Jessica's, for instance."

"Exactly," I said. "She's the one I was looking at in science lab when this whole idea came to me."

Jessica's dad's name is Charlie Mintz and her mom's name is Sylvia Pepper.

How hard could it have been to name her Jessica Mintz-Pepper instead of Jessica Pepper-Mintz? If they'd had a name expert around, trust me, it never would have happened.

"You know, I take back what I said about this idea being dumb," Lucas said. "I think maybe you're onto something big here."

"Yeah? You think?" I said.

"Yeah. And you know, once business takes off, you might even need a partner," Lucas said excitedly. "We could call it Experts, Incorporated."

"We?" I laughed. "I thought you were going to pitch for the Yankees."

Lucas smiled and shrugged.

"I doubt I'll get picked up; I can't even throw a slider. But if you want a partner who really understands why the world needs name experts, I'm your man, Rodd-o."

Mrs. Greenberg came down the aisle collecting the papers. As I handed her mine, I heaved a huge sigh of relief. Not only had I avoided ruining the pizza party, I'd managed to plan my entire future too, and it was looking pretty bright, if I do say so myself.

About the Author

SARAH WEEKS, Incorporated

For **Sarah Weeks,** the best thing about writing is that she gets to spend all day doing what she enjoys most. Sarah prefers writing books about things she knows or has experienced. She has written about animals and the environment as well as about kids and their experiences.

When Sarah is not writing picture books or novels, she loves to bake, watch movies and little league games, and spend time with family and friends. She also visits classrooms around the country to talk about her stories.

Matthew Peyton/Getty Images

Author's Purpose

The author uses a lot of dialogue in *Experts, Incorporated.* How does the dialogue make the story more realistic?

Respond to the Text

Summarize

Use details from *Experts, Incorporated* to summarize what happened in the story. Information from your Plot: Conflict Chart may help you.

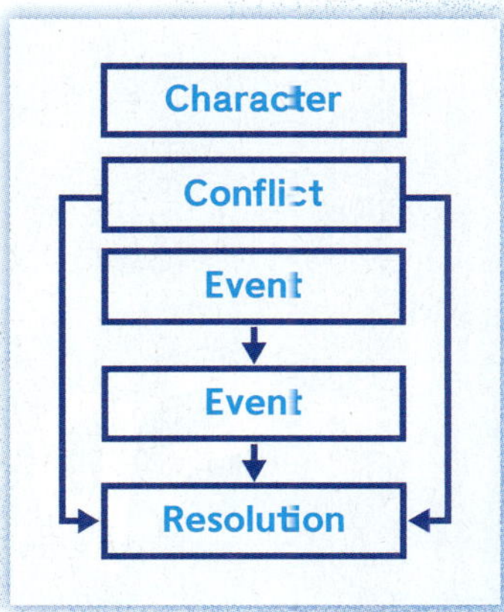

This chart can help you!

Write

What can readers learn from Rodney? Use these sentence starters to organize your text evidence.

One thing you can learn from Rodney is . . .
For example, Rodney . . .
This shows that . . .

Make Connections

How did Rodney's actions affect others in this story? **ESSENTIAL QUESTION**

Rodney saw a real-world problem in his school and turned it into a future career. Make a list of jobs in which people make a difference or solve problems. Talk with a partner about why people might do these special jobs. **TEXT TO WORLD**

Genre • Expository Text

Compare Texts

Read to find out about how people are standing up to bullying.

Speaking Out to STOP Bullying

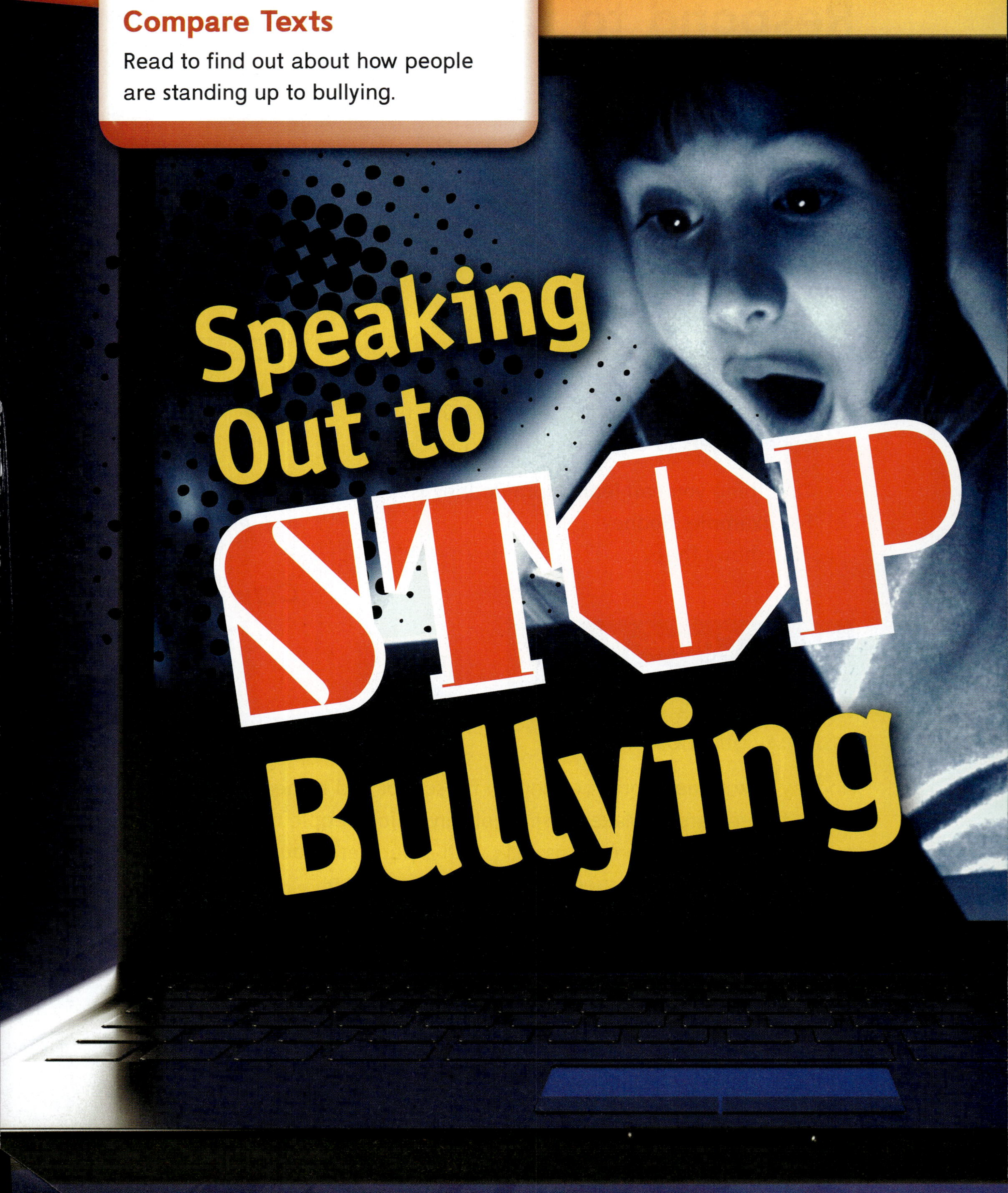

Victims of bullying often feel powerless, or unable to do anything about their problem.

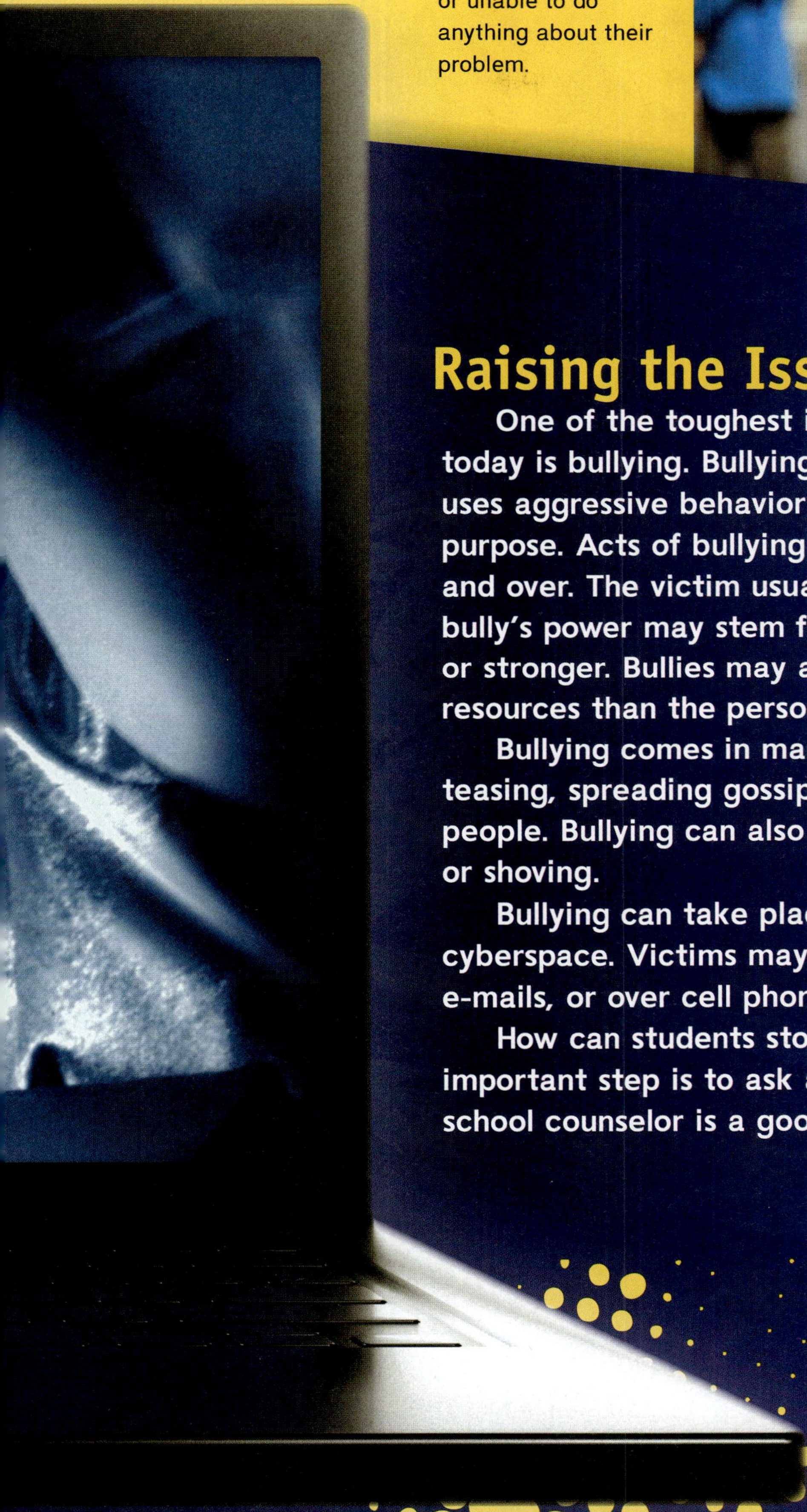

Raising the Issue

One of the toughest issues facing students today is bullying. Bullying occurs when a person uses aggressive behavior to hurt others on purpose. Acts of bullying often happen over and over. The victim usually feels powerless. A bully's power may stem from being older, bigger, or stronger. Bullies may also seem to have more resources than the person they target.

Bullying comes in many forms: name calling, teasing, spreading gossip, ignoring or excluding people. Bullying can also be physical, like hitting or shoving.

Bullying can take place anywhere, even in cyberspace. Victims may be targeted online, in e-mails, or over cell phones.

How can students stop bullying? The most important step is to ask an adult for help. The school counselor is a good resource.

(bkgd) Kutay Tanir/Photodisc/Getty Images; (c) Pat LaCroix/The Image Bank/Getty Images; (tr) Toby Maudsley/The Image Bank/Getty Images

Students should report any signs of bullying to an adult they trust.

He or she can set up a meeting with the bully, called a mediation, or do role-playing where the bully has to put him- or herself in the victim's place. Students who witness bullying should also report it. Additionally, they can be active bystanders by placing themselves next to the person being targeted. That move shows the bully that the target is not alone, without a direct confrontation.

Communities Take a Stand

New Hampshire passed a law to stop bullies. The law states that all school staff must be trained to know what bullying looks like. People learn to spot the signs of bullying. The law tells people who see bullying to report it. The state hopes that the law will create bully-free schools.

In Midland, Texas, the police take their message to the schools. Police officers make sure to tell students that bullying can be a crime. They want bullies to know that they are accountable for what they do. This means that bullies will be punished if they are caught. The officers tell students who have been bullied or who have seen bullying to report it right away. They make it clear that people have choices. They tell students that anyone can choose to stop being a bully.

an/Corbis

Left, Julia Kordon talks to students about how to stay safe from online bullying.

Television actress Lauren Potter speaks out about bullying of special-needs students.

Young People Speak Out

Julia Kordon from Phoenix, Arizona has a message for students. When she was 13, she started a group called The Bullying Ends Now. Julia wants all schools to be safe and fun. She travels all over the state talking to young people. She tells them how hurtful words can lower a person's **self-esteem**. Julia asks students to share their stories online. She wants people to stand up for others.

Actress Lauren Potter has a message for lawmakers. She has been speaking out about the bullying of special-needs students. Lauren was born with Down Syndrome. Because she did not look like her classmates, she was teased and called names as a child. She wants laws that will keep people safe from bullies.

Learning to Speak Up

It is important for people everywhere to recognize and stand up to all forms of bullying. Everyone has a right to feel safe and to be treated with respect. Likewise, each person has a responsibility to treat others with respect. Report anything that may get in the way of maintaining a safe environment.

Make Connections

How are people standing up to bullying? **ESSENTIAL QUESTION**

In what ways do actions make a difference? **TEXT TO TEXT**

Kids in Business

Hayleigh Scott/Hayleigh's Cherished Charms

Essential Question

How can starting a business help others?

Read how kid entrepreneurs are making a difference.

Go Digital!

Starting a business is a huge undertaking. That's why these young entrepreneurs who help others are nothing short of amazing.

Hayleigh Scott has been wearing hearing aids since she was 18 months old. Hiding the hearing aids behind her hair had become **routine**. At age 5, she decided that she wanted to be proud of them. So Hayleigh began drawing out her ideas to make charms that look like earrings. The charms would hang from her hearing aids and really stand out. Her mother helped Hayleigh bring those drawings to life. Her idea to highlight hearing aids launched a new **enterprise**.

At age 8, Hayleigh began a business with help from her family, including her twin sister. She now sells almost 400 charms in different styles. She even holds patents on her creations.

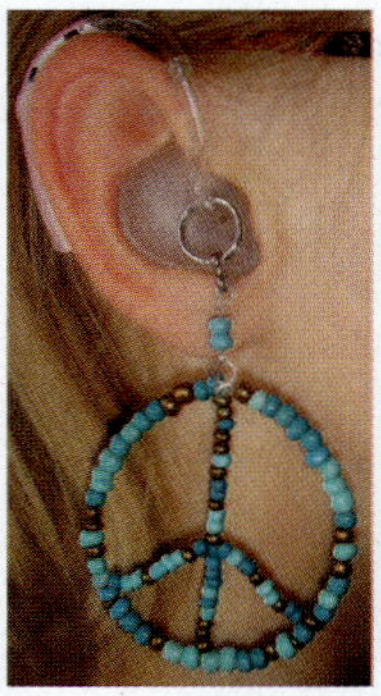

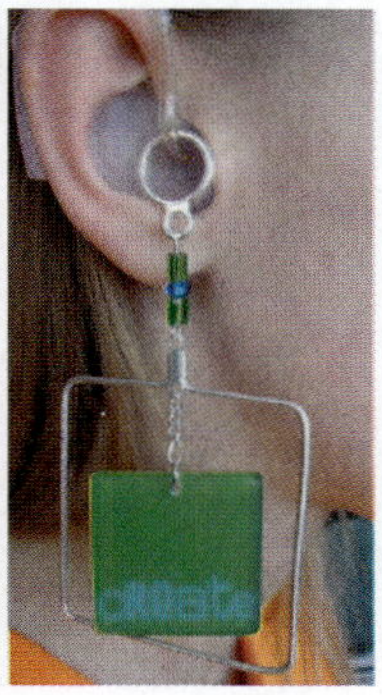

Joshua Williams has a message for kids: "You're never too young to make a difference." As head of Joshua's Heart Foundation, Joshua is one of the youngest foundation presidents in the world. His organization aims to help stamp out hunger in Miami, Florida. The **compassionate** group gathers and distributes food to people in need. Local businesses pitch in by providing food and helping hands.

Joshua's work includes a backpack program that is aimed especially at helping hungry children. He has plans to start a community garden too. That way, he says, "People can get more fresh food."

(t) Joshua's Heart Foundation; (c) D. Hurst/Alamy; (b) Hayleigh Scott/Hayleigh's Cherished Charms

Anna's plant business helps the environment.

Anna Azevedo is passionate about the environment. At age 10, she realized that most drinking glasses cannot be recycled. So, she found a nature-friendly way to reuse old drinking glasses. Anna's budding business, Sprout, sells "plants—in a glass."

Anna hatched her **innovative** idea based on biology. "Plants basically work for you. They purify the air and take out all the bad stuff," Anna says. Her **process**? She collects drinking glasses, grows plants in her backyard, and makes fertilizer. Then she transfers the plants, sand, and soil to the glasses to create a green product for indoors. Anna sells the plants on her website.

Cecilia Cassini is an **exceptional** young designer who makes clothes for kids and teens. For her sixth birthday, Cecilia asked for a sewing machine. She wanted to make her own clothes. Cecilia took two sewing lessons. Then, she says, she just started sewing, and she hasn't stopped since.

"I started making clothes for my sister and her friends, and word got around," Cecilia told *TIME For Kids*. Her mom's friend, a store manager, helped Cecilia start her business. Her dream is to have her clothes sold in stores around the world. Cecilia knows there's more to life than just pretty clothes, however. She also donates dresses to raise **funds** for charity. After all, trends come and go, but helping others never goes out of style.

Cecilia often donates dresses she has made to raise funds for charity.

For the Love of a Good Book

You don't need money to make a difference. If you have books that you no longer read sitting around your house, donate them to charity! Better World Books takes in unwanted books from people and libraries. They sell them at a discount or donate them to people in need. The money from their online sales goes to supporting global literacy. The bar graph shows the total amount of money Better World Books has collected for global literacy.

Cumulative Funds Raised for Global Literacy

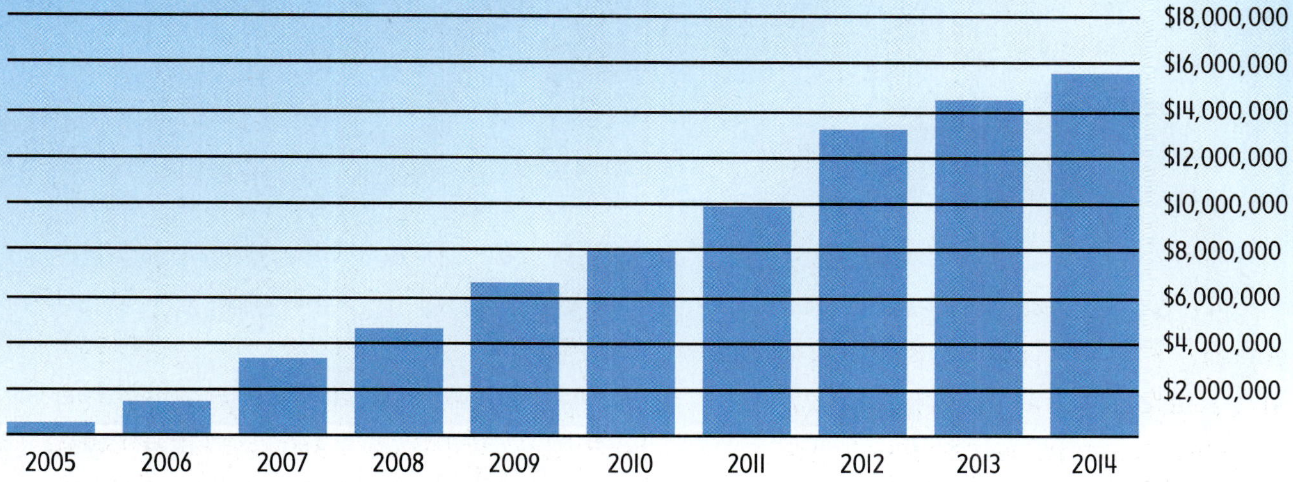

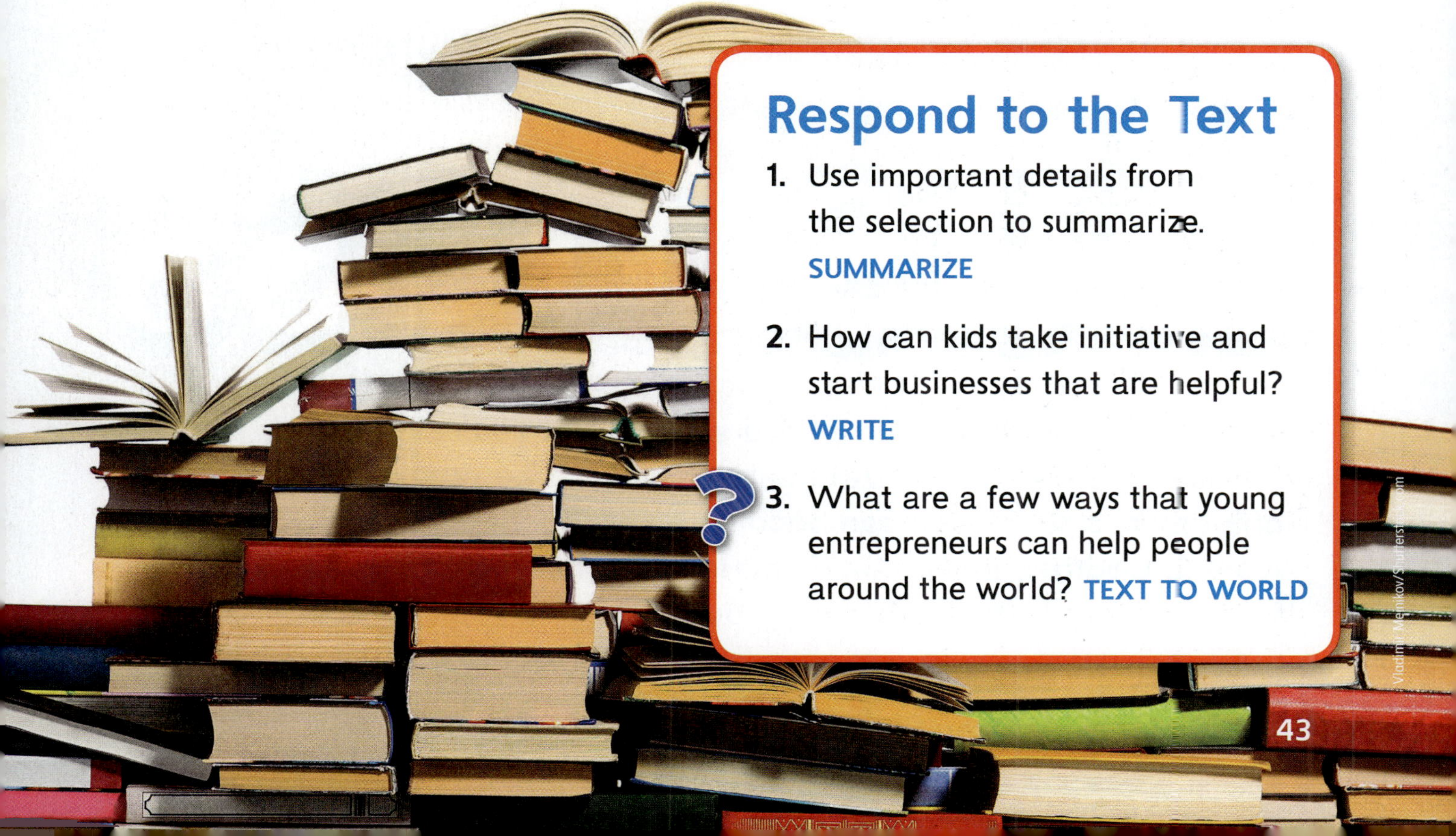

Respond to the Text

1. Use important details from the selection to summarize. **SUMMARIZE**
2. How can kids take initiative and start businesses that are helpful? **WRITE**
3. What are a few ways that young entrepreneurs can help people around the world? **TEXT TO WORLD**

Genre • Procedural Text TIME for KIDS

Compare Texts

Read about the steps you should take to start a business.

Starting a Successful Business

Becoming an entrepreneur is hard work. But if you're dedicated and have excellent organizational skills, it can be rewarding—sometimes, a small idea can become a very successful business! Neale S. Godfrey, author of *Ultimate Kids' Money Book,* shares these tips for starting a booming business.

Step 1 **Have an innovative idea.**

Suppose you like dogs, have free time, and feel compassionate towards people with busy schedules. Why not start a dog-walking service?

Step 2 **Find out if your business has a chance of succeeding.**

Come up with questions and do a market survey. Ask prospective clients about their likes and needs. Find out how much they would be willing to pay for your services. The responses to your questionnaire will help you decide if you should move forward with your plan. Also, check out the competition. If there's already another dog-walking service in your neighborhood, your business has a smaller chance at success.

Step 3 **Compile a business plan and a budget.**

A detailed business plan says what product will be sold, how it will be sold, whom the customers will be, and how much it will cost to start. A budget outlines your finances in detail.

Step 4 **Contact potential customers.**

Reach out to anyone who could need you. Then, set a work schedule for yourself. Finally, you have to actually start walking dogs!

Step 5 **Keep tabs on your business.**

Once your business is up and running, look at how it's doing. If you have money left over after your business expenses are paid, you've made a profit. You can consider yourself a successful entrepreneur!

Make Connections

What steps can you take to start a new business? **ESSENTIAL QUESTION**

How can an entrepreneur become successful? **TEXT TO TEXT**

Eric Larsen

Essential Question

How can science help you find out how things work?

Read how forces and motion affect our lives.

Go Digital!

A CRASH COURSE IN FORCES AND MOTION WITH MAX AXIOM SUPER SCIENTIST

About Max

Real Name: Maxwell J. Axiom
Hometown: Seattle, Washington
Height: 6' 1" **Weight: 192 lbs**
Eyes: Brown **Hair: None**

Super capabilities: Super intelligence; able to shrink to the size of an atom; sunglasses give x-ray vision; lab coat allows for travel through time and space.

Origin: Since birth, Max Axiom seemed destined for greatness. His mother, a marine biologist, taught her son about the mysteries of the sea. His father, a nuclear physicist and volunteer park ranger, schooled Max on the wonders of earth and sky.

One day on a wilderness hike, a megacharged lightning bolt struck Max with blinding fury. When he awoke, Max discovered a newfound energy and set out to learn as much about science as possible. He traveled the globe earning degrees in every aspect of the field. Upon his return, he was ready to share his knowledge and new identity with the world. He had become Max Axiom, Super Scientist.

BY Emily Sohn
ILLUSTRATED BY Steve Erwin and Charles Barnett III

FORCES THAT MOVE US

In fact, the world is full of all kinds of motion.
Everything that moves needs a force to get it moving.
Back for another jump, already?
You bet!
A force is any push or pull on an object. Bungee jumping depends on a force called gravity.
It pulls objects toward each other, and it keeps us on the earth.
Gravity is the reason I fall down, not up or sideways.

Whew!
Moving can be thrilling, but I need a break.
SNAP
SNAP

Hi, Rosita! What are you doing here?
Hello, Max! I'm taking notes for the physics class I teach. Why are you just sitting there? Is something wrong?
Once I sit, sometimes it's hard to get moving again. But once I get going, I often can't stop.

Isaac Newton

Isaac Newton (1643–1727) was the first person to realize that certain laws of nature explained all motion on earth and in space. He also was the first to explain the idea of gravity.

Here we go.
KLIK KLAK KLIK KLAK KLIK
I feel like I'm being pushed to the back of my seat.
That's inertia!
When the ride starts, your body is at rest. When the chair moves forward, your body wants to stay at rest, but the chair moves into you.
The chair's forward motion makes you feel like you're being pushed to the back of your seat.

Wow! How does this roller coaster go so fast?
The force of gravity is increasing our speed.
Speed is how fast we are going at any given moment. Acceleration is how much speed we pick up as we go down the hill. Acceleration causes us to move more quickly at the bottom of the hill than we did at the top.
That bar digging into my stomach must be inertia too.
You got it!
The ride comes to a stop, but your body wants to keep moving. The lap bar applies a force that keeps you from flying out of the car.

Friction in Space

In space, there is no friction. If you kicked a stone, it would keep going and going and going. That's why astronauts are tied to the space station when they do space walks. Otherwise, they'd just float away.

Brakes on the roller coaster used friction to slow us down too. Come on, I'll show you how.
BRAKE RAIL
Each roller coaster car has two brake fins attached to its underside. As the cars approach the station, these fins slide between two sets of brake rails.
I see. When the brake rails squeeze against the fins, friction stops the cars.
I had a great time, Rosita, but I've got to run. My nephew is having his birthday party over at Skater's Paradise.
See you later, Max!

MOTION IS A WEIGHTY ISSUE

Gravitational Pull

Weight is different from mass. Weight is determined by gravity's pull on an object. Each planet in our solar system has a different gravitational pull. If you traveled to each of the places below, your mass would always be the same, but your weight would be different. Multiply your weight by the number shown below each planet to find out how much you would weigh there. If you weigh 100 pounds on earth, you would weigh 38 pounds on Mars and 236 pounds on Jupiter.

(bc) NASA-ESA-J. Hester and A. Loll (Arizona State University)

I have another way to think about Newton's second law. I need two volunteers.
Pick me!
I'll do it!
I'm going to push both of them with the same amount of force on a level surface.
Who do you think will accelerate faster?
Johnny's bigger, he'll go faster!
Jenny's an awesome skater, she'll win!

Both of my arms are equally strong.
So the amount of force will be the same.
Let's see who gets a faster start.
Like the tennis ball, Jenny has less mass than Johnny, so she gets a faster start with the same push. Johnny would need a stronger force to get moving as quickly.
I'm like the tennis ball!
Does that make me a bowling ball?

Uncle Max, Jenny won the race on a flat surface. But I've noticed that the bigger kids always travel farther than the smaller kids when skating down a ramp.
Sometimes having more mass can give you an advantage. Let's have Johnny and Jenny race again.

In the last race, we wanted to see who would get a faster start. This race is for distance.
I'm going to release you at the same time. We'll see who travels farther without pumping.
Johnny's got it in the bag.
No way, Jenny will beat him easily.

Do you see that? Gravity pulls them down the ramp, but Johnny travels farther than Jenny.
Max, what happened? I got a good start, but Johnny just passed right by me.
Johnny's larger mass takes more force to slow down or stop than your smaller mass.
Friction between your wheels and the ground was the main force slowing both of you down. Johnny needed more friction to stop, so he traveled farther.
Time for cake!
I don't think these kids will let a little friction stand between them and chocolate cake.

About the Author and Illustrator

EMILY SOHN lives in Minneapolis, Minnesota. She writes mostly about science and health for kids and adults. Emily studied science in school. She even spent a few seasons following sea lions and seals to learn about them. When not writing and learning more about science, she loves rock climbing and running triathlons.

STEVE ERWIN is a comic book artist. Early in his career, Steve contributed art to many superhero comic series, including *Batman Returns* and *Superman: The Man of Steel*. For his accomplishments in comics, he was inducted into the Oklahoma Cartoonists Hall of Fame.

Author's Purpose

A Crash Course in Forces and Motion with Max Axiom, Super Scientist is an informational text written in the form of a graphic novel. This means that the information is presented graphically, or in words and pictures that tell a story, much like a comic book. Why would the author choose to teach science concepts in a graphic novel format?

Respond to the Text

Summarize

Summarize what you learned about forces and motion. Information from your Cause and Effect Chart may help you.

Cause	→	Effect
	→	
	→	
	→	
	→	

Write

Think about how authors explain complex ideas. Why does Emily Sohn use real-life examples to show how physical forces work together? Use these sentence starters to organize your text evidence.

Emily Sohn uses real-life examples . . .
This helps me understand that . . .
This makes complex ideas about force and motion easier to understand because . . .

Make Connections

How do forces and motion affect you? **ESSENTIAL QUESTION**

In what ways can understanding gravity help people? **TEXT TO WORLD**

NASA/JPL

Genre • Science Fiction

Compare Texts

Read how two futuristic robots use science to solve a problem.

The Box-Zip Project

The thirteenth sun of Xyport rose in the orange-tinted sky as Dr. Tank and his assistant, Shine, arrived for work.

"Good morning," Shine said, slipping into his lab coat. "Today's the day! I feel it in my battery!"

Dr. Tank smiled and said, "Now, Shine, we don't feel. We are robots, remember?"

Shine's robot laughter clattered like marbles inside a can. "You got me, Dr. Tank! But, honestly, I think we'll figure out the problem with this silly machine today."

The silly machine, known as Box-Zip, stood in the middle of the science laboratory looking like a ticket booth.

"Let's hope so, Shine. This project will be history if we're not successful pronto!"

For months, the robots had been attempting to travel in the Box-Zip to Earth. A voyage to planet Xto was no problem, and it was twice the distance. They could land on Grolon in a heartbeat. When they traveled to Vinzine, they returned ten minutes before they even left!

But Earth? Every time they attempted landing on that bizarre planet they could only get so close.

"Time for the morning checklist," Dr. Tank said.

"Ready-o," Shine answered.

"Inertia?" inquired Dr. Tank.

"Check," said Shine. "This baby is definitely at rest."

"Superb. Now let's apply force to move it," Dr. Tank said. Together, they pushed Box-Zip, which slid easily.

"Now use force to stop it," Dr. Tank said. Shine held out his enormous robot hand and immediately stopped the sliding Box-Zip.

"Let's do a trial run to Klugger and back," said Dr. Tank. Both robots stepped into Box-Zip and buckled up.

"Accelerate to warp times five blinkers," Dr. Tank advised. As Box-Zip moved faster, the seat belts kept the robots in place.

Lance Lekander

Almost instantly Box-Zip glided onto a dusty purple planet. Shine wanted a purple frozen beverage from the 7-0-12 store, but Dr. Tank explained that there was simply no time. In five blinkers, they were back in the laboratory.

"Klugger is no problem, yet we can't manage an Earth landing!" the frustrated Dr. Tank said. "It's ridiculous!"

"Come on," Shine encouraged. "Giving up is not an option."

Dr. Tank couldn't help but smile at his unfailingly cheerful assistant. Now he regretted not letting Shine get a purple frozen beverage on Klugger.

"You're absolutely right," said Dr. Tank. "Let's try Earth again."

Buckled safely in Box-Zip, Shine began to **accelerate** to warp times seven blinkers, then twelve blinkers. The world was a distorted blur of colorful motion. The robots' chrome teeth chattered as they whizzed through the galaxies, finally landing with a thud. They peered out the window.

"Drats!" Dr. Tank shouted in frustration. "It's happened again! We'll never make it all the way down."

Shine looked down. There was Earth below, yet Box-Zip remained at least fifteen feet above, stuck in the many arms of some enormous green and brown structure.

"Why can't we get to Earth?" Dr. Tank cried.

"Yoo-hoo, there!" came a voice from below.

The robots looked at each other. Something was attempting communication!

"Yoo-hoo!" the voice called again.

"Maybe 'yoo-hoo' means hello," said Shine. "Let's try to communicate!"

Shine leaned out the window, calling, "Yoo-hoo!"

"Might I possibly make an **inquiry**?" the Earth creature said.

"An inquiry?" asked Shine.

"A question, might I ask a question?"

"Certainly," answered Dr. Tank. "And then we'll ask you a question."

"Very well," said the creature. "Did you mean to land in a tree?"

"Tree!" said Shine. "What a hilarious name for this funny-looking thing!"

"Your tree prevents us from landing on your planet," said Dr. Tank. "Is there something we can do about it?"

The creature nodded his head. "I believe that gravity might offer a solution. Try rocking back and forth a bit. Once you start falling, I'm sure you'll come all the way down."

The robots looked at each other doubtfully. Still, they shifted from side to side until Box-Zip began to move. Then it moved down. In fact, it moved down rather quickly.

"Yes!" Dr. Tank shouted. "We've landed on Earth at last!"

To prove their successful landing, the robots had photographs made with the Earth creature, whose name turned out to be Mortimer. With some special sticky tape, Box-Zip was soon patched up and ready to go home. Before leaving Earth, Dr. Tank bought Shine a delicious green frozen beverage for the trip home.

Make Connections

How did science help the robots solve their problem? **ESSENTIAL QUESTION**

What are a few ways that science can help us answer questions and solve problems? **TEXT TO TEXT**

Genre • Fairy Tale

The Princess and the Pizza

by Mary Jane and Herm Auch

Essential Question

Where do good ideas come from?

Read to find out how a princess gets out of a difficult situation.

Go Digital!

Princess Paulina needed a job. Her father had given up his throne to become a wood-carver and moved them to a humble shack in a neighboring kingdom. Since the king was still learning, his carvings didn't sell, and Paulina's garden barely kept enough on the table.

Paulina missed princessing. She missed walking the peacock in the royal garden, surveying the kingdom from the castle tower, and doing the princess wave in royal processions.

Paulina tried walking a stray chicken around her shack, but it only pecked at her bare toes. Surveying the kingdom from the shack's leaky roof made even more holes. She tried princess-waving to the townspeople from her father's cart, but nobody bothered to wave back. They just thought she was swatting at flies.

One day, a page rode past the shack, announcing that Queen Zelda of Blom was seeking a true princess to become the bride of her son, Prince Drupert.

"This is my chance to get back to princessing," Paulina cried. She rummaged through her trunk of ex-princess stuff, brushed the wood shavings from her best ball gown, and blew away the bits of sawdust that clung to her diamond tiara. Then she tucked a piece of garlic into her bodice for good luck, snipped some fragrant herbs to cover up the garlic smell, and headed for the castle.

Paulina didn't expect much competition. There wasn't another princess for hundreds of miles. But when she got to Blom Castle, Paulina found she was only one of twelve princesses hoping to become the royal bride.

When she looked into her assigned room, Paulina saw her bed piled with sixteen mattresses. "Oh, for Pete's sake. The old princess-and-the-pea trick. That's so once-upon-a-time." Naturally, Paulina didn't sleep all night because she felt the lumpy pea through all of the mattresses.

When the twelve princesses gathered in the throne room the next morning, the seven who looked bright-eyed were sent home. Now only Paulina and four other sleepy princesses remained.

First, they were made to write essays entitled "Why I Want to Have the **Gracious** and Exquisitely Beautiful Queen Zelda for My Mother-in-Law."

Prince Drupert and Queen Zelda finally appeared on the balcony. Queen Zelda did all the talking. "Congratulations, ladies, you have written some lovely essays, which I will keep in my scrapbook. And you have all passed the mattress test. But to make absolutely sure you are of royal blood, there is a second test. Only a true princess can wear these glass slippers."

"For Pete's sake, you never heard of sneakers?" Paulina asked.

Queen Zelda gave Paulina a sharp look. "Nobody said you had to hike in them. Just try them on."

After the royal page made his way around the room with the slippers, two big-footed princesses were sent home. Now only Paulina and two others remained. One was followed around by seven strange little men, and the other had such a long braid dragging behind her, Paulina kept tripping over it.

"For Pete's sake, you never heard of scissors?" Paulina cried.

Queen Zelda glared at Paulina.

"You all have passed the second princess test. Your final task is to cook a feast that proves you worthy of being my dear Drupert's wife."

This set up a wail among the princesses, especially Paulina. "For Pete's sake. You have no royal chef?"

"Silence!" said the queen. "The table holds the makings for three fine feasts. Choose well, for the winner will become my dear Drupert's bride."

As Paulina started for the table, the long-haired princess tripped her, then loaded up with food. By the time Paulina got there, the seven strange little men had run off with everything but some flour, yeast, water, three overripe tomatoes, and a hunk of **stale** cheese.

"Hey, that's not fair! Queen Zelda, will you help me?"

"No," said the queen. "Because you have a big mouth."

A servant escorted Paulina to her room and locked the door. "Hey! How can I cook without a bowl or spoons or pots?"

There was no reply.

Paulina tried to make bread, kneading the flour, water, and yeast together; but it only stuck to the tray in a **flattened** mess. She squished the tomatoes over the dough to brighten it up. It looked awful. She sprinkled cheese gratings over the top. It was still a mess, and Paulina was exhausted.

"For Pete's sake, where's your fairy godmother when you need her? I'm going to take a nap." She reached under the pile of mattresses, pulled out the offending pea, and climbed into bed.

She hadn't been sleeping long when there was a knock at the door.

"Only twenty minutes left," called Queen Zelda. "I don't smell anything cooking."

"I'm not cooking," said Paulina. "I'm napping. Then I'm going home."

"You're not going anywhere," said the queen. "The losers will be beheaded."

Paulina sat bolt upright. "Beheaded! You didn't tell us that!"

"I forgot," said the queen.

"Can't I have a second chance? How about I try to spin straw into gold? Or maybe I could guess a weird little man's name?"

"No second chances," declared the queen.

"But that's not fair!" Paulina cried.

"Who needs to be fair? I'm the queen."

Paulina leaped out of bed and ran to the window, but it was an unbelievably long drop to the ground. The meal was her only hope. She rushed the tray over to the fireplace, stirred the few remaining hot coals, then crushed her garlic and sprinkled it over the mess for good luck. Finally, Paulina tossed on the herbs to cover up the garlic smell.

Paulina paced back and forth, planning her escape. Perhaps she could make a deal with the long-haired princess to climb down her braid. She didn't notice that the goopy dough had browned into a crust, the tomatoes were bubbling, the hard bits of cheese had melted, and the fragrance of garlic and herbs filled the room.

A page opened the door. "Time's up."

Paulina took a deep breath and carried her tray into the great dining room.

The other princesses had made lovely feasts, especially the one who had the seven strange little men to help her.

Prince Drupert went right to Paulina's tray. "It's not pretty, but it smells scrumptious." He helped himself to an unusually generous piece. "What do you call this dish?"

Paulina shrugged. "I don't know."

"It can't be an **official** entry in the contest if it doesn't have a name," said the queen.

"Oh, for Pete's sake," Paulina **muttered**.

"What's that?" snapped the queen. "Pete's what?"

Remembering the beheading threat, Paulina **frantically** tried to think of a name. "It's Pete's . . . ah . . ."

"Pizza?" The queen took a big bite. "Odd name, but it's tasty. The winner is Paulina's pizza."

"You mean I won't be beheaded?"

"I was only kidding about the beheading," said the queen.

"Then I was only kidding about wanting to marry Prince Drupert. Who needs him? I have other plans."

"Will you leave your recipe?" asked the queen.

"No way," said Paulina. "It's just become a family secret." She headed for the door.

"I liked you best," whined the queen, following close behind.

"Oh, for Pete's sake," muttered Paulina as she stomped across the drawbridge.

Princess Paulina's Pizza Palace opened a few weeks later. It featured unusual, carved furniture and fifty kinds of pizza.

Every Thursday, on the royal chef's night off, Queen Zelda and Prince Drupert came to Paulina's for popcorn-pineapple pizza. They often stayed to play cards with Paulina's father.

From then on, whenever Paulina drove her pizza delivery cart through town doing the princess wave, everybody waved back and ran after her, asking about the day's specials.

Life was good. Paulina was grateful not to have Queen Zelda for a mother-in-law, but she still worried about one little thing.

She worried about getting Queen Zelda as her stepmother!

About the Author and Illustrator

Mary Jane Auch and Herm Auch are a wife and husband author-illustrator team. Mary Jane's love for books and art began at an early age. She could always be found sketching characters from her imagination into notebooks. When a polio epidemic kept Mary Jane home from school for the first half of second grade, her mother taught her how to read. By the time she returned to school, her teacher was introducing her to books that excited and challenged her. Mary Jane believes, "The writer in me was probably born the year that I almost missed second grade."

Mary Jane began collaborating with her husband, Herm, after finishing a number of young adult novels. Before then, Herm had spent years working as a graphic artist, editorial cartoonist, and digital artist. He photographs Mary Jane's artistic creations and works on the images in his digital studio.

Author's Purpose

The Princess and the Pizza is a special kind of fairy tale called a fractured fairy tale. Fractured fairy tales are based on fairy tales you know, but they change the characters, setting, points of view, and/or events, usually for humor. Why would the author choose to write Paulina's story this way?

(t) Herm Auch

Respond to the Text

Summarize

Use your Plot: Conflict Chart to help you summarize the important events in *The Princess and the Pizza*.

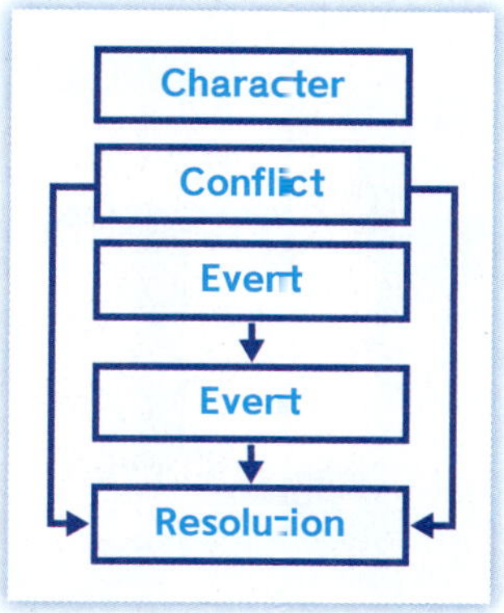

Write

How does the author show that winning the contest changes Paulina's life? Use these sentence starters to focus your text evidence.

In the beginning, Paulina . . .
Then the author . . .
This shows that Paulina's life . . .

Make Connections

How did Paulina get out of a difficult situation and win the competition? **ESSENTIAL QUESTION**

Fairy tales and fables often include characters who think of clever ideas to solve a problem. What can these tales teach us about where good ideas come from? **TEXT TO WORLD**

Genre • Fable

Compare Texts

Read to find out how Tomás and Maria come up with an idea to solve their problem.

TOMÁS AND HIS SONS

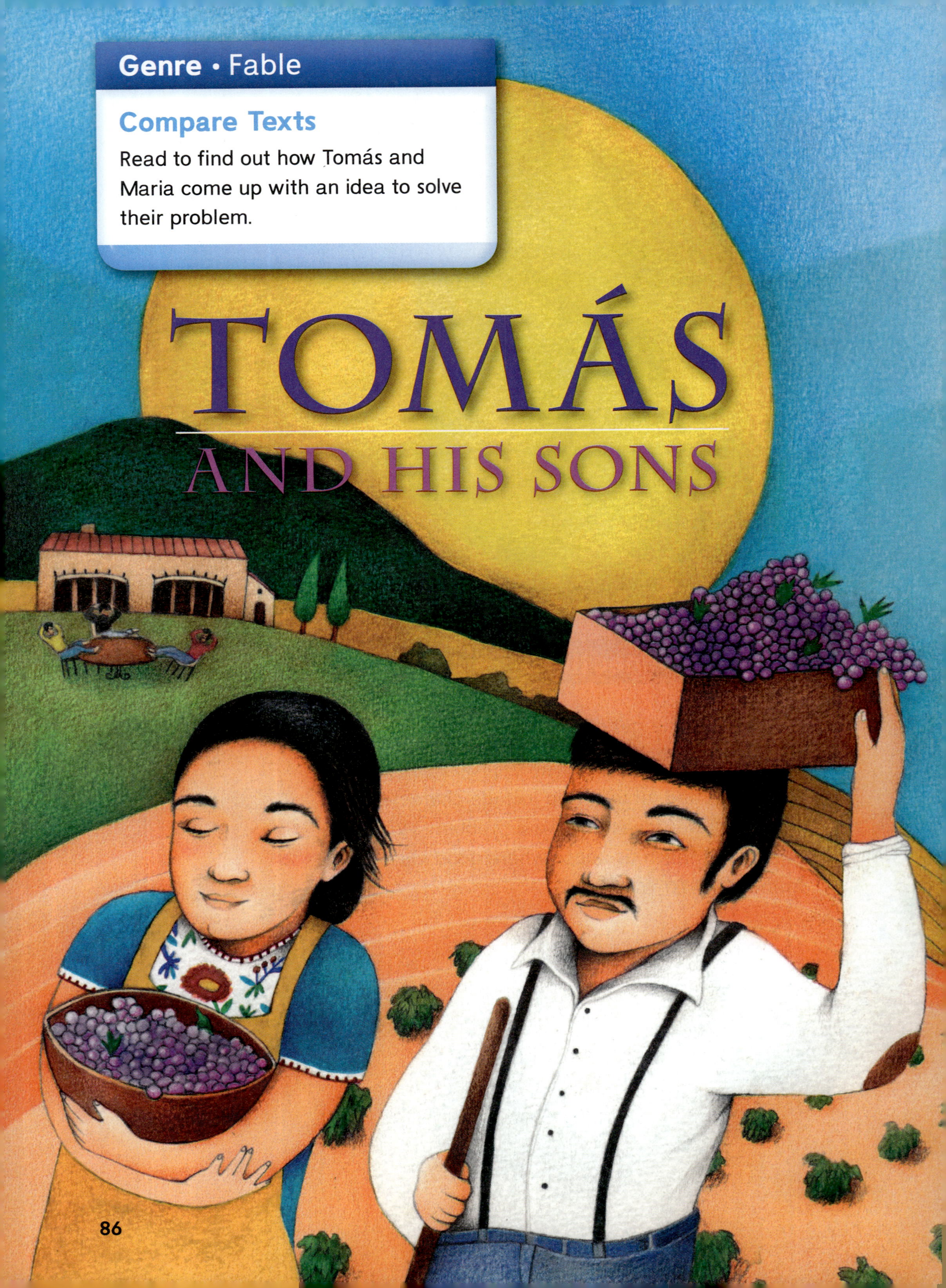

Tomás was a hardworking farmer. His vines produced the best grapes of any vineyard around. "It is the soil, which has been tilled for years," he told people if they asked him his secret. Other times, he said, "Mexico's sun gives the grapes no choice but to grow large and juicy."

Over the years, Tomás's stories became more inventive. But Tomás knew why his grapes were the best. Generations of hard work had kept the land plentiful.

Hard work was something Tomás knew well. But his sons, Eduardo, Miguel, and Luis, were the three laziest boys in all of Mexico.

While their parents tilled the earth under the hot afternoon sun, the boys slept. As the sun bent toward evening, the brothers rose. They stumbled into the kitchen. They filled their plates with eggs and tortillas. By nightfall they were wide awake. Soon, they were off to the village to sing and dance until morning.

Tomás worried about the land. What would happen once he and his wife, Maria, were too old to work? Their sons showed no interest in the vines. Once, Tomás had asked the boys to walk through the vineyard with him. He again told them about their ancestors bringing the vines from Spain.

"These vines tell our family's story," Tomás said. But he knew his words were lost on the boys. The farm's success was not as exciting as last night's fiesta.

One afternoon, under the calabash tree, Tomás brought his worries to Maria. "What can we do?" Tomás asked. "The vines will perish unless the boys learn to plow the earth."

Ester García Cortés

Maria knew the boys valued a warm night under the stars. Why would they want to work in the heat of the day?

"There must be a way to get the boys to plow," Maria said. "Let's **brainstorm** ideas to find one that will work."

Each day, Tomás and Maria sat under a calabash tree and talked over their problem. One day, when it seemed no **original** ideas would ever come to them, a gourd fell from the tree. Maria picked up the gourd. Turning it in her hands, she remembered something that had worked in the past.

"Of course, Tomás!" said Maria. "The boys need a purpose, a real reason for doing something. Last year, Luis could not find his gourd drum. His room was a mess. His clothes were lying all around. It was not possible to find his bed, much less a small gourd drum! The only way to find his drum was to clean his room."

"And did he?" asked Tomás.

Maria smiled. "He did. Once he had cleaned, Luis found his great treasure buried under a pile of shirts."

Tomás thought about this. "Maria," he said after a while, "what if the boys believe a treasure is buried in the vineyard? Would they dig to find it?"

"I think that's just the motivation they need," Maria said.

The next day Tomás told his sons he had been keeping a secret. "When our ancestors brought the vines to this land, they also brought a great treasure. I believe it is buried in the vineyard. For years I have tilled the earth to find it. We will be rich beyond belief once it is found." Right away his sons declared they would help Tomás find the treasure.

Many happy seasons passed with the family digging together in the vineyard. The sons were amazed each year to see the big, juicy grapes. Even more, they were thrilled by the wealth the crop had brought them.

One day, long after the farmer's sons had taken over the vineyard, Luis asked his brothers, "Have we found the great treasure yet?"

The three brothers began to laugh. They had forgotten that they were digging to find treasure. Yet all their hard work made them realize that their vineyard was a treasure.

Make Connections

How did Tomás and Maria come up with an idea to solve their problem? **ESSENTIAL QUESTION**

Compare the ways in which characters come up with ideas. **TEXT TO TEXT**

Genre • Expository Text

Essential Question

What helps an animal survive?

Read how spiders have adapted to survive.

Go Digital!

Spiders

by Nic Bishop

Some spiders are as small as a grain of sand. **The biggest, the Goliath birdeater tarantula from South America, is as big as a page in this book.** Yet all spiders share similar features. They have eight legs, fangs, spin silk, and eat other animals. At first you might confuse them with insects. But it is easy to tell the difference. Insects have six legs; spiders have eight. And spiders never have wings.

The Goliath birdeater tarantula likes to stay near its burrow on the rain forest floor. It waits for prey to come close enough to grab.

A spider's body has two main parts. The back part is called the abdomen. This contains the heart, which pumps pale blue blood (yes, blue!), and the spinnerets, which make silk. The front, or head part is called the cephalothorax. It has the spider's legs, eyes, fangs, brain, stomach, and two short arms, called pedipalps, which a spider uses to hold its prey.

The green lynx spider is perfectly **camouflaged** when it hides among leaves waiting to **pounce** on an insect. The long black spines on its legs are thought to help it trap its prey.

Spiders eat in an unusual way. They don't chew and swallow food like you do. They drink it. First the spider stabs its prey with its fangs and injects poisonous venom to stop it from moving. Then it dribbles digestive juices on its meal. This turns the animal's insides into soup, so the spider can slurp them out. Afterward, all that's left of the prey are empty bits of skin and some wings.

This black widow spider has just caught a wasp in her web. She will feed once she has wrapped it safely in silk.

Most spiders have eight eyes, so they can look several ways at once. But a spider cannot see as clearly as you. **Their eyes are usually very small and simple.** Spiders will notice if something moves nearby, but they often cannot see shapes very well.

A few spiders have no eyes at all. They live deep inside caves where it is completely dark all the time. But they have no trouble catching prey. That's because spiders have other amazing senses to rely on.

The long-jawed spider is a web builder. It gets its name from the very long jaws that hold the two thin fangs, which you can see folded underneath.

A spider does not have a nose or ears, at least not like you do. Even so, it has extraordinary senses all over its body. Take a close look. You will see this spider is covered with hairs. Many of these sense touch, vibrations, and sounds. **Hairs on a spider's legs can sense the sound of a flying insect.**

Other organs on the feet can smell and taste things just by walking on them. A spider can even recognize the taste of its own silk by touching it.

This huntsman spider is beautifully camouflaged on a rain forest leaf. Hairs on its body and legs will sense the vibrations made by the footsteps of an approaching insect.

Spider skin is made of tough stuff called chitin. It is the spider's personal body armor as well as its skeleton. Spiders don't have bones inside their body for support. Their hard skin is like a skeleton they wear on the outside. It protects and supports the spider's body.

This hard skin does not stretch, so a spider must molt now and then as it grows. **The spider finds a safe place and then slowly squeezes out of its old skin.** It can take an hour and is very stressful. The spider must even shed the skin covering its eyes and the inside of its mouth. Afterward, its new skin is damp and soft like putty. The spider rests until its new skin dries and hardens.

A cobalt-blue tarantula has to roll onto its back to molt. It is pulling the old skin off its legs. Its new fangs are pure white, but will turn dark later.

Silk is the secret of spider success. Spiders make several different types, which can be sticky, stretchy, strong, or fluffy. Each has a special use: for making egg sacs, wrapping prey, building webs, or making draglines that the spider trails as it walks along or jumps.

Silk is made by the spinnerets on the spider's abdomen. Liquid threads come out of dozens of tiny nozzles and turn solid as the spider pulls them. Spider silk is an amazing substance. It can be stronger than steel and can stretch twice its own length. Best of all, it's recyclable. A spider can eat its silk when it has finished with it.

A black-and-yellow garden spider will use its legs to turn its prey as it wraps it with silk from its spinnerets.

Spiderwebs are made of silk. Some webs look like old tissue paper draped on hedges. Others hang in messy tangles in the corner of your garage. But the best known is the orb web with its wonderful spiral of sticky threads. A large orb web may contain more than 100 feet of silk thread and can take about an hour to build.

Most spiders build their webs at night, working by touch. Once finished, the spider sits in the middle or at the edge and holds the web so it can feel the vibration of a trapped insect. If the prey is a dangerous wasp, the spider may cut it free. Otherwise it wraps the prey in silk and bites.

Orb web spiders have special claws and non-stick feet so they can walk on their webs without getting stuck.

About the Author

A Creepy-Crawly Kind of Guy!

Nic Bishop is an author and photographer of nature books for kids. He also happens to really love spiders! What some people find creepy and gross is utterly amazing and intriguing to Nic.

Born in England, Nic has lived and traveled around the world. Some of his trips have been in search of the most interesting spiders on the planet. Sometimes his wife, a biologist, comes along. He seeks out spiders and other creatures to show kids what the natural world is all about.

Nic has even raised his own spiders at home. He does this so that he can take photos of them doing things like molting and laying eggs. It is hard to get pictures of spiders doing these things in the wild. Most of Nic's spiders stay in their cages, but a few pesky ones have found ways to escape! Don't worry, though—Nic has always been able to find and catch the little runaways!

Author's Purpose

Nic Bishop includes dramatic photographs and captions alongside the text. How do these text features give you a better understanding of spiders?

Respond to the Text

Summarize

Use relevant details from *Spiders* to summarize how spiders have adapted in order to survive. Information from your Central Idea and Relevant Details Chart may help you.

Central Idea
Detail
Detail
Detail

Write

Do you agree with the author's perspective on spiders? Use these sentence starters to organize your text evidence.

The author thinks that . . .
I know the author's perspective on spiders because . . .
I agree/disagree that . . .

Make Connections

How have spiders adapted to survive? ESSENTIAL QUESTION

Explain how spiders in the rain forest and spiders in the desert might adapt in different ways. TEXT TO WORLD

Nic Bishop

Genre • Trickster Tale

Compare Texts

Read how a spider learns to use his own special ability to save himself.

ANANSI AND THE BIRDS

Anansi always welcomed a challenge. His attempts to fool merchants out of their riches and lions from their jungle thrones made for exciting adventures. Today he would show those haughty birds that he could fly with the best of them.

He begged a feather from every bird he could find to create his own pair of wings, and then he began to practice flying. Anansi's wings **camouflaged** him well, and he looked just like a bird.

"Hoot!" the old owl chided under the moon. "A spider is not meant for the sky. Why do you try to be something you are not?"

"Mind your business, owl," Anansi replied angrily. "You are a **predator**, so go hunt some mice!"

Anansi followed the birds to their feast on the top of a mountain peak. He helped himself to their fare, shoving birds aside to get his fill. When he was full, he fell into a deep sleep.

Michael Slack

Angrily, the birds took back the feathers from his wings and then left, all except for one crow. When Anansi awoke, he realized what had happened and begged the crow to help him get down the mountain.

"Of course," the crow replied slyly as he shoved Anansi over a cliff.

"Aaaayeeee!" shouted Anansi. Unable to fly, he tumbled helplessly through the air.

The old owl appeared before him, asking, "Why didn't you listen, Anansi? You are not a bird!"

"Please help me, owl!" pleaded Anansi.

The owl urged Anansi, "Push in your belly!" When he did, threads of silk shot out behind him. The owl caught them and tied them to a high branch. Dangling by threads, Anansi realized the owl was right. From that day on, he stuck to spinning webs instead of trying to be something he was not.

Make Connections

What helps Anansi survive?
ESSENTIAL QUESTION

In this story Anansi discovered that he had an amazing ability. Discuss some other amazing animal adaptations.
TEXT TO TEXT

Genre • Drama

Ranita
The Frog Princess

by Carmen Agra Deedy
illustrated by Renato Alarcão

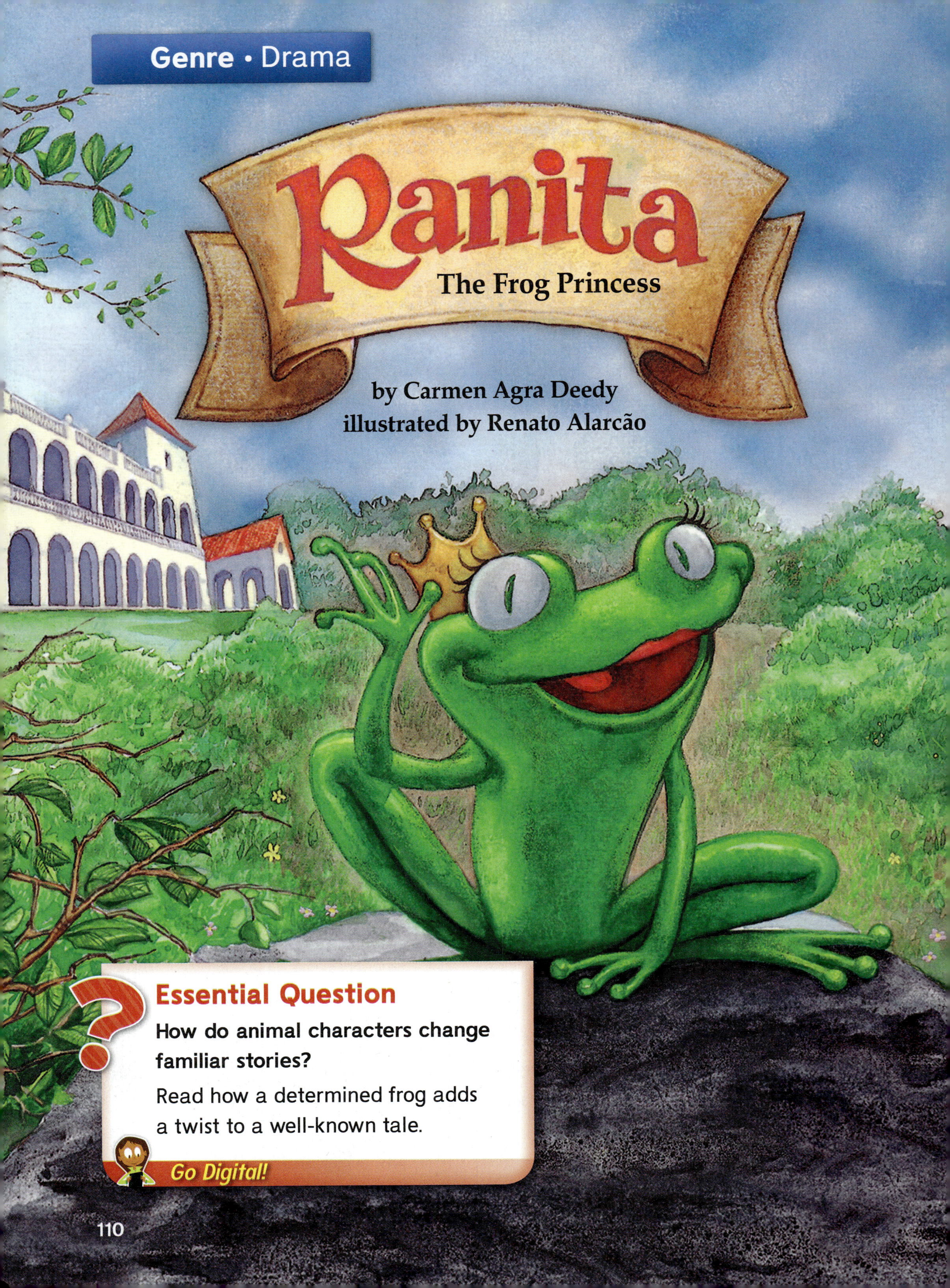

Essential Question

How do animal characters change familiar stories?

Read how a determined frog adds a twist to a well-known tale.

Go Digital!

Setting

Long ago in Mexico. The Viceroy's hunting lodge in Chapultepec forest.

Players

Felipe, the Viceroy's rotten son

Pepe, Felipe's mistreated servant

Ranita, a little frog with a mysterious past

Vieja Sabia, a wise but **cranky** old woman

Viceroy, the representative of the Spanish throne

Viceroy's Wife

Cook

Man One

Man Two

Servant One

Servant Two

Man Three

Extras: Members of hunting party, servants attending dinner, noblemen and ladies

Scene 1

In a forest clearing, men are frantically searching the ground. From a nearby stone well, Ranita watches but remains unnoticed.

Man One: *(Frustrated)* Keep looking! If we don't find that golden arrow—

Man Two: —we'll be on *tortillas* and water for the next month!

(Men, grumbling, all agree.)

(Enter Felipe.)

Felipe: *(Loud and demanding)* Well? Have you found my golden arrow yet?

Man Three: Not yet, Señor!

Felipe: *(Sweetly, hand over heart)* It was a gift from my dear mother. *(Turning suddenly and hissing)* Find it or I will feed you to the jaguars—starting with my bumbling servant, Pepe. It's his fault I missed my mark. Now, out of my sight, all of you!

(Men exit hurriedly.)

Felipe: *(Stomping foot and whining)* I want my golden arrow back!

Ranita: *(Sitting on top of well, holding the golden arrow)* You mean, *this* golden arrow?

Felipe: *(Joyously)* My golden arrow! You found it! You—*(Stops cold)*—you're a frog.

Ranita: You were expecting a Mayan princess, perhaps?

Felipe: *(Rolls eyes)* Well, I wasn't expecting a talking frog!

Ranita: *(Sighs)* I'm under a spell. I don't like to talk about it.

Felipe: *(Pauses to think)* Not my problem. Hand over the arrow.

Ranita: *(Plink! Drops it back down the well)* Hmm, looks like it's your problem now.

Felipe: N-n-noooo! *(Threateningly)* What have you done, you foolish frog?

Ranita: If I am so foolish, how come I am the one with the arrow while you are the one standing there talking to a *rana,* a frog?

Felipe: I would squish you right now—*(Sniffs)*—but you are only a frog.

Ranita: *(Warningly)* You want that golden arrow?

Felipe: *(Suspicious)* In exchange for what?

Ranita: A promise.

Felipe: *(Relieved)* Oh, is that all?

Ranita: A promise is a very serious thing.

Felipe: *(Coughing)* Yes, yes, of course—go on.

Ranita: If I rescue your golden arrow, you must promise to let me eat from your *plato*, sleep in your *cama*, and give me a *beso* when the sun comes up.

Felipe: *(Just stares)* Eat from my plate? Sleep in my bed? KISS you? *That* is disgusting!

Ranita: No promise, no golden arrow.

Felipe: *(Crossing his fingers behind his back)* I promise.

(Ranita fetches the arrow. Felipe bows and runs off.)

Ranita: *Espera*! Wait! I can't hop that fast! *(Hangs her head and begins to cry)* He's gone. Now I'll never break this evil spell.

(Enter wise woman, leaning on two canes.)

Vieja Sabia: It doesn't feel very good, does it?

Ranita: *(Blows nose)* Please, no lectures today, old woman.

Vieja Sabia: My name is Vieja *Sabia*.

Ranita: Sorry, *Wise* Old Woman. *(Sadly)* You've already turned me into a frog. Isn't that enough?

Vieja Sabia: You wouldn't be a frog if you hadn't refused to give me a drink from this well, so long ago.

Ranita: I was a **selfish** child then. I have paid for that, haven't I? I have learned what it is like to be alone and forgotten.

Vieja Sabia: Perhaps you have . . .

Ranita: *(Brightening)* Then, you will turn me into a girl again?

Vieja Sabia: No. But I will take you as far as the Viceroy's hunting lodge. You must make the leap from there.

(Exit Vieja Sabia and Ranita.)

Scene 2

Hunting lodge with Viceroy, his wife, noblemen and women, all seated at long banquet table. Servants scurry in and out with bowls of food.

Servant One: *(Placing bowl of soup before Viceroy) Sopa,* Señor?

Viceroy: (*Exasperated*) *Sí, sí*. Where is Felipe?

Viceroy's Wife: *(Wistfully)* Dear boy. He is probably feeding the birds.

Servant Two: *(Aside)* To the cat.

Servant One: *(Muffles laugh)*

(Enter Felipe.)

Felipe: I am famished. What a day I've had today. First, I lost my golden arrow—

(Shouting from the kitchen can be heard.)

Felipe: *(Louder)*–then I met this ridiculous, demanding–

(Enter Ranita, running from the kitchen chased by cook and servants.)

Felipe: *(Slack-jawed)*–frog.

Cook: You hop back here! *(To servant)* Stop her, right now!

Servant One: *(Tries to catch frog)* Aaaaayyyy! She's a slippery one!

Servant Two: Oooooeeeeee! She bit me!

Cook: Get her, Pepe. *(Pepe catches Ranita under the table, smiles, and lets her go. A* ***commotion*** *follows as the cook and servants chase Ranita.)*

Viceroy: *Basta!* Enough! Who *is* this creature?

Felipe: *(Sneering)* She's the nasty little frog who rescued my golden arrow.

Ranita: And in return he promised to let me eat from his *plato*, sleep in his *cama*, and give me a *beso* when the sun came up.

Viceroy: Did you make this promise?

Felipe: *(Sullen)* I don't remember.

Viceroy's Wife: *(Indignant)* Even if he did—he is the Viceroy's son!

Viceroy: *(Grave) Sí.* And THE VICEROY'S SON KEEPS HIS PROMISES. Pepe! Set a place for our guest.

Felipe: But, Father—

Viceroy's Wife: Ernesto!

Viceroy: *(Slams fist on table) Silencio!* Silence!

(Ranita hops on table. Felipe is too stunned to speak. Viceroy's Wife is glaring.)

Viceroy: Everyone—and I mean *everyone*—EAT!

(Pepe puts bowl down in front of Felipe.)

Felipe: *(Gives a yelp)* Pepe!

Pepe: *(Innocently) Sí?*

Felipe: *(Disgusted)* There is a fly in my soup!

Pepe: It's for the frog.

Viceroy: Excellent. Eat up, Felipe.

Viceroy's Wife: *(Revolted)* Arggh.

Scene 3

(Felipe's bedroom)

Felipe: *(On bed)* I refuse to sleep next to a FROG. Pepe!!!!!!!!

Pepe: *(Enters immediately) Sí,* Señor?

Felipe: *(Snappish)* What took you so long? Hurry—tell my father I can't do this. *(Desperate)* Tell him I'll get warts.

(Enter Viceroy.)

Viceroy: *(Annoyed)* With any luck, you will get one on your oath-breaking tongue, boy.

Felipe: *(Whining)* Father—

Viceroy: You made a promise, Felipe. *(To Pepe)* Help him keep his word, eh, Pepe?

(Exit Viceroy.)

Felipe: *(Throws pillow at Pepe. Falls on bed and begins to wail.)* AAAAAAAYYYYYYY!

Pepe: *(Blows out candle and sits in chair.) Hasta mañana . . .* until tomorrow. Sweet dreams, Felipe.

Felipe: *(Growls)* I will dream of roasted frog legs.

Ranita: I'm telling.

Felipe: Bug breath!

Ranita: Big baby!

Pepe: *(Sighs)* It's going to be a long night.

(Next morning)

Ranita: *(Cheerful) Despierta,* wake up! It's "beso time"!

[Felipe rubs eyes, sees Ranita, and shrieks.]

Felipe: *(Whimpers, clutching his blanket)* It wasn't a bad dream, after all. Forget it, frog! I am not kissing you!

Ranita: *(Stubbornly)* You promised.

Felipe: Well, *(Smiles slowly)* I've just had a better idea. *(Kicks chair to wake his servant)* Pepe!

Pepe: *(Groggy)* Señor!

Felipe: You are sworn to obey me in all things, *sí*?

Pepe: *(Confused) Sí,* Señor.

Felipe: *(Smug)* KISS . . . THE . . . FROG.

(Pepe shrugs and kisses Ranita's cheek.)

(No longer a frog, Ranita is now a beautiful Mayan princess.)

Felipe: *(Dazzled)* I–but who? *(Bowing)* Allow me to introduce myself, I am–

Ranita: –the Spanish Viceroy's Rotten Son. And I am . . . the Mayan Emperor's Lucky Daughter.

(Felipe and Pepe fall on their knees.)

Ranita: I have been enchanted for 200 years.

Felipe: *(Looks up)* You've been a frog for 200 years? What's so LUCKY about that?

Ranita: I'll tell you. As a princess, I could have ended up the wife of a spoiled brat like you. Instead, I found myself a prince . . . *(Takes Pepe's hand)* a prince of a husband, that is.

(Pepe kisses the Princess's hand, while Felipe has a screaming tantrum.)

Epilogue

The same clearing in the forest as in Scene 1

Felipe: *(Kicks a stone)* If they think I'm going to their ridiculous wedding . . . ha! May they have a dozen ugly tadpole children!

(Enter Vieja Sabia.)

Vieja Sabia: *Agua!* Water from the well, my son, before I die of thirst.

Felipe: *(Snarling)* I'm no water boy. I'm the Viceroy's son! Get your own water, you old *cucaracha!*

Vieja Sabia: *(With gentle concern)* Cockroach? It's very rude to speak to your elders that way. Has no one taught you manners?

Felipe: *(Puzzled)* No.

Vieja Sabia: *(Smiling wickedly)* Well *(pointing finger at Felipe),* that is my **specialty**.

*(**POOF** Felipe the Frog hops onto the top of the well.)*

Vieja Sabia: *(to audience)* And now you know how the Frog Prince ended up in that well.

About the Author and Illustrator

Carmen Agra Deedy came to the United States from Cuba in 1960, after a revolution made it dangerous for her family to live there. Hoping for a more peaceful life, Carmen and her family settled in Georgia. Carmen has not forgotten her Cuban heritage. She combines it with the heritage of the southern United States when writing her stories.

Renato Alarcão was born, raised, and currently lives in Rio de Janeiro, Brazil. Among his many art projects was the creation of 13 murals around Paterson and Passaic, New Jersey, all done with a team of artists and local teens.

Author's Purpose

Why did the author write *Ranita, The Frog Princess* as a drama? What do the dialogue and stage directions add?

Respond to the Text

Summarize

Summarize *Ranita, The Frog Princess*. Include the most important clues from the play. Information from your Theme Chart may help you.

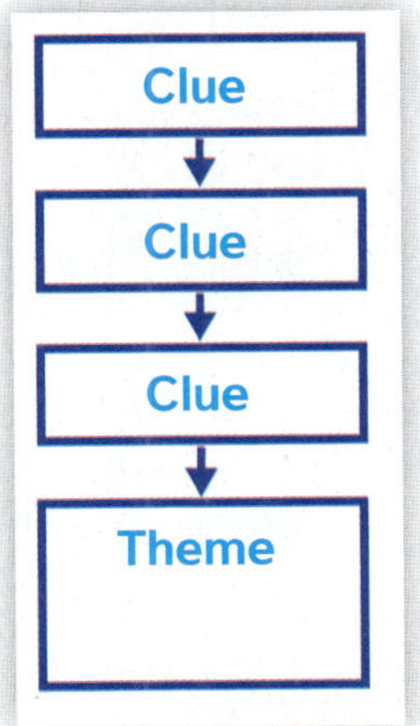

Write

Which character changes the most? Why is this change important to the story? Use these sentence starters to organize your text evidence.

> I think [character's name] changes the most . . .
> In the beginning, . . .
> By the end, . . .

Make Connections

How does the character of Ranita give the story a twist? **ESSENTIAL QUESTION**

Why do people relate to animal characters? **TEXT TO WORLD**

Genre • Tall Tale

Compare Texts

Read how Pecos Bill deals with a snake-like monster.

Pecos Bill and the Bear Lake Monster

Have you ever heard tell of Pecos Bill? The cowboy raised by coyotes for seventeen years? The one who lassoed a tornado out of the sky using a live rattlesnake as a lariat? And dug the Rio Grande because his cattle felt thirsty and needed water? Well, of course you have! But I bet you haven't heard this tale about Pecos Bill. It's not as **familiar**, but it's a doozy.

Pecos Bill was spending some time riding the range and herding cattle with a bunch of cowpokes. Late one night around a campfire, a cowpoke from Utah started telling stories about the Bear Lake monster. He said the monster looked like a snake with tiny legs and was over 100 miles long. One of the monster's favorite tricks was to suddenly appear in front of swimmers just to hear them shriek. Of course, it also ate a couple of those swimmers for lunch. Then there was the time a herd of pronghorn antelope went to drink from the lake. The snake slurped the whole herd down as if it was nothing more than a big gulp of sweet tea. Another time, the monster had an itch on its tail. It got so **frustrated** trying to scratch that itch, the waves from the lake flooded the shore for days.

Pecos Bill told the cowpoke that he'd go wrestle the Bear Lake monster until it promised to behave itself. "I do enjoy a good wrestling match," he said with a big grin. Bill had **attitude** to burn!

The next morning, Pecos Bill jumped on his horse, Widow-maker, and took off for Utah. Later that day, some ranchers swore they saw a comet shooting across the horizon, but it was just the sparks from Widow-maker's horseshoes as he galloped across the rocks.

When Bill got to Bear Lake he was mighty hot and thirsty. He waded right into the cool clear water and swam out a mile or two. All of a sudden, the water churned and foamed and ten-foot waves started crashing over Bill's head. A monster reared out of the water with its mouth open and roared. Its roar shook the surrounding mountains. Bill had seen caverns smaller than that snake's mouth. Without missing a beat, Pecos Bill jumped onto the monster's neck and slipped a loop of rope into its mouth. Then he held the ends like reins.

To say the snake was as **cranky** as a grizzly that's been stung by a swarm of hornets is understating the matter. The monster twisted and turned its scaly back trying to buck Bill off. But Bill didn't budge. The winds shrieked and howled around Bill, whipping up the waves to higher and higher peaks. So much water got splashed around that the whole lake turned into a giant waterspout!

Two days later, Bill wrestled the monster onto the shore of Bear Lake. He picked it up by its tail and flung it around and around his head, whirling it faster and faster. Then he let go. The monster flew through the air all the way across the Atlantic Ocean until it landed in Loch Ness, Scotland. A loch is a big stretch of water similar to a lake. The monster snake from Bear Lake, Utah, still lives in the loch to this day. Only now it's so shy and frightened that only a few people have ever seen it. People round those parts gave the monster a new name. They call it the Loch Ness monster, or "Nessie" for short.

Make Connections

How does the monster change from the beginning of the tale to the end? **ESSENTIAL QUESTION**

What character traits do Ranita and Pecos Bill share? **TEXT TO TEXT**

Genre • Poetry

The Sandpiper

At the edge of tide
He stops to wonder,
Races through
The lace of thunder.

On toothpick legs
Swift and brittle,
He runs and pipes
And his voice is little.

But small or not,
He has a notion
To outshout
The Atlantic Ocean.

–Frances Frost

Essential Question

How are writers inspired by animals?

Read how poets visualize animal characteristics and habits.

Go Digital!

Bat

All day bats drowse in houses' eaves
Like tents collapsed for storage,
But when dusk darkens, like fall leaves,
They loosen. Then they forage

For juicy June bugs, meaty moths,
Mosquitoes (eaten rare).
They're scary. But there's nothing like
A bat to clear the air.

–X.J. Kennedy

The Grasshopper Springs

The grasshopper springs
and catches the summer wind
with his outstretched wings.

—James W. Hackett

Fireflies at Dusk

Fireflies dance at dusk,
tiny lanterns in the dark
lighting my way home.

—Evelyn Rose

Respond to the Text

Summarize

Use details from "Bat" to summarize the poem. Information from your Character Perspective Chart may help you.

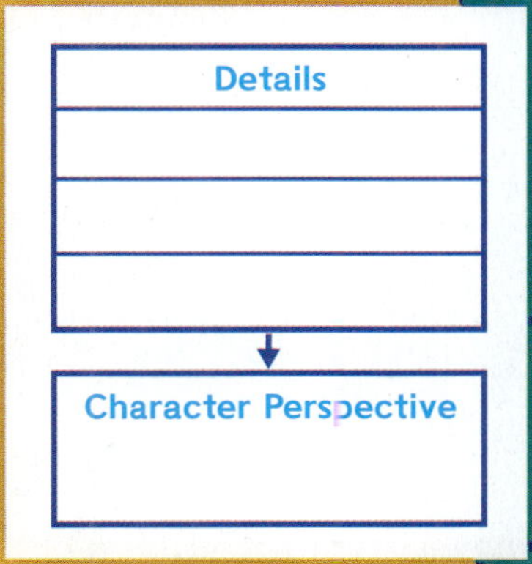

Write

What can you learn about the speakers in the poems from how they describe the animals? Use these sentence starters to help organize your text evidence.

In . . . the speaker says . . .
This shows that . . .
I think that the speaker . . .

Make Connections

In what ways did these animals inspire writers? ESSENTIAL QUESTION

What are some other animals around the world that deserve their own poems? Why do you think they would inspire writers? TEXT TO WORLD

Genre • Poetry

Compare Texts

Read how two poets compare weather conditions to animals.

Fog

The fog comes
on little cat feet.

It sits looking
over harbor and city
on silent haunches
and then moves on.

–Carl Sandburg

White Cat Winter

White cat Winter
prowls
the farm,
tiptoes
soft
through withered corn,
creeps
along low walls
of stone,
falls asleep
beside
the barn.

–Tony Johnston

Make Connections

In what ways are fog and winter like a cat? **ESSENTIAL QUESTION**

Writers often make comparisons. Talk about how each writer's creative comparisons helped you visualize an animal. **TEXT TO TEXT**

Reprinted by arrangement with the author and Writers House LLC, acting as agent for the author.

Genre • Narrative Nonfiction

Essential Question

How are all living things connected?

Read about the relationship between buffalo, humans, and the land.

Go Digital!

The BUFFALO *Are* BACK

by **Jean Craighead George** • *paintings by* **Wendell Minor**

In a time long ago, an orange buffalo calf was born. He wobbled to his feet and blinked. A lark flew to the top of a six-foot blade of grass and sang as sweetly as a panpipe. A town of prairie dogs barked. The green-gold grasses of the plains **rippled** like waves from horizon to horizon. On that day in the mid-1800s seventy-five million buffalo roamed in North America. In little more than fifty years, there would be almost none.

What happened? The answer is a story of the American Indians, the buffalo, and the grass.

The American Indians

On the day that the calf was born the air was smoky. The Indians who lived on the plains were setting the grasses ablaze, as they had for thousands of years. The fire was good for the prairie. The calf may have been afraid of the flames, but they kept the trees from taking over the grasslands. The fire's ashes put nutrients into the soil, making the grass healthier for the buffalo that ate it.

By taking care of the grass, the Indians took care of the buffalo. In return, the buffalo took care of the Indians and the plains. Buffalo were the Indians' food and were used to make their shelter and clothing. The buffalo never ate too much grass, and their sharp hooves helped rainwater reach into the soil, keeping the prairie healthy.

The orange calf learned to roll in a dust wallow. He watched the prairie chickens show off their exotic feathers. From the Mississippi to the Rocky Mountains and from the Gulf of Mexico up into Canada, the buffalo herds grazed the Great Plains.

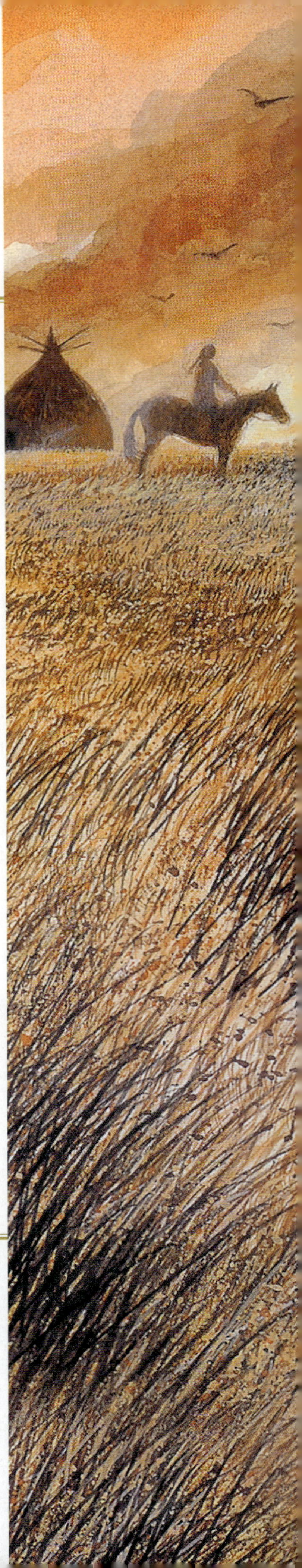

The Buffalo

In the mid-1800s, change came to the plains. First it was white fur hunters. They stacked the beautiful buffalo hides in pointed canoes and sold them east for profit. Then the American explorers came, who shot many animals for fun. Buffalo made good targets for the hunters because they are big and often stand still.

But it was settlers from the East and the American government that killed almost all of the buffalo herds. After the Civil War, the government bought huge tracts of land from the Indians. They forced many Indians to go to reservations and sold the land to settlers. Families from Europe and the East Coast rushed west to settle the rich black prairie land.

But there was trouble on the plains. The government broke its treaties with the Indians. So the Indians fought back and won several battles against the United States Army. Then the government saw another way to defeat the Indians. Soldiers and settlers were encouraged to shoot every buffalo they saw, or drive whole herds over cliffs. Without the buffalo for food, shelter, and clothing, the Indians could not survive on the plains.

Most of the last wild buffalo went down in dust and gunfire.

Said the great Sioux Chief Sitting Bull, who defeated General George A. Custer at the battle of Little Big Horn: "A cold wind blew across the prairie when the last buffalo fell—a death-wind for my people."

And, the settlers soon discovered, a death-wind for the prairie.

The Grass

With the death of the buffalo, the Indian Wars were over. The settlers faced a new fight—the battle of the grasses. Over the eons the prairie grasses had adapted to the Great Plains' frequent **droughts** by growing tough roots to hold in moisture. These roots were wide and deep and held the rich soil in place. The buffalo's sharp hooves, and the Indians' prairie fires, had helped keep the grasses healthy. But the new settlers did not understand the importance of the grass.

Early settlers were ranchers and cowboys. They brought fences and cattle to the plains. The cattle did not roam, so they ate too much of the grass within their fences. Their flat hooves packed the earth. Air and rainwater no longer reached into the soil.

Later settlers wanted to farm the land, so they tore out the grass and planted crops to sell. Steel plows and steam tractors were invented to conquer the grassland and "the great plow up" began. Wheat, corn, and soybeans were planted. These crops have shallow, **fragile** roots.

At first, the crops **flourished** in the prairie sunshine and timely rains. New railroads carried the harvests to distant markets.

Now not one orange buffalo wobbled to its feet. The larks that had once eaten the insects living in the grass did not sing. The prairie dogs were silent. Without the buffalo, without the grasses, and without the Indians to care for them, the prairie was in danger. The settlers would soon learn why.

Drought came, as it had before. Billions of grasshoppers swept down on the plains. Long ago, when drought came and grasshoppers chewed the healthy grass, the plants would grow back. Their tough roots always survived. But when the fragile crops were chewed by grasshoppers, nothing grew back.

Suddenly, the grasshoppers laid eggs and flew on. The farmers replanted their crops. They did not know they had begun to destroy the prairie.

When the buffalo lived on the prairie, their sharp hooves helped rain reach deep into the earth, and the tough roots of the grass held in the wet. Now, no moisture remained in the soil. The farmers' crops withered and died.

In the 1930s, the plowed earth finally **crumbled** to dust. The wind eroded the land, picking up the dust and boiling it into terrifying black clouds. The clouds rained dirt. Barns, farms, houses, and towns were buried beneath the dust. People coughed, choked, and grew ill. Many died.

Hungry and penniless, plains farmers and townsmen packed up their belongings and sold their worthless land to the government. The prairie soil had blown away. The land was no longer rich. The farmers climbed into old cars and left. The "great plow up" had been a disaster. In just over fifty years, it had destroyed the buffalo, the protective prairie grasses, and the Indians who had cared for both.

What could be done to save the prairie?

The Prairie Comeback

In the beginning of the 1900s, Americans elected a president who had once been a hunter on the Great Plains. He knew and loved the land and wanted to protect it for future generations. Nature-loving President Theodore Roosevelt especially wanted to save the buffalo. He was very fond of the great American grazer with its humped back and shaggy coat. So, he sent out scouts to look for wild buffalo.

The scouts came home with nothing—all the scouts but one. A naturalist named W. T. Hornaday looked and looked and would not give up. On a tip from a Crow Indian he rode his horse into a secluded meadow in Montana, a place that had been hidden away from the world. There before him grazed three hundred buffalo. A little orange calf wobbled to her feet and blinked. A lark flew to a blade of grass and sang as sweetly as a panpipe.

There had been seventy-five million buffalo on the plains. Now there were three hundred left in the wild. People who understood the land, led by Hornaday, knew the buffalo had to be saved. The president helped.

Roosevelt established the National Bison Range in Montana and made it illegal to shoot buffalo. Over the years, more land was set aside in western states for the great grazing herds, which were beginning to grow.

Thanks to Roosevelt, the orange calf in Montana romped with other calves and rolled in the dust. Her herd grew in numbers. Many were sent to national parks and wildlife refuges that had been established to start new herds.

As the dust storms attacked farms and cities, the government worked to save the prairie. Farmers were taught to plant and grow crops in curves, instead of straight lines. The contour plowing helped to prevent dirt from blowing away. Government workers planted trees with deep roots, to hold moisture in the soil and break the wind. When the rains returned, farmers planted grass between their curving rows of corn to hold the soil in place. Crops flourished again.

One day a young girl walked into her house in Kansas waving a six-foot blade of grass.

"Where did you find that?" her father asked. "That's buffalo grass. It's been **extinct** for years—or so we thought."

"In my schoolyard," she said.

"That is land that was never plowed," her father told her.

Like many older people living on the prairie, he longed to see the beautiful grasses again.

"Let's try to find more of these tall native grasses," he said. Perhaps the tall grass could come back to the plains.

People like the girl's father rounded up kids, parents, botanists, farmers, and merchants. They searched the places the plows had never reached—graveyards, old railroad beds, and crumbling fencerows. There they found small stands of the native grasses: bluestem, gamma, bunch, and buffalo grass. They raised them and sowed the seeds on abandoned farms and public lands. The grasses flourished, tall and graceful.

Groups that work to protect nature purchased thirty-thousand acres where native grasses had been grown. This nature preserve, in Kansas, is called the Tall Grass Prairie Preserve. Into the tall grass they released three hundred buffalo.

One morning not too long ago, a young man just out of graduate school galloped his horse across the Prairie Preserve, counting buffalo for the buffalo census. Suddenly he reined in his horse. An orange calf wobbled to his feet and blinked.

"Welcome, little calf," the Wichita Indian youth called. "You are America's two hundred thousand and eighty-first buffalo."

A lark flew to the top of a six-foot blade of grass and sang as sweetly as a panpipe. The buffalo are back.

ABOUT THE AUTHOR AND ILLUSTRATOR

Jean Craighead George started writing when she was in the third grade, and she's been writing ever since. As a child she enjoyed camping and hiking, and soon she found a love for reading and writing about the great outdoors. In all, she's written more than 100 books! George says that a young person who wants to be a writer should "read, write and talk to people, hear their knowledge, hear their problems. Be a good listener. The rest will come."

Wendell Minor grew up on a farm in Illinois on flat land much like the plains described in *The Buffalo Are Back*. One of his earliest memories is of watching a mother robin feed her babies outside his classroom window. He was supposed to be reading, but watching nature was more fascinating to him. Now he illustrates nature scenes in books and hopes they will keep young people reading instead of looking out the window—at least for a little while.

Author's Purpose

Did the author write *The Buffalo Are Back* mainly to inform, entertain, or persuade? Use details from the selection to support your response.

(t) Jean Craighead George, (b) Wendell Minor

Respond to the Text

Summarize

Summarize *The Buffalo Are Back.* Information from your Central Idea and Relevant Details Chart may help you.

Central Idea
Detail
Detail
Detail

Write

Think about how the author uses repetition. Why does she begin and end the selection with the birth of an orange buffalo calf? Use these sentence starters to organize your text evidence.

Jean Craighead George states, ". . ."
Her point is that . . .
This point is important because . . .

Make Connections

Tell how humans, buffalo, and the land are connected. **ESSENTIAL QUESTION**

How would people be affected if certain animals were removed from our ecosystem? **TEXT TO WORLD**

Genre • Expository Text

Compare Texts

Read how a barred owl is part of the food chain in the forest.

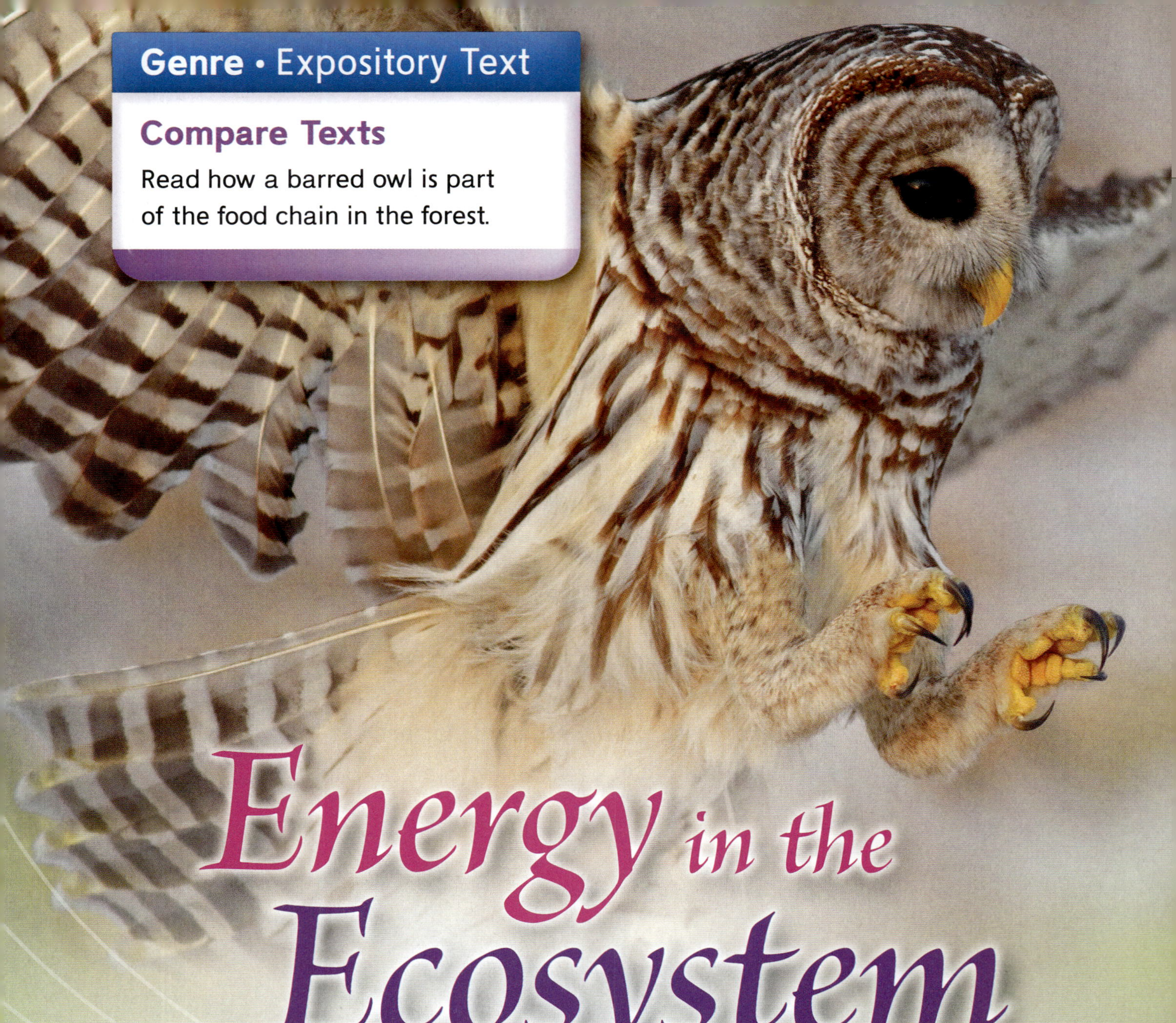

Energy in the Ecosystem

In spring, the climate of the eastern woodlands warms up after the cold winter. Daylight lasts longer. By the middle of spring, the sun's energy has awakened forests. Trees bud and put forth leaves. Grasses and ferns pop up from the forest floor. Songbirds return. The woods come alive with sound. At night the forest echoes with peepers, bullfrogs, and the *yip-yip* of the red fox. One call can be heard often from the forest. It sounds like, "Who cooks for you? Who cooks for you all?"

HOO HOO Hoo-hoo! HOO HOO Hoo awww!

This is the call of the barred owl, the night hunter of the forest. From its perch high in oak or hickory trees, the owl studies the forest floor. Far below, voles and mice eat grasses and grubs. They do not see the hunter watching them.

The Living Woodlands

All forest plants, animals, and other *organisms*, or living things, depend on nonliving elements. A forest's **ecosystem** needs a balance of sunlight, moisture, temperature, and soil nutrients. Any **imbalance** in these nonliving elements will harm the forest. For example, a **drought**, or long period without rain, will kill plants. Without plants, animals die.

In forests of the eastern United States, energy from sunlight and nutrients in water and soil allow plants to grow. These plants form the first link in the forest food chain. A food chain is the path that energy takes from one organism to another in the form of food. Energy from the sun flows through the food chain, joining all the plants and animals in an ecosystem. Several links in the chain join plants with the creature that sits in the treetops, the barred owl. The energy from this bird's feeding plays an important role in the first links of the food chain. How?

Below: Layers of plant life in a forest produce food by using energy from the sun and nutrients in soil and water.

Forest Food Chain

The forest food chain begins with organisms that make their own food. They are called *producers*. Grasses, trees, and other green plants are producers that feed forest animals. Organisms that cannot make their own food are known as *consumers*. Any animal that eats plants or plant products is a consumer. Some forest consumers, such as rabbits, are *herbivores* that eat only plants. Other mammals, such as voles and mice, are *omnivores*. They eat plants as well as insects, worms, and grubs.

Higher up on the food chain are organisms that eat other consumers. In the forest, birds of prey such as owls occupy this link in the chain. Owls are *carnivores*, which means they eat only other animals. Since owls cannot make their own food, they are also consumers in the food chain.

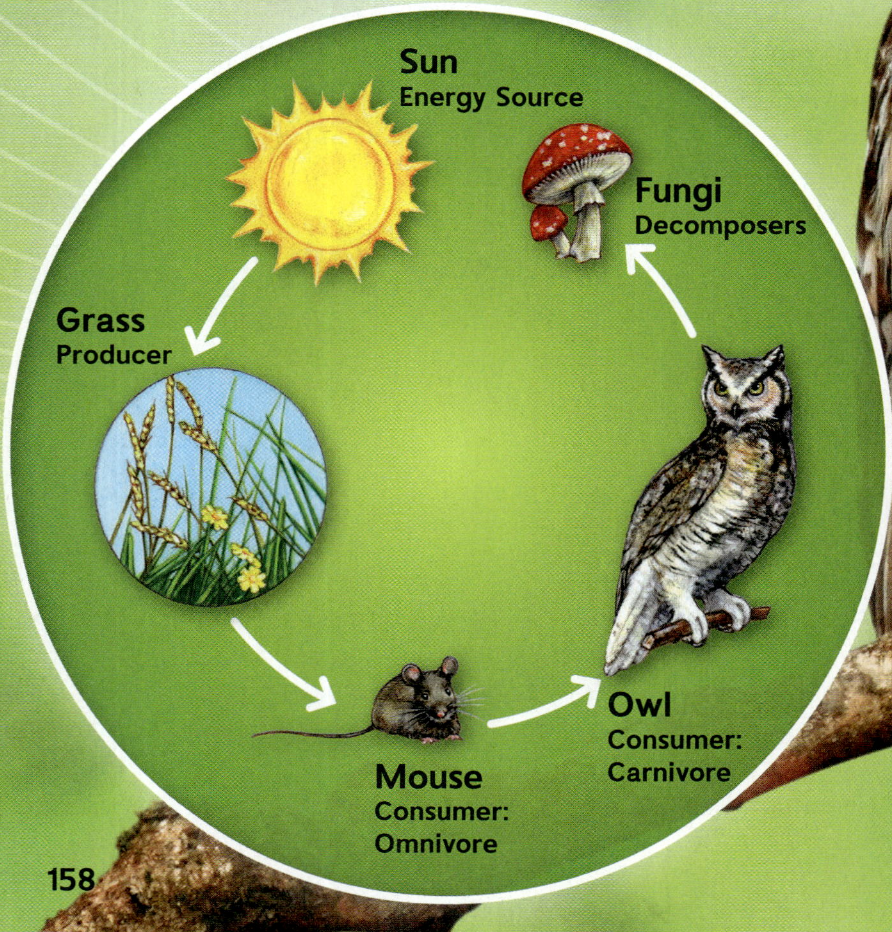

(l) Linda Ayriss; (r) Corbis Super RF/Alamy

Back to the Cycle

Fungi play a different role in the food chain. They are *decomposers*. Decomposers recycle all wastes and remains from plants and animals back into the ecosystem. The dead material becomes soil nutrients, which help plants grow. With sunlight and water, the cycle begins again.

When an owl eats a mouse or vole, it digests the meat and organs of those animals. However, owls cannot digest fur, teeth, or bones. These are formed into oval pellets. The owl throws up these balls of fur and bone after every meal. Owl pellets are often found on the ground around owl nesting places. They provide food and shelter for moths, beetles, and fungi.

If you are near a forest at night, listen carefully. Do you hear it?

"Who cooks for you? Who cooks for you all?"

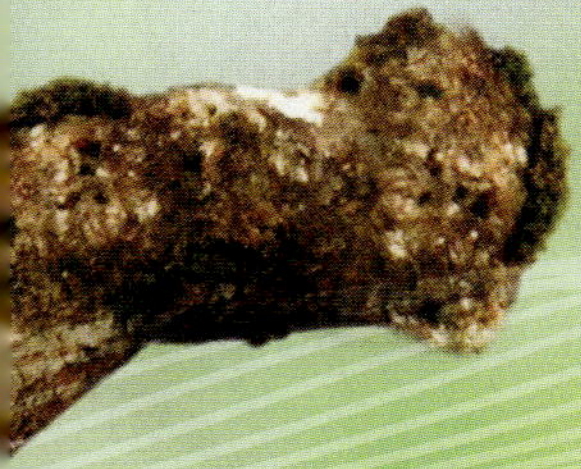

Right: Owl pellets are an important source of food and shelter for some insects and fungi. The bones, teeth, and fur that make up each pellet cannot be digested by owls.

Make Connections

How does a food chain connect all living things? **ESSENTIAL QUESTION**

How is a forest's ecosystem similar to other ecosystems? **TEXT TO TEXT**

Genre • Folktale

THE Secret Message

Based on a poem
by Rumi

BY
Mina Javaherbin

ILLUSTRATED BY
Bruce Whatley

Essential Question

What are some messages in animal stories?

Read about a merchant who, without realizing it, delivers a secret message.

Go Digital!

Many years ago, a wealthy Persian merchant kept a parrot from India in his shop at the bazaar. The bird, who once flew free in the Indian forests, now lived in a small cage.

Colorful tiles covered the shop's domed ceiling and walls, but the parrot preferred the beauty of the forest. All day the bird sang of longing. But the merchant would not let him go, because the parrot could sing and talk, and his bright feathers **attracted** customers to the shop. The parrot had helped the merchant become rich and famous.

One day, a group of wealthy traders walked by. Their sparkling cloaks reminded the parrot of the forest stars, and he called out to them. Enchanted by the bird, the traders entered the shop. Once inside, they purchased all the merchant's goods. The merchant rewarded the parrot with a large, golden cage.

That night at home, the merchant announced, "I'm going to India to buy more goods for my shop."

Everyone wanted something from India. The cook asked for extraordinary spices; the merchant's daughters asked for **dazzling** silk robes; and his wife **requested** brilliant jewels. The merchant promised to buy all the gifts.

Before he left on his trip, the merchant asked the parrot if he wanted anything from the place that had been his home. "An exotic flower or a silver cup, perhaps?"

"I don't want any gifts," the parrot said with a sigh. "But when you pass through the forest and see other parrots like me flying free, tell them I live far away. Tell them I miss flying with them, I miss their sweet voices, I miss the smell of the trees—"

The merchant interrupted, "But, Parrot, you live inside this wonderful golden cage with three swings."

"You're right," said the parrot. "Tell them about this cage."

"I will," said the merchant.

On the Silk Road, the caravan **trudged** over dry sand dunes, passed through steep green valleys, and braved dangerously narrow mountain paths. After a long journey, the travelers crossed the Indus River.

At the city of Gilgit, they saw temple dancers, monkeys, elephants, and cows enjoying a river festival. When they noticed the yogis who stayed calm in twisted poses, they knew they had arrived in India.

After the merchant made his purchases for the shop, he found brilliant jewels for his wife and sent men to the far corners of the market to buy rare spices for the cook. At the silk market, the merchant could not make up his mind—**fabrics** waved on display in a carnival of colors. Finally, the merchant picked a soft shade of pink with small red flowers and a bold blue fabric with a yellow leaf pattern for his daughters.

On the way back to Persia, the merchant's caravan passed through a thick tropical forest. He heard voices like his parrot's. He saw beautiful birds like his, flying free among the trees.

"Stop the caravan," ordered the merchant. He stepped down and asked the birds to gather around. "I have a message from your friend," he said. The parrots sat on twisted banyan tree branches and listened.

"Far away from India, I own a parrot that looks like you. He sent a message: he remembers flying in the forest, hearing your sweet voices, and smelling the trees. He lives inside a beautiful cage that I bought for him. It has three golden swings inside."

The birds listened carefully. Suddenly, one by one, they fell off the branches with their backs on the ground and their feet in the air. Their bodies lay still under the shadow of the banyan canopy.

The shocked merchant could not believe his eyes. The parrots stayed stiff on the ground. After a while, the merchant ordered his caravan to move on.

Once he was back in Persia, the merchant's family and friends celebrated his arrival with delicious food prepared by the cook, using his new Indian spices. Dancers paraded in the courtyard to tambourines and harp as the merchant told tall tales about his journey. He left out the part about the parrots in the forest.

At his shop, the merchant busied himself with storing the new goods. He avoided the parrot.

One quiet afternoon the parrot asked, "Merchant, when you were in India, did you deliver my message?"

"Parrot, something bad happened in the forest. I don't wish to talk about it."

"For years I have sung for you in a cage," said the parrot. "I didn't ask for jewels or spices. I only asked you to deliver a message for me. Is this how you repay me?"

"Well, if you insist, I will tell you. I did indeed deliver your message to the birds. They listened, and then, suddenly, they all fell off the tree branches, not one breathing a single breath."

The parrot listened. Then, as soon as the merchant stopped talking, he fell off his golden swing with his feet pointing up to the sky. Not a single breath came out of him.

The merchant ran to the cage. "What have I done?" he cried. "Have I caused your death?"

The parrot stayed still at the bottom of the cage. The merchant knew that this parrot would never bring another customer to his shop.

He took the stiff bird out of the cage and placed him on the counting table.

In an instant, the parrot fluttered his wings and **soared** up to the shop's domed ceiling.

"You're alive!" the merchant said.

"More alive than ever, Merchant, thanks to the message from my friends in India!"

Then the parrot flew away through the hole in the domed ceiling, and all the way to India, to fly free among his friends.

About the Author and Illustrator

Mina Javaherbin would rather read than do anything else in the world, but she also enjoys eating, talking, and writing. As a child, she filled journals and diaries with songs, poems, and stories. *The Secret Message* is based on a bedtime story her father told her when she was growing up in Iran. "Years later, when I studied Persian literature," says Mina, "I discovered my favorite bedtime story was actually an ancient poem."

Bruce Whatley loves how characters sketched on paper come to life in his illustrations. His favorite stories to illustrate are those with an unexpected twist at the end. Old movies and television shows have a great influence on his work, as do early American artists. Always interested in learning new art techniques, Whatley hopes to try animation in the future.

Mina Javaherbin

Bruce Whatley

Author's Purpose

Mina Javaherbin based *The Secret Message* on a poem that was written long ago. Did she write this story mainly to inform, persuade, or entertain? How do you know?

Respond to the Text

Summarize

Use details from the selection to summarize *The Secret Message*. Information from your Theme Chart may help you.

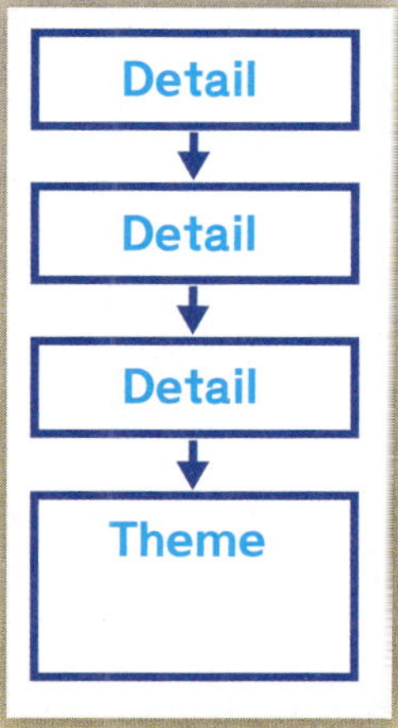

Write

Think about how the author structures the events in this folktale. How does the secret message change things for both the parrot and the merchant? Use these sentence starters to organize your text evidence.

> The author begins the folktale by describing . . .
> She uses cause and effect to show . . .
> This helps me figure out that the parrot . . .

Make Connections

Tell how the merchant delivered a secret message even though he did not know it. **ESSENTIAL QUESTION**

Folktales often include a central message for the people who read them. What lesson does this folktale teach about the importance of freedom? **TEXT TO WORLD**

Genre • Fable

Compare Texts

Read how a goat learns an important lesson.

The Fox and the Goat

Francis Fox had already gobbled one mouse, but one was never enough to fill his stomach. His greed got him into trouble as he chased the second mouse. He did not see the old well and tumbled nose over tail down into the cold water. Looking up, Francis saw a blue circle of sky and jumped as high as possible—but he could not reach the top.

"How will I get out?" howled Francis.

Just then, the sound of chewing echoed down in the well, and Francis saw Gordo Goat at the edge of the well's opening. Francis knew that Gordo would do anything for food and water. He made loud slurping sounds to attract the old goat's attention.

"This water is delicious," the sly fox shouted. "Don't you want a thirst-quenching drink?"

Richard Downs

Gordo had been chewing on thorns and weeds, and he definitely needed water to wash down his food. "Sure," he said, "but how will I get out?"

"We'll help each other," said Francis with a smile that showed all of his teeth.

Gordo was not sure whether Francis was being honest, but the goat was very thirsty. He jumped into the well, and when his thirst was quenched he looked up.

"Now . . . how do we get out of here?" he asked.

"Easy," said Francis. "Put your front hooves on the wall, and I'll climb on your back and jump out of the well. Then I'll go get help for you," said Francis, grinning. "Honest."

"Okay, but hurry back," said Gordo, placing his hooves against the stones.

In a flash, Francis leaped onto Gordo's back and then climbed onto the goat's horns to spring out of the well. Francis looked back down at the goat and waved. "Didn't anyone ever tell you to look before you leap?" The fox chuckled as he ran off, leaving Gordo to find his own way out of the well.

Make Connections

What lesson does the goat learn in the fable? **ESSENTIAL QUESTION**

What lessons can we learn from animal characters? **TEXT TO TEXT**

Genre • Realistic Fiction

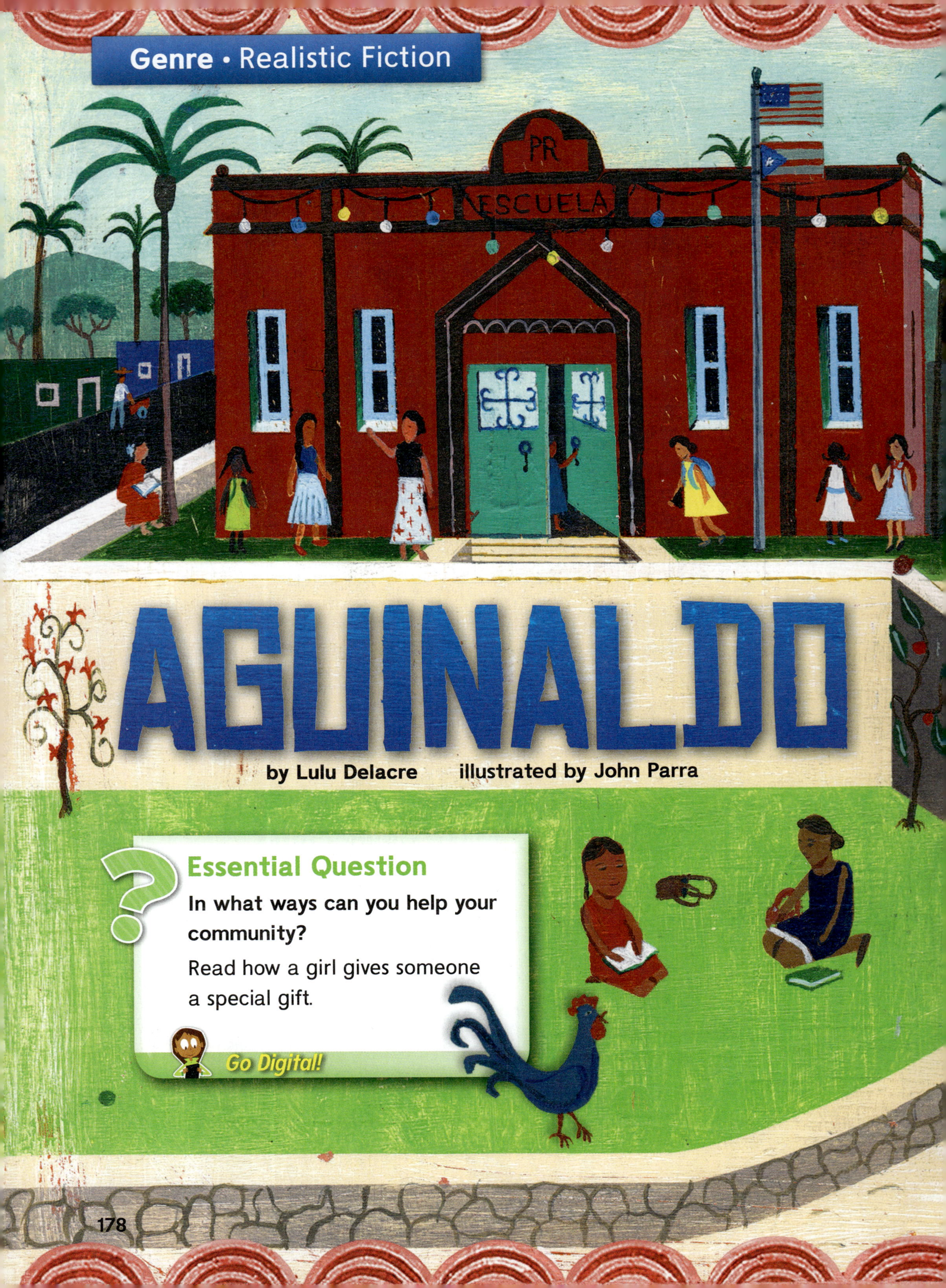

AGUINALDO

by Lulu Delacre illustrated by John Parra

Essential Question

In what ways can you help your community?

Read how a girl gives someone a special gift.

Go Digital!

When I was growing up in Puerto Rico, I went to a small girls' school. Every December, Señorita Antonia, our teacher, insisted that the sixth grade visit the nursing home in Santurce. Bringing Christmas cheer to the old and infirm was an experience she felt all sixth graders should have. But the year I was in fifth grade, Señorita Antonia decided our class was **mature** enough to join the older girls and have that experience, too.

"I'm not going," I whispered to my friend Margarita.

"You have to, Marilia," she said. "Everyone has to go."

All of my classmates looked forward to the trip. Some, because they liked the rackety bus ride to anywhere. Some, because they could skip school for the day and that meant no homework. And others, because they believed that to do a sixth-grade activity in fifth grade was very special. But ever since my only grandma died in a nursing home, the thought of going back to one made me feel sad. I didn't want to go.

As I sat at my desk coloring the Christmas card that I was **assigned** to make for a resident, I tried to figure out how I could skip this field trip. Maybe they would let me help at the library. Maybe I could write a special book report at school while they were out. Or better yet, I could wake up ill and stay home from school. As soon as the recess bell rang, I ran over to the library to try out my first plan.

"*Hola*, Marilia," Señora Collazo greeted me.

"*Hola*, Señora Collazo," I said, smiling sweetly. "I came to ask you if I could stay here tomorrow to help you paint posters for the book fair. I really don't mind spending the whole day at the library."

"Aren't you going on a field trip tomorrow?" Señora Collazo asked.

"My class is going. But I could be excused if you need my help." The librarian thanked me and said that if I wanted to help I could join the other students who had already volunteered to stay after school to do the posters. Biting my lower lip, I left the library in a hurry. It was time to try my second plan.

Outside, seated on the polished tiles of the covered corridor, my friends were having a tournament of jacks. But I didn't join them. Instead, I marched right to the sixth-grade classroom. Señorita Antonia was grading papers at her desk as I went in.

"Señorita Antonia," I said softly.

"Yes, Marilia," Señorita Antonia answered.

I stared for a moment at the buckles of my shoes. Then without looking up, I took a deep breath, swept back my black curls, and asked, "May I stay in school tomorrow to do an extra book report?"

"I'm afraid not, Marilia," Señorita Antonia said firmly. "Tomorrow is our trip to the nursing home. Both the fifth and sixth grades are going. But if you want to do an extra book report, you can do it over the weekend."

I glanced across the room to the trays of *besitos de coco,* the coconut sweets that the sixth graders had prepared to bring to the nursing-home **residents** as an *aguinaldo*. *Aguinaldos,* surprise Christmas gifts, were fun to receive. But still, I wasn't going, so it wasn't my concern. I whispered thank you to the teacher, and left.

That evening at dinnertime, I put my third plan into action. To my parents' surprise, I had two big helpings of rice and kidney beans, two helpings of Mami's *tembleque* for dessert, and three glasses of mango juice. I *never* ate so much. I figured that with all this food, I was sure to get indigestion. I went to bed and waited. I tossed and turned. I waited for several hours expecting a stomachache any second, but instead, the heavy meal made me tired and I fell sound asleep.

"Marilia, get dressed!" Mami called early the next morning. "We have to leave soon for school!"

How unlucky. I woke up feeling quite well. There was only one thing left to do, I ran to the bathroom, let the hot water run, and drank a full glass of it. Then I went back to bed.

"Marilia," Mami came in. "Get up! What is going on with you?"

"I feel warm, Mami," I mumbled.

Mami looked at me with concern. She touched my forehead and my neck. Then she left the room and in a few minutes came back with the thermometer in her hands. I opened my mouth and she slipped it under my tongue.

When the time was up, Mami pulled the thermometer out and read it.

"One hundred and six degrees?" she exclaimed. "That's impossible. You look perfectly fine to me."

After a little questioning, I confessed what I had done. I told Mami how much I didn't want to go on the field trip.

"You know, Marilia," she advised, "you might enjoy yourself after all. Besides, I've already promised Señorita Antonia two trays of *tembleque* to bring as an *aguinaldo* to the residents of the home."

There was no way out. I had to go.

* * *

In the big lobby of the nursing home, paper streamers hung from the tall windows. The residents were **scattered** everywhere. Some were seated on the couches. Some were in wheelchairs. Some walked clutching onto their walkers. A nurse hovered over a group of men as she dispensed pills. Señorita Antonia took out her guitar and at the sound of the first bar we began to sing a medley of carols. Several of the girls accompanied with *maracas*, *güiro*, and *palitos*.

Meanwhile, the residents clapped and sang along while a sixth grader passed around our cards for us to give to them later. As I watched how happy our music made the residents, memories of my grandma rushed to me, making me dizzy with sadness. Suddenly, I saw that everybody was visiting with the residents. I was alone. I didn't feel like joining one of the groups. Maybe I could quietly slip away until the visit was over. I hoped it would be soon. Then I noticed a chair against the yellow wall. I sat there still holding the card I had made.

Across the room there was a frail old lady in a wheelchair. She was alone, too. I looked at my card again. It was rather pretty. I had painted it with shades of blue and gold. Maybe I could just hand it to her and leave. It might brighten her day. So **gingerly**, I crossed the lobby and stood next to her.

"Who is there?" the old lady asked as she coquettishly fixed her silver bun with the light touch of her manicured hand.

"My name is Marilia," I said. "I brought you a card."

"*Dios te bendiga,*" the old woman said. "God bless you."

She reached for the card but her hand was nowhere near it. Her gaze was lost in the distance, and I knelt down to place the card in her hand. It was then that I saw the big clouds in her eyes. She was blind. *What was the use of a card if you couldn't see it?* I felt cheated. I stood up to go back to my chair.

"My name is Elenita," she said as I tried to slip away. "Tell me, Marilia, what does your card look like?"

I knelt down beside her and, in as vivid detail as I could, described the three wise men I had drawn. Then, Elenita's curious fingers caressed every inch of the card. She couldn't have enjoyed it more if she had seen it.

When the coconut sweets were passed around, she mischievously asked for two.

"I bet you are not supposed to eat one of these," she giggled.

"No," I replied. "Señorita Antonia told us that the sweets were just for residents."

"Well," she whispered. "Nobody said I couldn't give you one of *mine*."

I liked Elenita. I placed the *besito de coco* in my mouth and relished it even more. Especially since I wasn't supposed to have it. I enjoyed being her partner in mischief. After that, she asked me if I liked music and if I knew how to dance.

"*Ay*," I said. "I love to listen to music and dance."

Then she told me how, when she was young, she had been a great dancer.

"I used to dance so well that men would line up for a chance to dance with me. I had many, many suitors at one time," she said. "I had suitors that serenaded me in the evening and others that brought me flowers. But I didn't go out with all of them. You have to be **selective**, you know."

Too soon we were interrupted by Señorita Antonia. It was time to get on the bus and return to school. I didn't want to leave.

"Thank you for the card, Marilia," Elenita said. She opened her hand and gestured for me to give her mine. "I'll keep this card to remember you by."

"I'm sorry you can't see it," I said as I squeezed her hand. For a moment it felt as warm and giving as my own grandma's. "I wished I had brought you a better *aguinaldo*."

"The best *aguinaldo,*" Elenita said, "was your visit, Marilia."

As I left, I felt light and warm and peaceful. On the bus ride back, I told my friend Margarita all about our visit. I couldn't wait to come back next year when I was in the sixth grade. I already knew what I would bring Elenita. I would make her a collage. That way she would be able to feel the many textures of my picture, even if she couldn't see it. And maybe I could make the picture of her dancing. I knew she had been very pretty when she was young.

"Are you going to wait until next Christmas to give her your collage?" Margarita asked.

I thought for a moment. "Maybe Mami could bring me back sooner," I said.

As I looked out the window, I remembered how good Elenita's hand felt to touch. It's funny how sometimes things change unexpectedly. Just that morning I didn't want to go at all. But then, I couldn't wait to visit my new friend again. We had gone to the nursing home to give *aguinaldos*. And what a very special *aguinaldo* I had been given—Elenita's friendship.

ABOUT THE AUTHOR

Lulu Delacre's childhood in Puerto Rico has inspired her as both a writer and an artist. Climbing tamarindo trees, catching lizards, and drawing at her grandmother's house are memories that are close to her heart and her work. Now a well-known author and illustrator of children's books, Lulu has received many awards. She proudly celebrates Latino heritage and traditions in words and color.

ABOUT THE ILLUSTRATOR

John Parra is an illustrator as well as a designer, teacher, and painter. When he was young, John liked drawing what was around him—the beautiful California landscapes, wild animals, cities, and families. His Hispanic roots influence his art. John has received numerous awards for his work, including a Pura Belpré Honor for *Gracias/Thanks*.

(t) Lulu Delacre, (b) John Parra

Author's Purpose

Why does the author include Spanish words and phrases throughout *Aguinaldo*?

Respond to the Text

Summarize

Use the most important details from *Aguinaldo* to summarize the story. Information from your Character Perspective Chart may help you.

Details

Character Perspective

Write

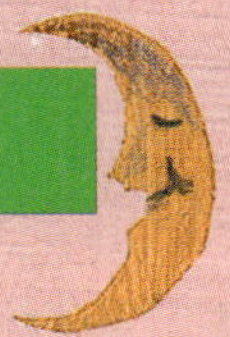

How does the class field trip to the nursing home affect Marilia? Why do Marilia's feelings about the nursing home change from the beginning of the story to the end? Use these sentence starters to help organize your text evidence.

> Marilia doesn't want to go to the nursing home because . . .
> Marilia eventually approaches Elenita because . . .
> Marilia says she likes Elenita after . . .

Make Connections

What is so special about Marilia's gift? **ESSENTIAL QUESTION**

Marilia and her classmates brought gifts to the residents at the nursing home. Why do people often say, "It is better to give than to receive"? **TEXT TO WORLD**

Genre • Expository Text

Compare Texts

Read about kids who are making a difference in their communities.

Partaking in Public Service

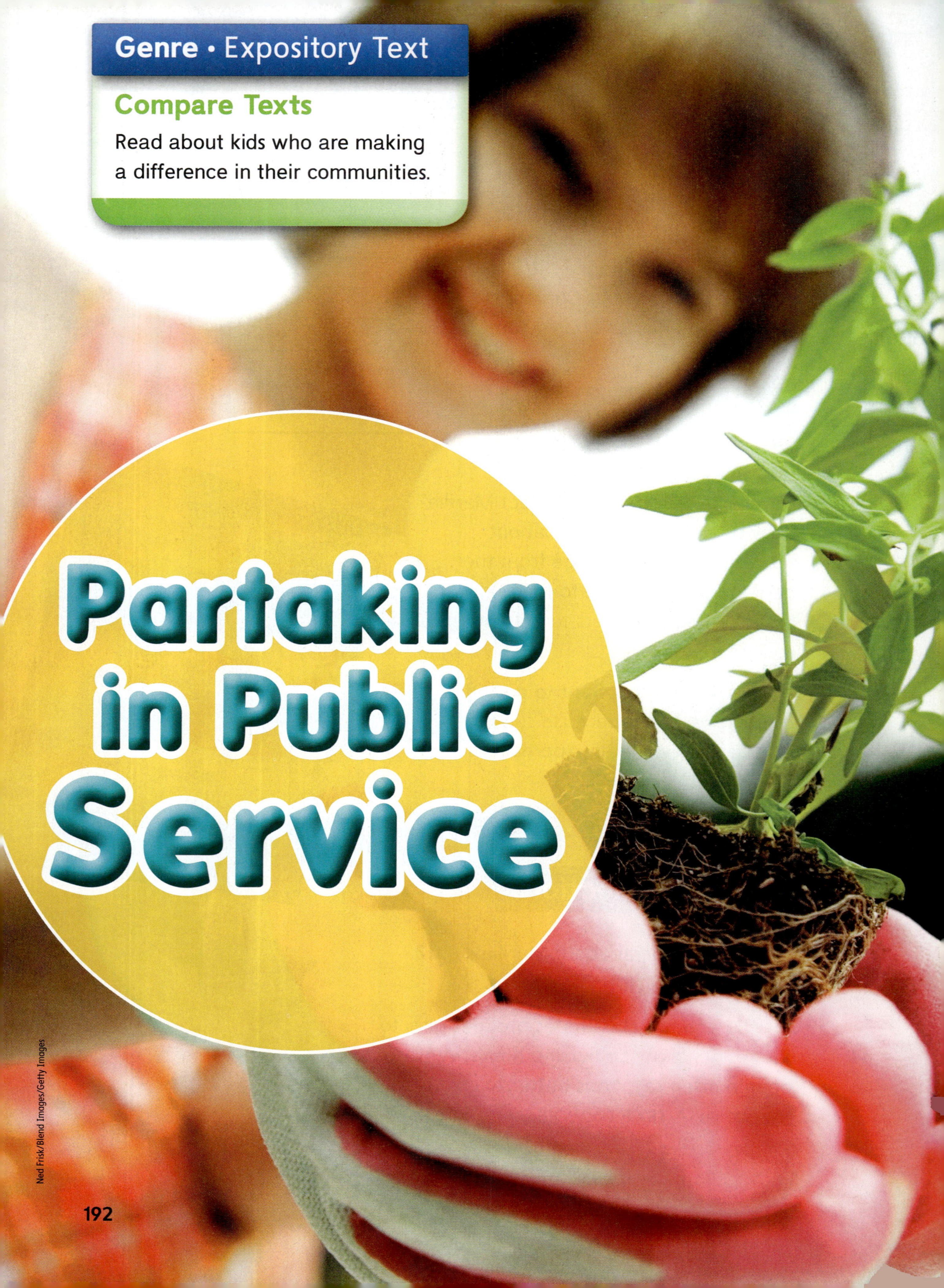

Ned Frisk/Blend Images/Getty Images

There is no doubt about it:

Volunteering is an important part of American life. About 27% of us volunteer in some way. This means that one American out of every four is performing a public service. Many volunteers are teens and children. In fact, in the last 20 years, the number of teen volunteers in this country has doubled. Youth service **organizations**, such as 4-H clubs, have grown in popularity.

Kids join local volunteer groups to give back to their communities. They work together to help others and to improve their schools and neighborhoods. Community projects may include planting gardens or collecting food and clothing. Some kids raise money for local charities. The volunteer opportunities are limitless.

Top Four Volunteer Activities for Kids

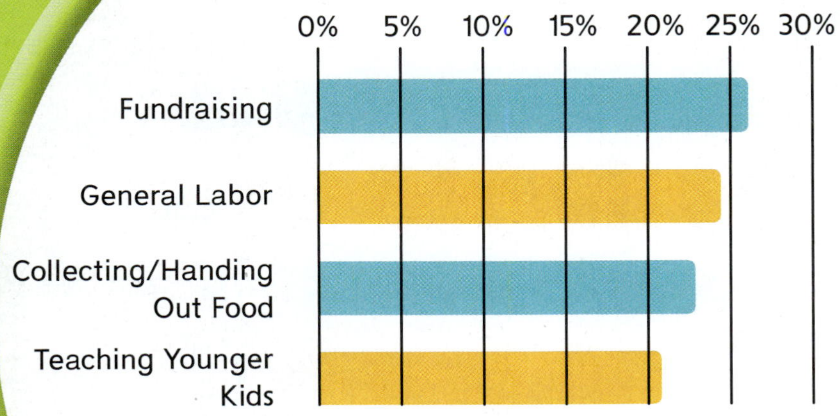

(l) Jill Tindall/Flickr/Getty Images; (c) Jamie Grill/Tetra Images/Getty Images; (r) George Doyle/Stockbyte/Getty Images

Some amazing young people have truly taken volunteering to the next level. They show the rest of us what public service is all about.

Alex Lin supports the idea of recycling. But he's not concerned with the kind that involves bottles and cans. Instead, he urges others to recycle e-waste, which is electronic garbage. Electronics, such as computers and game systems, have chemicals that can hurt the earth. They must be recycled and stored safely.

Alex was just nine years old when he formed the WIN community service team to recycle electronics. By the time he was 16, he had recycled 300,000 pounds of e-waste. He also helped to write a law against e-waste in his home state of Rhode Island.

Alex soon realized that reusing was an even better solution to e-waste. Working with his school, he set up a program that fixed old computers and donated them to students in need. Eventually, this program grew. Now it sends computers to people around the world.

Erica Fernandez also cares about the environment. She was 16 years old when she heard that a natural gas plant would be built near her hometown. Erica learned that the plant would pollute the air. It would bring harmful chemicals to nearby towns.

Erica decided to do something about it. She organized groups to protest the plant. They spoke out publicly. They wrote letters to the government. Eventually, the state agreed to cancel the plans for the plant. Thanks to Erica, the local environment was saved.

(t) Westerly Innovations Network; (b) Indrajit Das

Diana Lopez lives in San Antonio, Texas. Diana, along with other members of her community, started the Roots of Change community garden. The garden provides free organic produce to the community and also operates as an educational center. Two years later, Diana received a Brower Youth Award for her work as an environmental and community activist. Diana believes that, "Everyone deserves the right to a clean, healthy environment regardless of your color or economic status."

Evan Green was only seven years old when he started the Red Dragon Conservation Team. Its purpose was to protect the tropical rain forest. It has since become an international group of kids who want to save the planet. The kids collect community donations and send them to the Center for Ecosystem Survival (CES) in California. CES uses the donations to buy land in the rain forest and in coral reef areas around the world. This protects the land and sea nearby from being destroyed by humans.

Simple Ideas Solve Problems

All of these kids started with a simple idea. They worked to help their community in important ways. Their **generosity** has affected people around the world. Kids have the power to make a positive change through volunteering. In the words of Evan Green, "You don't have to be an adult to make a difference."

Make Connections

In what ways are these young people making a difference? **ESSENTIAL QUESTION**

Describe the role of public service. Use examples from the selections. **TEXT TO TEXT**

Genre • Biography

Essential Question

How can one person make a difference?

Read how one man became a Civil Rights leader in his community.

Go Digital!

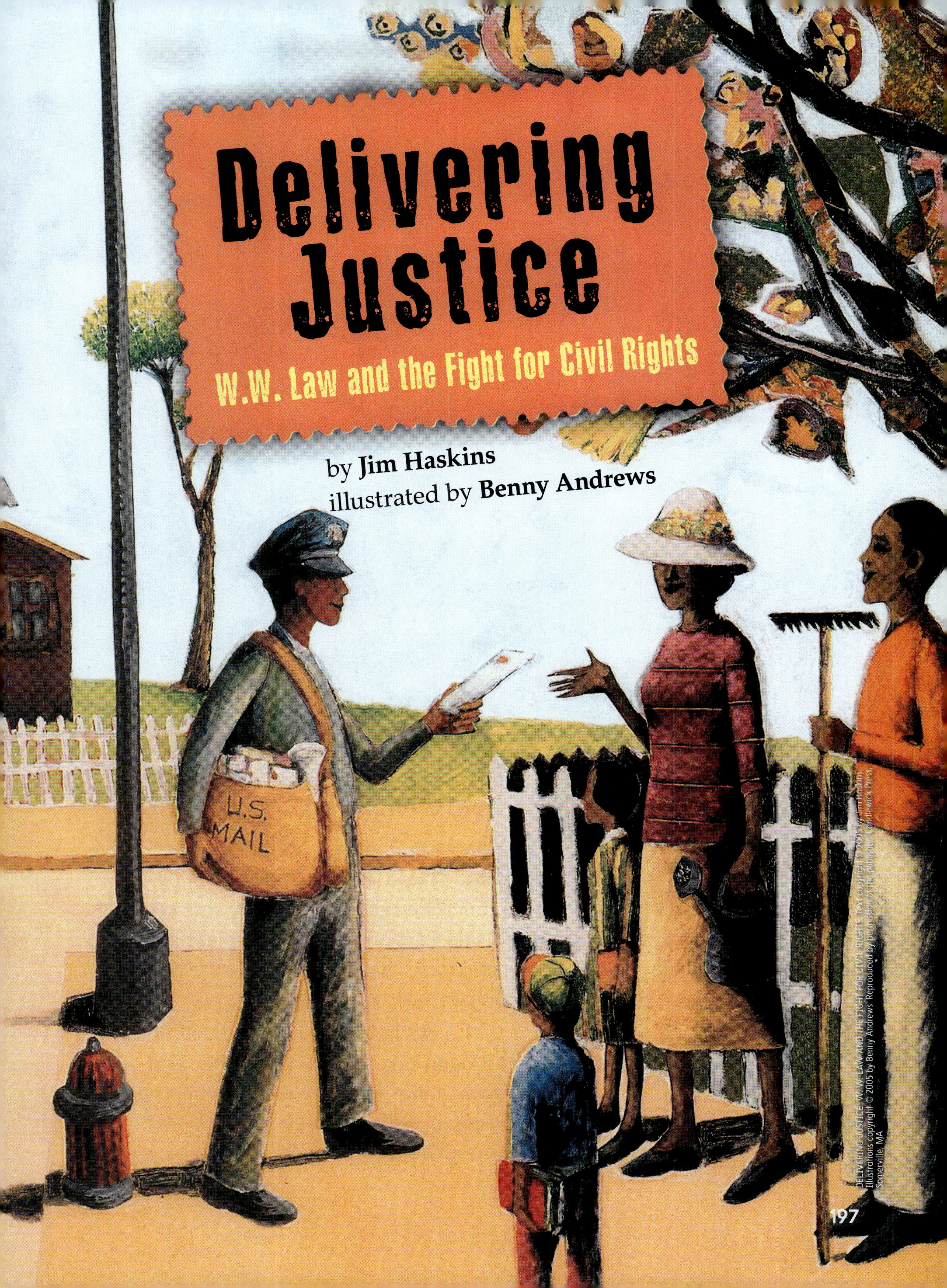

Delivering Justice

W.W. Law and the Fight for Civil Rights

by **Jim Haskins**
illustrated by **Benny Andrews**

Savannah, Georgia, 1932

The smell of his grandma's biscuits lured Westley to the kitchen. Westley was excited because today was Thursday, the day he would see his mother. The rest of the week, she worked for a white family just outside Savannah, cooking, cleaning, and taking care of their children. This was her day off.

Grandma's friend Old John was sitting at the table. Westley loved listening to the old man's stories. Old John had been born a slave. He had been taken from his mother and had never known her. He was nine—Westley's age—when he and all the slaves were freed in 1865. Westley felt lucky—at least he saw his own mama once a week.

Easter Shopping at Levy's

Once a year, sometime before Easter, Grandma would take Westley downtown to Levy's Department Store on Broughton Street to buy one nice outfit. They used a Levy's charge card and then paid a little bit each month.

On one shopping trip, the saleswoman would not serve them until after all the white customers had been helped. Westley had heard the saleswoman politely call the white women customers "Miss" and "Mrs." But she treated his grandma as if she were a child, a nobody.

Westley's grandma pretended not to notice. She was polite. But she was also proud. "Come on," she said, "it's time to go home." They left the store without buying a thing.

COLORED

Segregation

Back then, black people weren't treated as well as white people. Most of the time, they were kept segregated from whites. Westley went to a separate school for black children. He had to drink from water fountains marked "Colored." He could not sit and eat at the Levy's lunch counter.

His Grandma's Prayers

Sometimes Westley got angry that black people were **mistreated** and that no matter how hard his mother worked, they were still poor. But his grandma was always there to talk with him. She understood why he was upset, but she didn't want him to have bad feelings about himself.

She said that no matter how he was treated, he had no excuse not to "be somebody." She told him again about the day he was born. She said, "I got on my knees and prayed that you would grow up to be a leader of our people."

Westley promised himself that he would **fulfill** his grandma's prayer. He also promised himself that he would work hard so that one day his mother would not have to work in someone else's house.

Voter Schools, 1942

Westley knew that many black people didn't vote because they had to pass a test to register. The test was designed to be difficult for black folk to pass. It was intended to keep them from voting.

Westley was a member of the Youth Council of the NAACP—the National Association for the Advancement of Colored People. The Youth Council started a special "voter school" in the basement of a church.

With his friend Clifford, Westley talked to everyone, even passersby, about voting. When he found someone who, scared by the test, had never **registered** to vote, he took them to the voter school. When they felt ready to take the test, Westley went with them to the courthouse and stayed until they were registered. With Westley's help and **encouragement**, many black people in Savannah became registered voters.

Working as a Mailman, 1949

After college and the army, Westley wanted to be a teacher. But because of his membership in the NAACP, no one in Savannah would hire him.

So Westley became a mailman. The postal service hired **qualified** people, regardless of their color. As it turned out, this job suited Westley just fine.

"Good morning, Miss Sally Lawrence Jenkins," Westley sang out to a young woman in her garden. "Here's a letter from your sister."

Westley liked to address people by their full names. He could trace a person's history in their name. And history was important to Westley. "If you don't know where you've been, how do you know where you're going?" he loved to ask.

At the NAACP Office, February 1960

After work, Westley spent long evenings at the NAACP office. One night, he was visited by a group of students who were excited about what was happening in Greensboro, North Carolina. Young black people there had staged a sit-in at a lunch counter in a local store. They had refused to leave until they were served.

The students standing in front of Westley wanted to do the same thing at the department stores on Broughton Street. But they needed a leader. Westley remembered how his grandma had been treated at Levy's, and he agreed to help. But first, the students had to be trained. They had to **protest** without ever using violence, even if the other side did. If they were attacked and they fought back, Westley told them, their cause would be lost.

Levy's Lunch Counter

After weeks of training, small groups of students made their way downtown, entered the big stores along Broughton Street, and sat down at the lunch counters. The stores refused to serve them. At Levy's, the manager called the police, who arrested the students for breaking the city's segregation laws.

Throwing Down Their Cards

Westley called a mass meeting the next Sunday at the Bolton Street Baptist Church. People filled the pews and balconies. Westley opened the meeting with a hymn. All the voices singing together made a thunderous sound. And the mighty noise made people think that perhaps working together, they could really make something happen. Westley spoke about the arrests of the young people at Levy's. He said that things had to change, and he asked if people were ready to fight for their rights.

Someone shouted, "I'll never shop at that store again!" Then someone in the balcony threw down a Levy's charge card. Soon, everyone was tossing charge cards into a big pile in the church.

TORE

The Boycott Begins
March 17, 1960

The next morning, Westley led a group downtown. They carried baskets full of charge cards.

At Levy's, Westley and his group dumped the baskets of charge cards onto the sidewalk. Then Westley announced that no black people would shop at any store on Broughton Street until they were treated equally.

The Great Savannah **Boycott** had begun!

Picket Lines

Westley and other members of the NAACP organized a picket line every day in front of Levy's. White people yelled and jeered at the protesters and tried to force them off the sidewalk. But day after day, the protesters returned.

One day a large, burly white man punched one of the demonstrators in the face and broke his jaw. But everyone remembered what Westley had taught them. They didn't yell or fight back, no matter how much they wanted to.

Westley organized other protests. There were kneel-ins at the white churches on Sundays and wade-ins at the all-white beach at Tybee. Westley wanted to end segregation everywhere in Savannah—in libraries, theaters, public pools, beaches, and restrooms, as well as at lunch counters.

Talking About Peaceful Change

Large meetings were held every Sunday at different churches. Protestors talked about their activities; some gave fiery speeches. The meetings became so popular that no church was big enough to hold everyone who wanted to get in.

For a year and a half, no one from the black community shopped on Broughton Street.

Westley walked down the street and started counting: One, two, three, four, five GOING OUT OF BUSINESS signs. The white storeowners couldn't stay in business without black customers.

When he delivered mail to white people, Westley told them how much he loved Savannah. He wanted the city to be a better place for everyone. They respected Westley. They saw how peaceful and committed to change the protestors were. Little by little, more and more white people began to sympathize with the protestors.

Desegregation Without Violence

White people in the community who supported Westley asked what they could do to end segregation and stop the boycott. Together, leaders from the white and black communities worked out a plan. Each evening after delivering the mail, Westley organized a group of students to sit in a different kind of business or facility the next day. The theaters would be first, then the restaurants, then the library, and on down the line until every business had been desegregated.

Sometimes angry crowds would gather, or white people would leave in protest when the black students arrived. But most of the white and black leaders stuck together. The mayor made sure that all the signs marking separate facilities for blacks and whites at City Hall, the courthouse, health department, and hospital were taken down. City officials took the segregation laws off the books. Unlike desegregation efforts in other cities and towns in the South, there was very little violence in Savannah.

Justice Delivered

On a Sunday in September 1961, Westley greeted the hundreds of people who arrived at a downtown Savannah church. Inside, their voices joined together to sing out, "We are Soldiers in God's Army." When the song ended, Westley stood in front of the crowd. He saw his mother sitting in the front row. He saw students who had been arrested. He saw faces beaming with pride. Then he announced in a loud clear voice, "We have triumphed!"

Savannah was the first southern city in the United States to declare all its citizens equal, three years before the federal Civil Rights Act made all segregation illegal. People, both black and white, saw Westley as Savannah's hero. He had kept the protest disciplined and peaceful, even in face of the violence. Modestly, he would say, "I was just doing what every black American should be doing."

Westley Wallace Law delivered more than just the mail to the citizens of Savannah; he delivered justice, too. His grandma's prayers had been answered.

About the Author and Illustrator

Jim Haskins was born in 1941 in Alabama at a time when the South was segregated. Jim loved to read, but African Americans were not allowed to use the library. A white woman who knew Jim's mother agreed to check out books for him. Like Westley Law, Jim fought for civil rights. As an author, he has won many awards for his books.

Benny Andrews's early days were spent picking cotton in Georgia with his parents and nine siblings. His father painted in his free time and passed his love of art to his son. Benny became a world famous painter and was a teacher for many years. Like Westley Law and Jim Haskins, Benny Andrews fought for equal rights for all people.

Author's Purpose

Why does the author often start a section with the year in which the action took place?

(t) Jane Dominguez; (b) The Benny Andrews Estate

Respond to the Text

Summarize

Use important information from *Delivering Justice* to summarize the selection. Details from your Author's Perspective Chart may help you.

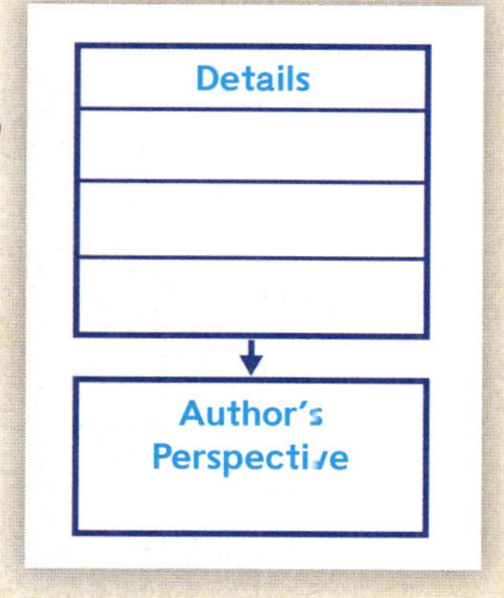

Write

What can readers learn from Westley Law and his actions? Use these sentence starters to help organize your text evidence.

Westley Law needed to help people register to vote because . . .
People boycotted shops on Broughton Street because . . .
Westley Law worked with other members of the NAACP to . . .

Make Connections

How did Westley Wallace Law become a leader in his community? ESSENTIAL QUESTION

Describe another individual in history who made a significant difference in the lives of others. TEXT TO WORLD

Genre • Autobiography

Compare Texts

Read how the events of the Civil Rights era changed a girl's life.

Keeping Freedom in the Family:

Coming of Age in the Civil Rights Movement

by Nora Davis Day

The Davis family at a rally for peace in New York City. From left to right: Mom, Dad, La Verne, me, and Guy. Guy made our picket signs!

"What do we want? Justice! When do we want it? Now!"

As I held on to my father's hand, we joined the line of people chanting and walking back and forth in a picket line in front of Lawrence Hospital. The year was 1965, and the hospital workers needed more money and better working conditions. So there we were on a cold Saturday afternoon to protest. When I looked up, I saw soldiers on the roof of the hospital. I squeezed Daddy's hand a little tighter. The soldiers were there to protect us, he said. We were American citizens, and we had the right to gather and to protest. I raised my picket sign as high as I could. I wasn't afraid. I had Daddy and the American Constitution to protect me.

I couldn't wait to get back home to tell my brother and sister, Guy and La Verne, about my day on the picket line. Dinnertime was always special at our house. We would sit around the table filling our mouths with food and our minds with ideas. Mom and Dad encouraged us to talk about anything we wanted to–anything. Sometimes we talked about our family. About Dad's childhood in segregated Waycross, Georgia, and Mom's love for Harlem, the part of New York City where she grew up. Other times we talked about big ideas like democracy, freedom, justice, and civil rights.

HE'S THEIR MAN! — Little Nora Davis and Guy Marshall Davis, son and daughter of Mr. and Mrs. Ossie Davis, pay tribute to former Federal Judge J. Waties Waring, at a testimonial luncheon given in his honor by the Tau Omega Chapter of the AKA Sorority at the Hotel Roosevelt last Sunday. Judge Waring was cited for his historic court decisions, pa... the way for school desegregation and ope... up the vote to Negroes in the South. Mrs. ... Davis is actress Ruby Dee, who is co-star... with her husband, Ossie, in the Broadway "Raisin in the Sun."

I was in fourth grade when I met Judge J. Waties Waring. His court decisions paved the way for school desegregation and voter registration in the South.

Some days, Mom and Dad weren't home for dinner. They were actors—Ossie Davis and Ruby Dee—but because they were black, they didn't have the same opportunities and rights as other citizens. They decided to use their lives as actors to make a difference. They wanted to make America a place where **injustice** was not welcome and where Guy, La Verne, and I would always feel like we belonged.

And so it was that my ordinary life of chores and homework and hopscotch soon became extraordinary. Every day there were new ideas to talk about at dinner. We learned new words like *nonviolence, sit-in*, and ***boycott***. Whenever they could, Mom and Dad took us with them to programs, **protests**, and picket lines.

Two years earlier, in 1963, we had moved into our new house and had gotten our first television set—just in time for one of the most important years in American history. We weren't allowed to watch TV during the school week, unless something really important was going on—like the March on Washington. When Martin Luther King, Jr., gave his famous "I Have a Dream" speech, I wished I could be there with Mom and Dad. I asked myself what kids like me could do to make a difference. Later that year, I had an answer to my question.

When four black girls were killed in a church bombing in Alabama, we realized that the fight for change would be hard, long, and dangerous. Mom and Dad encouraged us to think about how we could protest the bombing. Some people said we should boycott Christmas. This was our first Christmas in the new house, and the spirit of giving was important to us.

Daddy at the March on Washington for Jobs and Freedom in 1963. He and Mom were emcees.

So, instead of boycotting Christmas, our family decided to boycott Christmas shopping. Instead of buying gifts, our family gave the money to civil rights groups. Guy, La Verne, and I gave each other gifts we had made with our own hands. And when the time came to hang the home-made paper holiday chain, I wrote the names of the girls in the last four loops. In our own small way, we learned the true meaning of giving.

When we gathered for dinner that night, we said a special prayer for the girls and for our country—and I knew that Christmas at the Davis house would never be the same.

My sister, my brother, and me at the White House in 1995. Mom and Dad got the National Medal of Art.

1950 Nora Davis is born in New York City.

1959 Nora and Guy meet Judge J. Waties Waring, a champion of civil rights.

1962 The family marches for peace in New York City.

1963 The 16th Street Baptist Church in Birmingham, Alabama is bombed.

1965 Hospital workers picket in Bronxville, New York for 55 days.

1972 Nora votes in her first presidential election.

1985 Nora boycotts U. S. companies doing business in segregated South Africa.

2001 Nora speaks to students at her local high school about social justice.

Make Connections

How did the events of the Civil Rights era influence Nora Davis Day's life? **ESSENTIAL QUESTION**

Compare Nora Davis Day's experiences with those of others who made a difference. Contrast how each selection presents information. **TEXT TO TEXT**

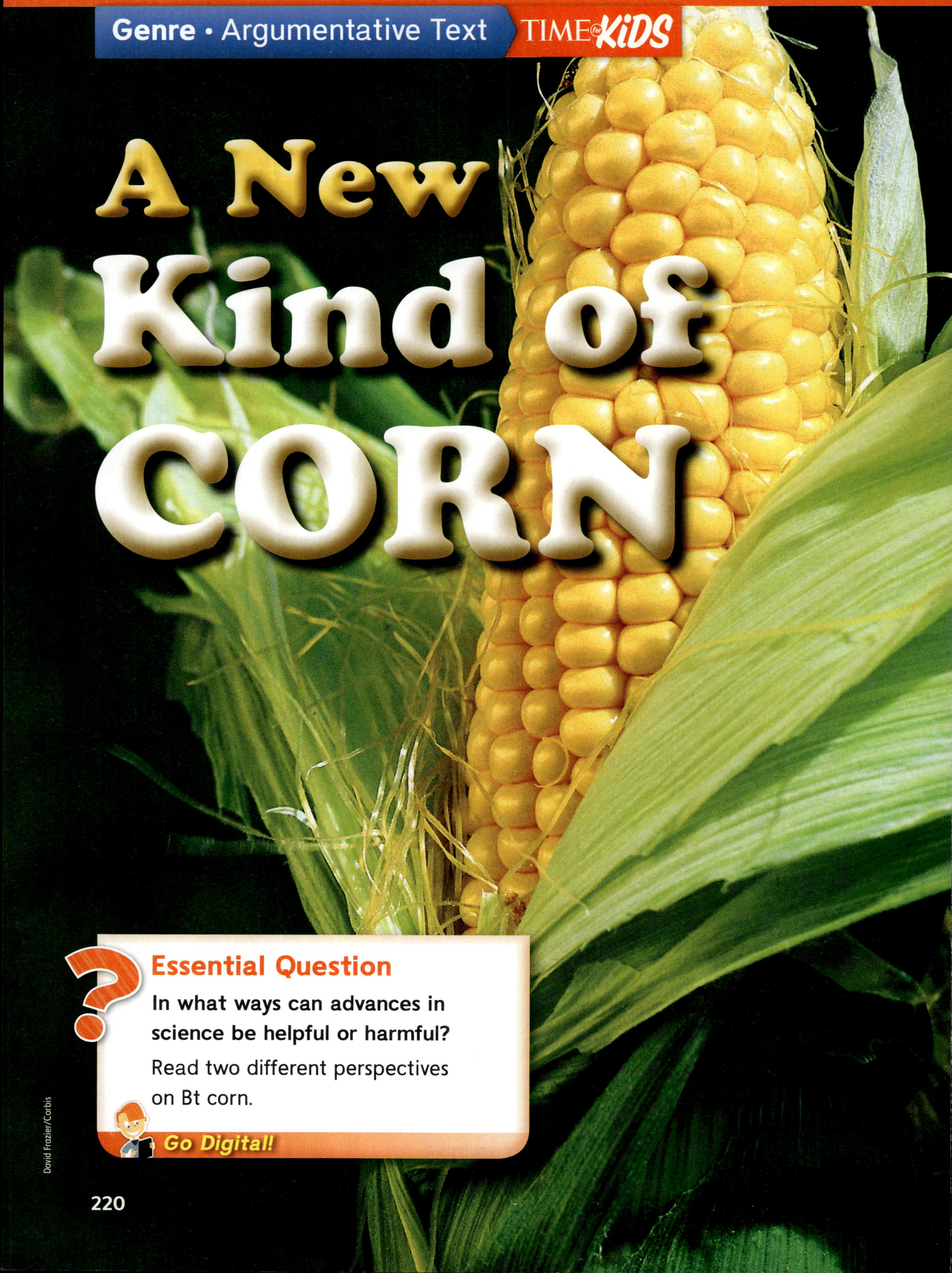

Genre • Argumentative Text TIME for KIDS

A New Kind of CORN

Essential Question

In what ways can advances in science be helpful or harmful?

Read two different perspectives on Bt corn.

Go Digital!

David Frazier/Corbis

A European corn borer feeds on an ear of sweet corn. Some farmers are turning to Bt corn to keep pests like corn borers from damaging their crops.

Advances in science have changed the way farmers grow corn. These advancements have also made consumers think about what they eat.

Have you heard of Bt corn? Probably not. But you have probably eaten it. Bt corn is grown all over the world. The crop is used in many foods, including tortilla chips and cornmeal. It is also used to make high fructose corn syrup, an unnecessary sweetener **prevalent** in many foods and drinks.

Bt corn is a genetically modified food. To make Bt corn, scientists change the genetic code of corn. This code sets which **characteristics** the corn will **inherit**. Bt corn contains an insect-killing gene. The gene comes from a bacterium called *Bacillus thuringiensis,* or Bt. These changes make the corn produce poison. The poison kills only insects that are harmful to it, such as rootworm beetles or caterpillars called European corn borers. This characteristic makes it unnecessary for farmers to spray pesticide in their cornfields.

Uses of Corn

When you think of corn, it might call to mind fresh corn on the cob. But how much do humans actually consume? The pie chart below shows the uses of corn in the United States according to the United States Department of Agriculture.

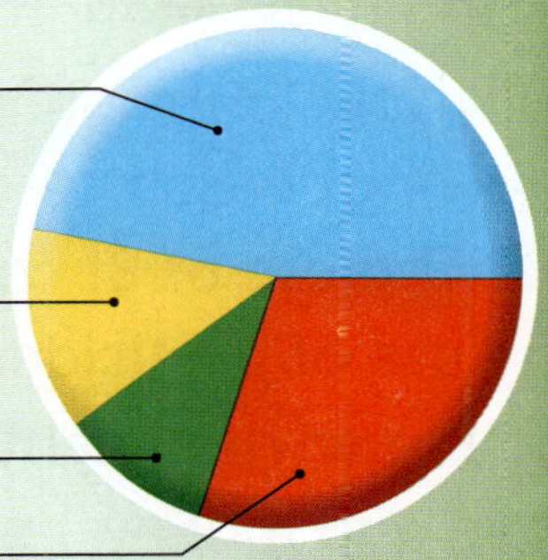

A scientist examines root damage from pests on a normal corn plant (left) and on Bt corn (right).

Where Is GM Food Grown?

Though the United States is the biggest producer of genetically modified foods, enhanced crops are grown all over the world.

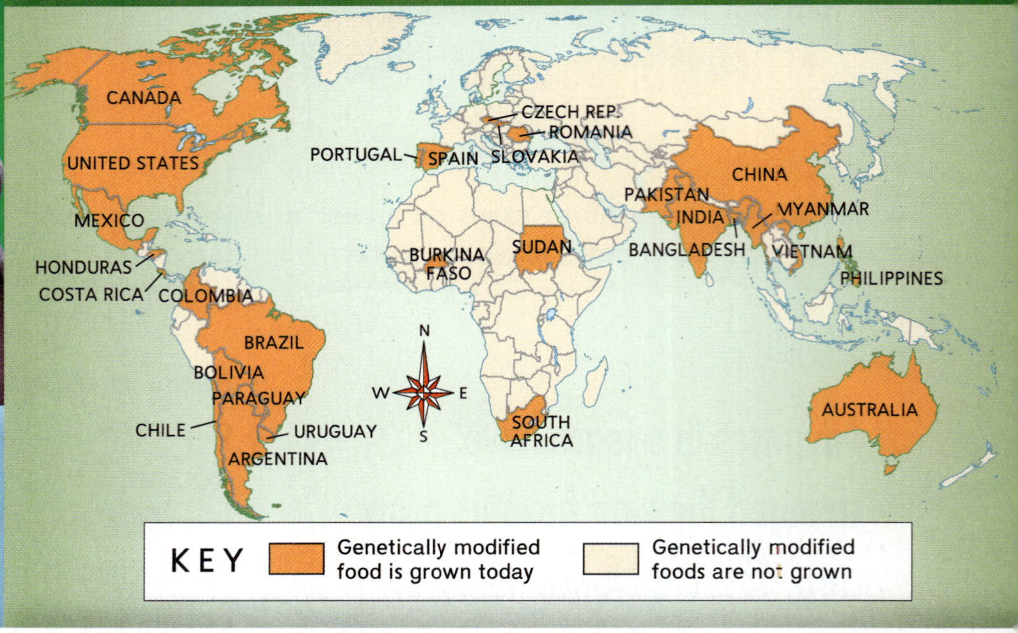

POINT COUNTERPOINT

Bt Corn Is Better

A Farmer's Perspective

I began growing Bt corn in 1996. Until that point, I never knew if I would have enough of a crop to sell. Now I am confident about each growing season.

The use of Bt corn has lessened the use of pesticides. That is great for the environment and saves time and money. I no longer have to spray the fields with costly pesticides. Further, I no longer worry about being exposed to the toxic chemicals.

Many people have raised **concerns** about the poison in Bt corn. So far, it is only fatal to rootworm beetles and corn borers. Other insects are able to survive where sprayed pesticides are not used.

Planting Bt corn has increased both profit and productivity on farms around the world. This is especially good for developing countries where corn is a staple. The savings to farmers are passed on to people who buy the corn. Plus, having more food available in hungry nations is a good thing. The benefits of Bt corn continue to grow. That is why more farmers are planting it in the fields.

COUNTERPOINT POINT

Bt Corn Could Be Bad

A Consumer's Concern

Bt corn has been on the market since the 1990s with little research on the consequences. Yet farmers are producing genetically modified (GM) crops at an alarming rate. I can't help but wonder about these recent advancements in **agriculture**—what are the long-term effects of GM foods? Is Bt corn really safe to grow and eat?

Much of the testing of GM foods has been done on lab rodents. The results have been alarming. In some reports, mice have developed lesions in their stomachs from eating GM foods. Rats have died prematurely for "unstated reasons." These results may happen to humans, so we should rethink stocking our supermarkets with unlabeled GM foods. Consumers should know what they are buying and eating.

Also, although the use of Bt corn has lessened the need for pesticides, a 2016 study found that continued growth in herbicide use pollutes our air and water and can harm biodiversity. Additionally, as of 2014, root worms have begun to develop a **resistance** to Bt corn.

Clearly, farmers have a responsibility to ensure their crops do not harm the environment and its inhabitants. To protect future generations, we need more research on the effects of Bt corn.

A consumer who **disagrees** with the sale of Bt corn attends a protest.

Respond to the Text

1. Use important details from the selection to summarize. SUMMARIZE

2. What is your opinion about Bt corn? Why do you feel that way? WRITE

3. What are some ways that genetically modified crops might be able to help people around the world? TEXT TO WORLD

Genre • Procedural Text

TIME for KIDS

Compare Texts

Read how you can grow a giant pumpkin.

The Pick of the Patch

This world record-breaking pumpkin tipped the scales at more than 1,810 pounds. What is the secret to growing a giant gourd? According to record-breaker Chris Stevens, "Sunshine, rain, cow manure, fish [fertilizer], and seaweed." Read on for a recipe you can recreate at home.

Chris Stevens

Growing a giant pumpkin takes knowledge and skill. Follow these six simple steps to grow your own great gourd.

1. Study up on seeds.

Some popular pumpkin seeds that get big results include Prizewinner Hybrid, Atlantic Giant, Mammoth Gold, and Big Max. Many are sold online for just $1.

2. Take your time.

Giant pumpkins need time to grow. May is a good month to plant seeds in a pot. Let them make **advancements** in that safe space before you transplant them outside. Plant them in good quality soil and fertilize them well.

3. Protect your pumpkin plants.

Watch out for bugs and other pests that could attack the plants. Prevent wind from damaging them by putting up a fence or plastic tarp.

4. Help your gourd grow.

Agriculture is a science that is not always automatic. Hand-pollinating the flowers will increase your chances of growing a giant gourd. Use a small paintbrush or cotton swab to spread pollen from the male flower to the female flower. A female flower has a little pumpkin at the base of its petals.

Before pollinating, make sure the flowers are open.

5. Pick your best bet.

Pumpkins compete with each other to get the best nutrients from the vine. In order to give your gourd a better chance to grow, select the best and biggest pumpkin on each vine and remove all other pumpkins.

Keep a daily record of your gourd's growth.

6. Continue with care.

Water and fertilize your pumpkins regularly until it is time to harvest. Weigh to grow!

Make Connections

What steps can you take to grow a giant pumpkin? **ESSENTIAL QUESTION**

How can advances in science be helpful or harmful? **TEXT TO TEXT**

Genre • Fantasy

THE CRICKET IN TIMES SQUARE

By George Selden

DRAWINGS BY Garth Williams

Essential Question

What makes a new friend feel welcome?

Read how two unlikely friends make a cricket feel at home in a strange place.

Go Digital!

Chester

Tucker Mouse had been watching the Bellinis and listening to what they said. Next to **scrounging**, eavesdropping on human beings was what he enjoyed most. That was one of the reasons he lived in the Times Square subway station. As soon as the family disappeared, he darted out across the floor and scooted up to the newsstand. At one side the boards had separated and there was a wide space he could jump through. He'd been in a few times before—just exploring. For a moment he stood under the three-legged stool, letting his eyes get used to the darkness. Then he jumped on it.

"Psst!" he whispered. "Hey, you up there—are you awake?"

There was no answer.

"Psst! Psst! Hey!" Tucker whispered again, louder this time.

From the shelf above came a scuffling, like little feet feeling their way to the edge. "Who is that going 'psst'?" said a voice.

"It's me," said Tucker. "Down here on the stool."

A black head, with two shiny black eyes, peered down at him. "Who are you?"

"A mouse," said Tucker, "Who are *you*?"

"I'm Chester Cricket," said the cricket. He had a high, musical voice. Everything he said seemed to be spoken to an unheard melody.

"My name's Tucker," said Tucker Mouse. "Can I come up?"

"I guess so," said Chester Cricket. "This isn't my house anyway."

Tucker jumped up beside the cricket and looked him all over. "A cricket," he said admiringly. "So you're a cricket. I never saw one before."

"I've seen mice before," the cricket said. "I knew quite a few back in Connecticut."

"Is that where you're from?" asked Tucker.

"Yes," said Chester. "I guess I'll never see it again," he added wistfully.

"How did you get to New York?" asked Tucker Mouse.

"It's a long story," sighed the cricket.

"Tell me," said Tucker, settling back on his haunches. He loved to hear stories. It was almost as much fun as eavesdropping—if the story was true.

"Well, it must have been two—no, three days ago," Chester Cricket began. "I was sitting on top of my stump, just enjoying the weather and thinking how nice it was that summer had started. I live inside an old tree stump, next to a willow tree, and I often go up to the roof to look around. And I'd been practicing jumping that day too. On the other side of the stump from the willow tree there's a brook that runs past, and I'd been jumping back and forth across it to get my legs in condition for the summer. I do a lot of jumping, you know."

"Me too," said Tucker Mouse. "Especially around the rush hour."

"And I had just finished jumping when I smelled something," Chester went on, "liverwurst, which I love."

"You like liverwurst?" Tucker broke in. "Wait! Wait! Just wait!"

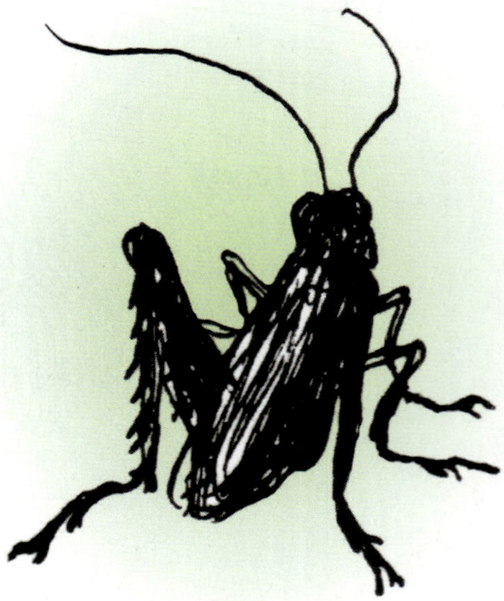

In one leap, he sprang down all the way from the shelf to the floor and dashed over to his drain pipe. Chester shook his head as he watched him go. He thought Tucker was a very excitable person—even for a mouse.

Inside the drain pipe, Tucker's nest was a **jumble** of papers, scraps of cloth, buttons, lost jewelry, small change, and everything else that can be picked up in a subway station. Tucker tossed things left and right in a wild search. Neatness was not one of the things he aimed at in life. At last he discovered what he was looking for: a big piece of liverwurst he had found earlier that evening. It was meant to be for breakfast tomorrow, but he decided that meeting his first cricket was a special occasion. Holding the liverwurst between his teeth, he whisked back to the newsstand.

"Look!" he said proudly, dropping the meat in front of Chester Cricket. "Liverwurst! You continue the story—we'll enjoy a snack too."

"That's very nice of you," said Chester. He was touched that a mouse he had known only a few minutes would share his food with him. "I had a little chocolate before, but besides that, nothing for three days."

"Eat! Eat!" said Tucker. He bit the liverwurst into two pieces and gave Chester the bigger one. "So you smelled the liverwurst—then what happened?"

"I hopped down from the stump and went off toward the smell," said Chester.

"Very **logical**," said Tucker Mouse, munching with his cheeks full. "Exactly what I would have done."

"It was coming from a picnic basket," said Chester. "A couple of tuffets away from my stump the meadow begins, and there was a whole bunch of people having a picnic. They had hard boiled eggs, and cold roast chicken, and roast beef, and a whole lot of other things besides the liverwurst sandwiches which I smelled."

Tucker Mouse moaned with pleasure at the thought of all that food.

"They were having such a good time laughing and singing songs that they didn't notice me when I jumped into the picnic basket," continued Chester. "I was sure they wouldn't mind if I had just a taste."

"Naturally not," said Tucker Mouse sympathetically. "Why mind? Plenty for all. Who could blame you?"

"Now, I have to admit," Chester went on, "I had more than a taste. As a matter of fact, I ate so much that I couldn't keep my eyes open—what with being tired from the jumping and everything. And I fell asleep right there in the picnic basket. The first thing I knew, somebody had put a bag on top of me that had the last of the roast beef sandwiches in it. I couldn't move!"

"Imagine!" Tucker exclaimed. "Trapped under roast beef sandwiches! Well, there are worse fates."

"At first I wasn't too frightened," said Chester. "After all, I thought, they probably come from New Canaan or some other nearby town. They'll have to unpack the basket sooner or later. Little did I know!" He shook his head and sighed. "I could feel the basket being carried into a car and riding somewhere and then being lifted down. That must have been the railroad station. Then I went up again and there was a rattling and roaring sound, the way a train makes. By this time I was pretty scared. I knew every minute was taking me farther away from my stump, but there wasn't anything I could do. I was getting awfully cramped too, under those roast beef sandwiches."

"Didn't you try to eat your way out?" asked Tucker.

"I didn't have any room," said Chester. "But every now and then the train would give a lurch and I managed to free myself a little. We traveled on and on, and then the train stopped. I didn't have any idea where we were, but as soon as the basket was carried off, I could tell from the noise it must be New York."

"You never were here before?" Tucker asked.

"Goodness no!" said Chester. "But I've heard about it. There was a swallow I used to know who told about flying over New York every spring and fall on her way to the North and back. But what would I be doing here?" He shifted uneasily from one set of legs to another. "I'm a country cricket."

"Don't worry," said Tucker Mouse. "I'll feed you liverwurst. You'll be all right. Go on with the story."

"It's almost over," said Chester. "The people got off one train and walked a ways and got on another—even noisier than the first."

"Must have been the subway," said Tucker.

"I guess so," Chester Cricket said. "You can imagine how scared I was. I didn't know *where* I was going! For all I knew they could have been heading for Texas, although I don't guess many people from Texas come all the way to Connecticut for a picnic."

"It could happen," said Tucker, nodding his head.

"Anyway I worked furiously to get loose. And finally I made it. When they got off the second train, I took a flying leap and landed in a pile of dirt over in the corner of this place where we are."

"Such an introduction to New York," said Tucker, "to land in a pile of dirt in the Times Square subway station. Tsk, tsk, tsk."

"And here I am," Chester concluded forlornly. "I've been lying over there for three days not knowing what to do. At last I got so nervous I began to chirp."

"That was the sound!" interrupted Tucker Mouse. "I heard it, but I didn't know what it was."

"Yes, that was me," said Chester. "Usually I don't chirp until later on in the summer–but my goodness, I had to do *something*!"

The cricket had been sitting next to the edge of the shelf. For some reason–perhaps it was a faint noise, like padded feet tiptoeing across the floor–he happened to look down. A shadowy form that had been crouching silently below in the darkness made a spring and landed right next to Tucker and Chester.

"Watch out!" Chester shouted, "A cat!" He dove headfirst into the matchbox.

Harry Cat

Chester buried his head in the Kleenex. He didn't want to see his new friend, Tucker Mouse, get killed. Back in Connecticut he had sometimes watched the one-sided fights of cats and mice in the meadow, and unless the mice were near their holes, the fights always ended in the same way. But this cat had been upon them too quickly: Tucker couldn't have escaped.

There wasn't a sound. Chester lifted his head and very **cautiously** looked behind him. The cat–a huge tiger cat with gray-green eyes and black stripes along his body–was sitting on his hind legs, switching his tail around his forepaws. And directly between those forepaws, in the very jaws of his enemy, sat Tucker Mouse. He was watching Chester curiously. The cricket began to make frantic signs that the mouse should look up and see what was looming over him.

Very casually Tucker raised his head. The cat looked straight down on him. "Oh, him," said Tucker, chucking the cat under the chin with his right front paw, "he's my best friend. Come out from the matchbox."

Chester crept out, looking first at one, then the other.

"Chester, meet Harry Cat," said Tucker. "Harry, this is Chester. He's a cricket."

"I'm very pleased to make your **acquaintance**," said Harry Cat in a silky voice.

"Hello," said Chester. He was sort of ashamed because of all the fuss he'd made. "I wasn't scared for myself. But I thought cats and mice were enemies."

"In the country, maybe," said Tucker. "But in New York we gave up those old habits long ago. Harry is my oldest friend. He lives with me over in the drain pipe. So how was scrounging tonight, Harry?"

"Not so good," said Harry Cat. "I was over in the ash cans on the East Side, but those rich people don't throw out as much garbage as they should."

NO SALE
Musical America

"Chester, make that noise again for Harry," said Tucker Mouse.

Chester lifted the black wings that were carefully folded across his back and with a quick, expert stroke drew the top one over the bottom. A *thrumm* echoed through the station.

"Lovely—very lovely," said the cat. "This cricket has talent."

"I thought it was singing," said Tucker. "But you do it like playing a violin, with one wing on the other?"

"Yes," said Chester. "These wings aren't much good for flying, but I prefer music anyhow." He made three rapid chirps.

Tucker Mouse and Harry Cat smiled at each other. "It makes me want to purr to hear it," said Harry.

"Some people say a cricket goes 'chee chee chee,'" explained Chester. "And others say, 'treet treet treet,' but we crickets don't think it sounds like either one of those."

"It sounds to me as if you were going 'crik crik crik,'" said Harry.

"Maybe that's why they call him a 'cricket,'" said Tucker.

They all laughed. Tucker had a squeaky laugh that sounded as if he were hiccupping. Chester was feeling much happier now. The future did not seem nearly as gloomy as it had over in the pile of dirt in the corner.

"Are you going to stay a while in New York?" asked Tucker.

"I guess I'll have to," said Chester. "I don't know how to get home."

"Well, we could always take you to Grand Central Station and put you on a train going back to Connecticut," said Tucker. "But why don't you give the city a try. Meet new people—see new things. Mario likes you very much."

"Yes, but his mother doesn't," said Chester. "She thinks I carry germs."

"Germs!" said Tucker **scornfully**. "She wouldn't know a germ if one gave her a black eye. Pay no attention."

"Too bad you couldn't have found more successful friends," said Harry Cat. "I fear for the future of this newsstand."

"It's true," echoed Tucker sadly. "They're going broke fast." He jumped up on a pile of magazines and read off the names in the half-light that slanted through the cracks in the wooden cover. "*Art News–Musical America*. Who would read them but a few long-hairs?"

"I don't understand the way you talk," said Chester. Back in the meadow he had listened to bullfrogs, and woodchucks, and rabbits, even a few snakes, but he had never heard anyone speak like Tucker Mouse. "What is a long-hair?"

Tucker scratched his head and thought a moment. "A long-hair is an extra-refined person," he said. "You take an Afghan hound—that's a long-hair."

"Do Afghan hounds read *Musical America*?" asked the cricket.

"They would if they could," said Tucker.

Chester shook his head. "I'm afraid I won't get along in New York," he said.

"Oh, sure you will!" squeaked Tucker Mouse. "Harry, suppose we take Chester up and show him Times Square. Would you like that, Chester?"

"I guess so," said Chester, although he was really a little leery of venturing out into New York City.

The three of them jumped down to the floor. The crack in the side of the newsstand was just wide enough for Harry to get through. As they crossed the station floor, Tucker pointed out the local sights of interest, such as the Nedick's lunch counter—Tucker spent a lot of time around there—and the Loft's candy store. Then they came to the drain pipe. Chester had to make short little hops to keep from hitting his head as they went up. There seemed to be hundreds of twistings and turnings, and many other pipes that opened off the main route, but Tucker Mouse knew his way perfectly—even in the dark. At last Chester saw light above them. One more hop brought him out onto the sidewalk. And there he gasped, holding his breath and crouching against the cement.

They were standing at one corner of the Times building, which is at the south end of Times Square. Above the cricket, towers that seemed like mountains of light rose up into the night sky. Even this late the neon signs were still blazing. Reds, blues, greens, and yellows flashed down on him. And the air was full of the roar of traffic and the hum of human beings. It was as if Times Square were a kind of shell, with colors and noises breaking in great waves inside it. Chester's heart hurt him and he closed his eyes. The sight was too terrible and beautiful for a cricket who up to now had measured high things by the height of his willow tree and sounds by the burble of a running brook.

"How do you like it?" asked Tucker Mouse.

"Well—it's—it's quite something," Chester stuttered.

"You should see it New Year's Eve," said Harry Cat.

Gradually Chester's eyes got used to the lights. He looked up. And way far above them, above New York, and above the whole world, he made out a star that he knew was a star he used to look at back in Connecticut. When they had gone down to the station and Chester was in the matchbox again, he thought about that star. It made him feel better to think that there was one familiar thing, twinkling above him, amid so much that was new and strange.

HOTEL
ASTOR
CHEVROLET
KINSEY

About the Author and Illustrator

George Selden got the idea for *The Cricket in Times Square* after hearing a cricket chirp at a busy subway stop in New York City. "The story formed in my mind within minutes," he said. In his writing, Selden created animal characters that reflect what he called "human truth," or the way that humans should behave. Like Chester Cricket, Selden grew up in Connecticut and then later lived in New York City.

Like Tucker Mouse and Harry Cat, **Garth Williams** was born in New York City. His parents were both artists. He spent his childhood on a farm in New Jersey, where he spent hours drawing animals. "Everybody in my home was always either painting or drawing," he said. Williams's illustrations brought to life some of the best-known characters in children's literature. In addition to *The Cricket in Times Square*, Williams illustrated *Charlotte's Web* and *Stuart Little*, two classic novels by E. B. White.

Author's Purpose

Think about the three different animal characters in *The Cricket in Times Square*. How does the author use these characters to show the importance of friendship?

Respond to the Text

Summarize

Summarize the most important events in *The Cricket in Times Square*. Information from your Character Perspective Chart may help you.

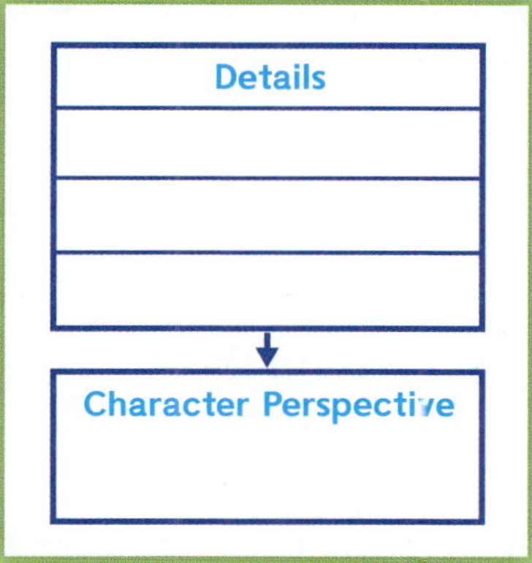

Write

How does George Selden use dialogue to show how Chester and Tucker's friendship develops throughout the story? Use these sentence starters to help organize your text evidence.

George Selden uses Chester and Tucker's first meeting to . . .
He shows how they feel by . . .
This helps me understand that their friendship . . .

Make Connections

How do Tucker and Harry make Chester feel at home in a strange place? ESSENTIAL QUESTION

Why is welcoming newcomers to a community important? TEXT TO WORLD

Genre • Fantasy

Compare Texts

How can you make new friends feel welcome?

At the Library

Rick Dodson waved good-bye to Mrs. Rio and locked the library door. Seeing a jumble of books, he sighed and began to gather them.

"No," he stated firmly, and returned the books to the table. "It's my birthday; these books can wait until tomorrow."

That evening Rick talked to friends who had called to wish him a happy birthday. If only this job had not required a move halfway across the country. After six months, he had several **acquaintances** here but no real friends.

"Books are my friends," he thought, which reminded him of the pile of books at the library. "I might as well go tonight and shelve them," he decided.

He entered the library and flicked on the lights, noticing a book face down on the floor. "What's going on?" he muttered as he cautiously lifted up the book. "Ahhh!" he yelled, flinging the book.

Four miniature figures scrambled out of the way as the book landed on the floor with a thud.

"Mr. Dodson," exclaimed a breathless voice, "we are enchanted to make your acquaintance."

"What . . . who . . . ? " Rick stammered.

"We're the Bookers! I'm William. This is Emily and our children, Harry and Clementine. By the way, happy birthday!"

"You know it's my birthday?"

"Naturally, we read your file when you arrived six months ago."

"You were scrounging through my files?" Rick said, collapsing into a nearby chair. He rubbed his eyes, but the tiny figures were still there—looking up at him expectantly.

"Haven't you heard of Bookers?" William asked. "Every library has Bookers!"

“We ensure everything runs smoothly,” said Emily. “Seen any mice around? They love to gnaw on everything.”

“I do nightly rodent patrols, and mice run at the sight of me,” Harry stated proudly.

“Do your chairs ever squeak?” inquired Clementine. “No! That’s because we oil them!”

Rick considered the past six months. He hadn’t seen one mouse and his chairs never squeaked.

“But why?” asked Rick.

“Look around!” exclaimed William. “We work and read. Bookers and libraries are **complementary**. We belong together.”

“To be honest, Mr. Dodson,” said Emily, “we wanted to meet you because we thought that we could be friends.”

Rick Dodson grinned. “Call me Rick. And I’d love to be friends,” he said.

Rick eventually made other new friends, but he still spent many evenings with the Bookers. He bought a toy car for Harry’s rodent patrol, and he read scary stories aloud to Clementine. Every year on his birthday, he brought cupcakes for his friends to share with him.

Make Connections

How do the Bookers make Rick Dodson feel welcome? ESSENTIAL QUESTION

Compare the different ways in which friendships form. TEXT TO TEXT

Genre • Biography

Essential Question

How can words lead to change?

Read how Lincoln's words made a lasting impact.

Go Digital!

Abe's Honest Words

The Life of Abraham Lincoln

by **Doreen Rappaport**
illustrated by **Kadir Nelson**

In the slave state of Kentucky, deep in the wilderness, young Abraham learned to hunt for nuts and currants and fish for trout and bass and tend to soil and seed.

He learned sorrow at age nine when his mama died. But he found great joy with a loving stepmother, who encouraged him to read and learn.

Abraham Lincoln is my name, and with my pen
I wrote the same, I wrote in both haste and speed
and left it here for fools to read.

The family moved deeper into the wilderness, to the free state of Indiana. Panther screams and prowling bears filled Abraham's nights with fear.

He had just a mite of schooling, yet he loved words the way his papa, a master storyteller, did. He stuffed books inside his shirt. In between splitting wood and plowing, he stood in the field and read. He read some books so many times, he knew whole parts by heart.

The things I want to know are in books; my best friend is the man who'll get me a book I ain't read.

Another move, to New Salem, a village in Illinois. The long, lanky boy was a man now. He ferried people and goods down the Ohio and Mississippi rivers.

In between the pull of the pole and the splash of the water, he listened to hunters spin tall tales of a mighty marksman, "half man, half alligator," and sailors describe giant mosquitoes that could kill a man.

He heard lawyers tell how they used words to gain justice for ordinary folks. He heard preachers quote from the Bible: "A house **divided** against itself cannot stand."

He stored these different voices in his heart and wove them into his own words.

The long, muddy Mississippi River brought Lincoln south to New Orleans.

He walked on cobblestone paths and along canals, past flowers spilling over lacy iron balconies. He saw men and women in fancy clothes, eating fancy foods and sipping wine. French, Spanish, and English words filled his ears. But a hideous sight **shattered** his joy.

Twelve Negroes, chained six and six together. Strung together like so many fish upon a trotline, being separated forever from their childhood, their friends, their fathers and mothers, and brothers and sisters, from their wives and children, into perpetual slavery.

(bkgd) Ryan McVay/Photodisc/Getty Images

Lincoln worked at many jobs—farmhand, store owner, postmaster, surveyor, rail-splitter.

Wherever, whatever, he always had a book in hand. Elocution, grammar, mathematics, biography, history, poetry, plays.

Upon the subject of education, I view it as the most important subject which we as a people can be engaged in.

America was growing. Farmers needed new waterways and railroads to ship their crops. Everyone needed better education. If he became a lawmaker, he could help people get these things, so he ran for the Illinois state legislature.

He spoke in public squares and country stores and hayfields.

I am young and unknown to many of you. I was born and have ever remained in the most humble walks of life. I have no wealthy or popular relations to recommend me.

He lost the election. But people liked what he said and how he said it.

He ran again. This time he won. He ran three more times and won.

He became a lawyer. His clients praised "'Honest Old Abe,' the lawyer who was never known to lie." He didn't like the nickname Abe, but it stuck.

Resolve to be honest at all events and if you cannot be an honest lawyer, resolve to be honest without being a lawyer. Choose some other occupation.

(bkgd) Ryan McVay/Photodisc/Getty Images

Nearly four million black men, women, and children were enslaved in southern states. Lincoln thought slavery a great evil. If he became a United States senator, more people would hear him speak out against it.

In speech after speech, he reminded people that slavery did not fit with the ideals of the Declaration of Independence.

As a nation, we began to declare that "all men are created equal." We now practically read it "all men are created equal, except Negroes."

He lost the election. But again, his words got much attention. People felt he spoke from his heart.

In the next two years, **tension** over slavery grew between the South and North. Lincoln ran for president and spoke out against this evil practice. He won this election.

But a month before he took office, seven southern states left the Union. They formed their own government with their own president. In his first inaugural **address**, Lincoln reminded Americans that they were *one* people.

We are not enemies, but friends.
We must not be enemies.

(bkgd) Ryan McVay/Photodisc/Getty Images

On April 12, 1861, Southern troops attacked Fort Sumter, a federal fort in South Carolina. Lincoln knew he had no choice now. The North had to fight the South to bring it back into the Union.

I hold that the Union of these states is perpetual. No state can lawfully get out of the Union.

Families were torn apart, as husbands, fathers, and sons went off to war, many never to return.

(bkgd) Ryan McVay/Photodisc/Getty Images

Many Northerners worried that Lincoln did not have the skills to lead the nation in this terrible time:

"He's too backwoods."

"He's unpresidential."

"He tells too many silly jokes."

"He's had too little experience in government."

If I were to try to read, much less answer, all the attacks made on me, this shop might as well be closed for any other business. I do the very best I know how—the very best I can; and I mean to keep doing so until the end.

(bkgd) Ryan McVay/Photodisc/Getty Images

Lincoln believed that true liberty could not permit slavery. He decided to use his wartime powers as commander in chief to end slavery.

In the third year of the war, he issued the Emancipation **Proclamation**. It freed over three million black men, women, and children and called for black men to join the Union army.

In giving freedom to the slave, we assure freedom to the free.

Most white Northerners **opposed** Lincoln's proclamation. But he stood firm.

I never, in my life, felt more certain that I was doing right, than I do in signing this paper. My whole soul is in it.

The war dragged on. Lincoln grew sadder and sadder as more Americans died.

He went to the Gettysburg battlefield and again reminded the nation why these men had sacrificed their lives.

Four score and seven years ago our fathers brought forth on this continent, a new nation, conceived in liberty, and dedicated to the proposition that all men are created equal.

The Emancipation Proclamation had freed slaves only in the states and territories that were in rebellion. Lincoln wanted slavery ended in the entire nation.

Most white lawmakers did not want this. He called them to the White House to convince them of what he knew was right.

The moment came when I felt that slavery must die that the nation might live!

Finally, they agreed.

In the fourth year of the war, victory seemed close for the North. But Lincoln felt no joy. Hundreds of thousands of men on both sides had died in battle. The country was deeply divided. Many Northerners wanted to punish the South for starting the war. Southerners were furious that the Union army had destroyed their cities and homes and crops. Could the nation ever be one people again?

(bkgd) Ryan McVay/Photodisc/Getty Images

In his second inaugural address, Lincoln shared his vision of how the country could heal itself.

With malice toward none; with charity for all; with firmness in the right, as God gives us to see the right, let us strive on to finish the work we are in; to bind up the nation's wounds.

The South finally surrendered. The job of healing the nation began. But Lincoln was not there to help. An assassin's bullet ended his life.

But his words were there to guide those who chose to remember.

It is for us the living, rather that we here highly resolve that these dead shall not have died in vain–that this nation, under God, shall have a new birth of freedom–and that government of the people, by the people, for the people, shall not perish from the earth.

(bkgd) Ryan McVay/Photodisc/Getty Images

About the Author and Illustrator

Words have always been important to **Doreen Rappaport**. Growing up, she wanted to be a singer and learned the words to many songs. She was also quite talkative in school. In fifth grade, Doreen memorized the Gettysburg Address—and she still remembers much of it. Doreen finds ideas all around her and likes the challenge of writing a good book.

Kadir Nelson began drawing at age three and began painting at age ten. When he was in fourth grade, his uncle, an artist and art teacher, made Kadir his art studio assistant. Before Kadir created the paintings for *Abe's Honest Words*, he took photographs of Lincoln's home and law offices in Springfield, Illinois.

Author's Purpose

Why did the author use the actual words of Abraham Lincoln throughout the biography?

Respond to the Text

Summarize

Summarize *Abe's Honest Words*. Include key historical details from the text that explain Lincoln's impact as the 16th president of our nation. Use your Author's Perspective Chart to help you.

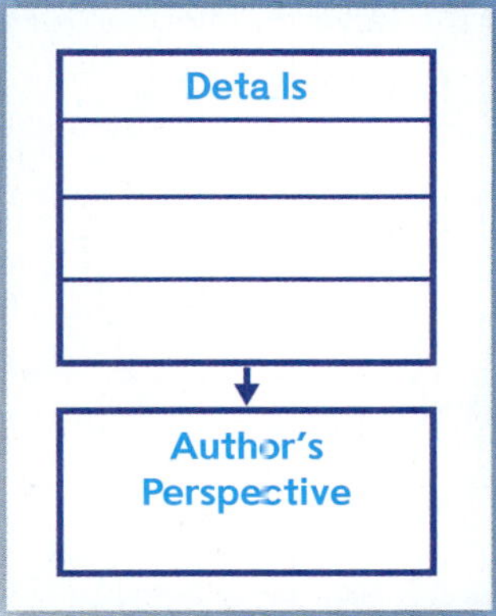

Write

Do you think the author's use of Abraham Lincoln's quotes throughout this selection helps you understand the events that lead to change? Use these sentence starters to help organize your text evidence.

The author uses Lincoln's quotes to . . .
They also tell about . . .
This helps me understand how . . .

Make Connections

Why did Lincoln's words leave such a lasting impression on people? **ESSENTIAL QUESTION**

Words have the power to make people think and act differently. How can words create change in the world today? **TEXT TO WORLD**

Genre • Speech

Compare Texts

Read Abraham Lincoln's most famous speech.

A New Birth of Freedom

The Battle of Gettysburg, Pennsylvania, in July 1863 was a turning point in the Civil War. Thousands of soldiers on both sides lost their lives. After the battle, a proclamation created a national cemetery there. President Lincoln came to Gettysburg on November 19, 1863 to honor the soldiers who had died. In his address, Lincoln praised their courage and asked people to honor them by working toward a "new birth of freedom." At the time, reactions to his speech were mixed. It has since become one of the most famous speeches in our nation's history.

The Gettysburg Address

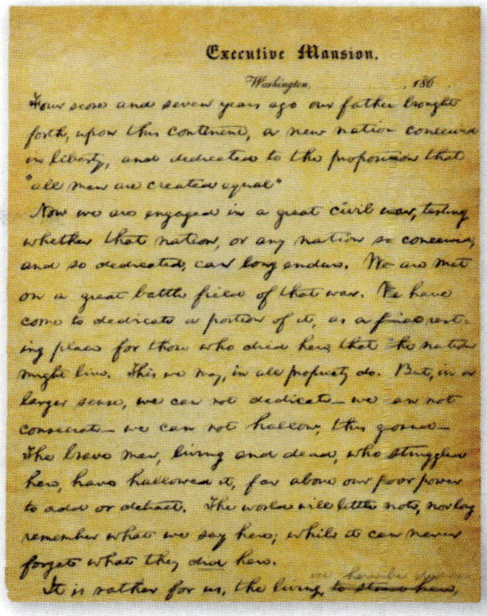
Executive Mansion.
Washington, , 186 .
Four score and seven years ago our fathers brought forth, upon this continent, a new nation, conceived in liberty, and dedicated to the proposition that "all men are created equal"
Now we are engaged in a great civil war, testing whether that nation, or any nation so conceived, and so dedicated, can long endure. We are met on a great battle field of that war. We have come to dedicate a portion of it, as a final resting place for those who died here, that the nation might live. This we may, in all propriety do. But, in a larger sense, we can not dedicate—we can not consecrate—we can not hallow, this ground—The brave men, living and dead, who struggled here, have hallowed it, far above our poor power to add or detract. The world will little note, nor long remember what we say here; while it can never forget what they did here.
It is rather for us, the living, ~~to stand here,~~

Four score and seven years ago our fathers brought forth on this continent, a new nation, conceived in liberty, and dedicated to the proposition that all men are created equal.

Now we are engaged in a great civil war, testing whether that nation, or any nation so conceived and so dedicated, can long endure. We are met on a great battlefield of that war. We have come to dedicate a portion of that field, as a final resting place for those who here gave their lives, that that nation might live. It is altogether fitting and proper that we should do this.

But, in a larger sense, we cannot dedicate—we cannot consecrate—we cannot hallow—this ground. The brave men, living and dead, who struggled here, have consecrated it, far above our poor power to add or detract. The world will little note, nor long remember what we say here, but it can never forget what they did here. It is for us the living, rather, to be dedicated here to the unfinished work which they who fought here have thus far so nobly advanced. It is rather for us to be here dedicated to the great task remaining before us—that from these honored dead we take increased devotion to that cause for which they gave the last full measure of devotion—that we here highly resolve that these dead shall not have died in vain—that this nation, under God, shall have a new birth of freedom—and that government of the people, by the people, for the people, shall not perish from the earth.

Make Connections

What purpose did "The Gettysburg Address" serve for people saddened by the terrible cost of war? **ESSENTIAL QUESTION**

Describe other leaders whose words have made an impact on our nation's history. **TEXT TO TEXT**

Genre • Narrative Nonfiction

SEE HOW

Essential Question

Why do we need government?

Read about the history of our government and the role of citizens.

Go Digital!

THEY RUN

BY SUSAN E. GOODMAN ★ ILLUSTRATED BY ELWOOD H. SMITH

★ A SHORT HISTORY OF DEMOCRACY ★

The Beginnings...

When was the first election? It's impossible to tell. For all we know, people voted in prehistoric times.

FLINT, FLINT, HE'S OUR MAN. IF HE CAN'T CAVE PAINT, NO ONE CAN.

ELECT GROG, KEEPER OF THE FLAME.

A VOTE FOR HOMO SAPIENS IS A VOTE FOR PROGRESS.

Early people may have had elections; we just can't be sure. They didn't have a written language, so they couldn't leave us records—let alone campaign posters or bumper stickers.

Beware of Greeks Bearing Gifts

The ancient Greeks get credit for inventing democracy, probably because they had the best word for it. The "demo" part comes from *demos,* which means "the people." "Cracy" comes from *kratein,* meaning "to rule."

Rule by the people.

Starting in 510 B.C., the citizens of Athens, Greece, gathered in the Assembly and voted on important community issues. Each one had an equal voice in deciding what would happen. This was the purest democracy of all time—sort of. Only adult males, born in Athens with Athenian parents, could be citizens with full legal rights. That meant only one out of eight Athenians could vote on decisions that affected all their lives.

There's No Place Like Rome

Around the same time and a little to the west, the city of Rome began working on its **version** of democracy. That is, when its citizens or armies weren't too busy conquering everyone else around them.

Roman democracy was different from the Greek version, in which ordinary citizens voted on major issues. Instead Romans voted to pick the people who would make decisions for them. They elected senators, who held their jobs for life. They also elected leaders called consuls, who controlled the army and created laws. But a Roman citizen's best **privilege** was being the only one in the Empire who could wear a toga!

Eventually Roman leaders became a little too power hungry. Julius Caesar got himself declared Dictator for Life. Augustus took the title of Emperor. Then he went all out and declared himself a god.

So far our presidents have shown more self-control.

A Place in History

Talk about power—both Julius Caesar and Augustus named months after themselves (July and August).

1,800 Years Later—Here Comes American Democracy

George Washington and the rest of our Founding Fathers borrowed bits and pieces from past democracies to create our own. They named our Senate after the Roman Senate. They adopted a British idea from the thirteenth century, saying that the government must respect a citizen's legal rights.

George and his crew wanted a government where people had some say in how to rule the country—but not too much. They didn't trust all their fellow Americans, especially those without much education. So they rejected the Greek method of having citizens vote directly on laws. Decisions would be made by people who "represented" the citizens instead, just like in the Roman Republic.

In 1787, the Founding Fathers locked themselves up for four months to write our Constitution. Coming up with this description of our new government wasn't easy. They all had different ideas and had to **compromise**. George Washington's face often wore its "Valley Forge look."

Here's what they came up with—a national government with three branches. Our Congress (the legislative branch) has two parts or houses: the Senate and the House of Representatives. Congress can make laws to raise taxes, improve citizens' lives, and defend the country. The president heads the executive branch. He (and someday soon, maybe she) carries out laws and is head of the military. He also appoints judges to the Supreme Court, part of our judicial branch. The court's job is to enforce existing laws and decide if the other two branches are obeying the Constitution.

What Did Ben Say?

Shortly after the Constitutional Convention ended, a woman asked Benjamin Franklin what kind of government the Founding Fathers created. Franklin's answer? "A republic, madam, if you can keep it." In other words, our kind of government needs citizens who care enough to stay informed and take part. In other, other words... *VOTE*!

Getting Better All the Time

Is the Constitution a perfect plan? Nope, but the people who wrote it were smart enough to know that. They improved it right away by writing the Bill of Rights, the first ten **amendments** (additions) to the Constitution. We've been making it better ever since.

The Good News: The United States was the first modern democracy with an elected government protecting the freedom and rights of its citizens.

The Bad News: In the beginning, only white men who owned land could vote.

The Good News: In 1856, white men who didn't own land got that right.

The Bad News: Everyone else was still left out in the cold. Changing beliefs and values isn't easy; it takes lots of thought and struggle.

The Good News: African American and other nonwhite men began voting in 1870.

The Bad News: People's beliefs and values change too slowly. An African American's right to vote was often denied in the South and parts of the North until the civil rights movement of the 1960s.

The Good News: American women of all races got the vote in 1920.

The Bad News: Women in New Zealand, Australia, Finland, Norway, Canada, Estonia, England, Ireland, the Soviet Union, Austria, Czechoslovakia, Germany, Hungary, Armenia, Azerbaijan, Poland, Luxembourg, and Holland were able to vote before them. At least the United States beat Switzerland, where women couldn't vote until 1971!

The Good News: Native Americans began voting in 1924.

The Bad News: Seems like a long wait, given that they were here first. What's more, some states banned them from voting until the 1940s.

The Good News: In 1971, the voting age was reduced to eighteen years old.

The Bad News: You've still got a while before you can vote.

The Good News: You have other ways to make your opinion heard. Keep reading to find out what they are!

★ Uncle Sam Wants You ★

Rx for Voting

When people are involved with their communities, their knowledge of politics grows. Their interest and **commitment** does too. That's true for kids as well as grown-ups.

Okay, you aren't old enough to vote, not even close. But you can still have a voice in our democracy.

Four million kids already cast ballots on Election Day. They're part of a program called Kids Voting USA in schools in twenty-eight states and Washington DC. True, their votes aren't counted in official tallies. But they're announced in schools and on local TV stations.

This program has another advantage. Kids get so excited that 3 to 5 percent more of their parents end up voting too.

That's where you come in, even if Kids Voting USA isn't in your school. You can make sure your parents are registered to vote. And you can make sure they actually do it.

How? Oh, come on. How do you get your parents to do anything? Drive you somewhere? Buy a new game? Let you stay up late?

You bug 'em!

So bug them about voting. Plaster a countdown calendar on the front door. Put reminders on their voice mail. E-mail too. If they say they're too tired on the Big Day, try a bribe (it works when they want something from you!). Offer to do the dishes if they go—but only if you're desperate!

Kids to the Rescue!

Bugging your parents is a good first step. Some kids are going even further. They are identifying issues and working on them. A recent report found that 55 percent of American kids volunteer. That's almost twice as many as adults.

Kids are becoming leaders. . .

Talk about bugging, a group of second graders decided that Massachusetts needed an official state insect. When they learned that any state resident could give legislators ideas for new laws, they got busy. Maybe it was the ladybug costumes they wore while visiting the state capitol. Maybe it was their speech saying ladybugs could be found all over the state. Whatever the reason, the legislature approved their bill and the governor signed a law proclaiming the ladybug as Massachusetts's state insect.

Third and fourth graders did something similar for New Hampshire, which didn't have a state fruit. The hardest thing about that process was convincing legislators that the pumpkin IS a fruit.

At age seven, Shadia Wood learned that the Superfund bill would clean up New York's worst toxic waste sites. For seven years, Shadia and a group called Kids Against Pollution tried to convince lawmakers to pass this bill. She had a lemonade stand on the steps of the state capitol, selling drinks and "toxic dump" cake. Then she'd send the profits to the governor to help pay for the Superfund. Eventually TV and newspaper reporters noticed what she was doing. The Superfund bill became law in 2003. (There's nothing wrong with shaming grown-ups into good behavior.)

Imagine getting $135 to skip school and do good work? When Massachusetts's governor signed a bill to let sixteen- and seventeen-year-olds work at the polls, Boston-based students began helping voters with computerized equipment on Election Day. It's a win-win-win-win situation: kids know computers better than many adult voters; they get involved with voting; they get money. They are also being trained for the job. Our country will need them soon. The average poll worker is currently seventy-two years old.

In Boise, Idaho, kids ages fifteen and up are on committees governing the city. Some towns, like Linesville, Pennsylvania, have had eighteen-year-old mayors. Mayor at eighteen seems pretty great. But in California, Ohio, Rhode Island, Vermont, Washington, and Wisconsin, an eighteen-year-old can be governor.

Sending a Message

If you see a problem in your community or have an idea of how to make things better, get active. Give a government leader a piece of your mind (the best part, please!).

- Speak up at a town meeting.
- Invite your mayor or another official to speak to your class about an important issue. Be ready to ask good questions and give your opinions.
- Set up a class trip to visit him or her.
- Write a letter or e-mail that identifies a problem. Tell how the problem affects you and your community. Write about the changes you'd like to see. Send your letter to the appropriate official in your town or to your state representative and senator or to your representative and senator in Congress or even to the governor or president.
- Write a letter and get people who agree with you to sign it too. Make sure you write your names and addresses clearly.
- Make a survey about the problem, write it up, and send it to the right official.

ABOUT THE AUTHOR AND ILLUSTRATOR

Susan E. Goodman loved reading as a kid, but reading did not make her a good writer. That happened when she got a D- on a school paper. Goodman's teacher allowed her to rewrite it. That taught Goodman the importance of reviewing and revising anything she writes. And Susan Goodman has written a lot–more than 700 articles and several books!

Elwood Smith grew up with a love of cartoon characters and comic books. When he began drawing humorous illustrations as an adult, he remembered the comics he had loved as a child and tried to draw in that style. Smith also plays guitar in a rock band with other artists.

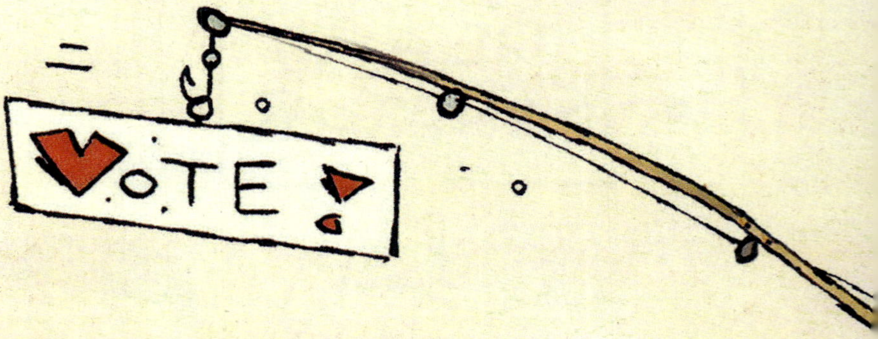

Author's Purpose

Why did the author explain the types of government used long ago before she explained the way that American democracy works?

(t) Michael J. Maloney/Courtesy of Susan E. Goodman; (b) Matt Petricone

Respond to the Text

Summarize

Summarize *See How They Run*. Include the most important events. Information from your Cause and Effect Chart may help you.

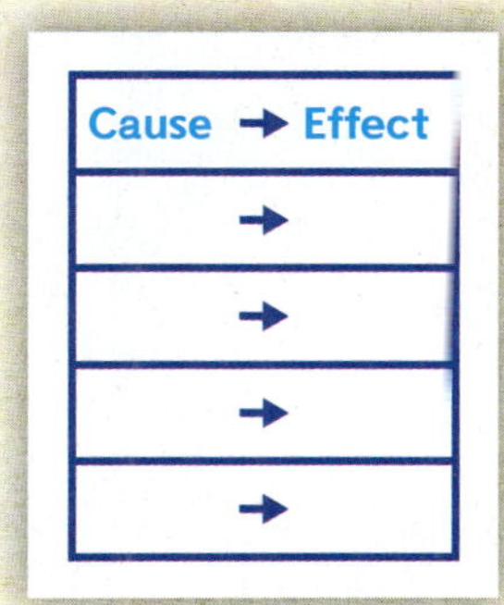

Write

Why is it important for people to participate in government? Use these sentence starters to help organize your text evidence.

> It is important to participate in government because . . .
> One way to participate is . . .
> Another way to participate is . . .

Make Connections

How would our lives be different if we did not have a government? **ESSENTIAL QUESTION**

How does the government of the United States compare to other types of government around the world? Why do you think many people want to be part of a democracy? **TEXT TO WORLD**

Genre • Expository Text

Compare Texts

Read about the Founding Fathers' plan for our government.

The Birth of American DEMOCRACY

I am apt to believe that it will be celebrated, by succeeding Generations, as the great anniversary Festival. It ought to be commemorated, as the Day of Deliverance. . . . You will think me transported with Enthusiasm but I am not. I am well aware of the Toil and Blood and Treasure, that it will cost Us to maintain this Declaration, and support and defend these states. Yet through all the Gloom I can see the Rays of ravishing Light and Glory. I can see that the End is more than worth all the Means.

Written by John Adams to his wife Abigail about the signing of the Declaration of Independence on July 4, 1776

Every Fourth of July, Americans celebrate the birthday of the United States. Fireworks and parades remind us that the thirteen colonies declared independence from Great Britain on July 4, 1776. That birthday took place in Philadelphia, Pennsylvania. There, the Second Continental Congress approved the Declaration of Independence. This document formed a new nation, the United States of America. The Declaration is almost like our country's original birthday card.

Our Founding Fathers

Five men, including John Adams, Thomas Jefferson, and Benjamin Franklin, wrote the Declaration of Independence. Jefferson wrote the first draft. His famous words sum up a basic American belief—"all men are created equal."

The men who signed the Declaration are called the Founding Fathers of our country. Signing the Declaration put the founders' lives in danger. They knew that their signatures made them traitors to Great Britain. They also knew that, if the colonies won the war, their names would go down in history.

Led by General George Washington, the colonists fought passionately for their freedom. After a long, bloody war, the British surrendered in 1781, and a peace treaty was signed in 1783. Our new nation was still a work in progress, however. Americans disagreed about how much power a federal, or central, government should have. Given that they had just won freedom from a powerful British king, Americans did not want their government to have too much power.

The Constitutional Convention

By 1787, the states were like separate countries. Each state printed its own money and made its own trade laws. The national government was weak and in debt from the war. In May 1787 each state sent delegates, people who represent others, to Philadelphia to attend a meeting called the Constitutional Convention. The delegates were to create a new plan for our government. George Washington was chosen as the president of the convention.

One young delegate, James Madison, proposed ideas. After many debates, he compromised with the other delegates on the United States Constitution as the plan for our government. Thus, today James Madison is known as the "Father of the Constitution." Delegates from large and small states argued most about the power to pass legislation, or laws. States with large populations wanted more votes in a legislature. Small states did not think this was fair. By September of 1787, the states agreed on a system of checks and balances known as the three branches of government. In this system, no branch has too much power.

THREE BRANCHES OF GOVERNMENT

The Legislative Branch creates laws.	The Executive Branch carries out laws.	The Judicial Branch settles disputes about laws.
Includes: • Congress – House of Representatives – Senate	Includes: • President • Vice President • Cabinet Members	Includes: • Supreme Court • Lower Federal Courts

The Three Branches

The Legislative Branch, or Congress, is made up of the Senate and House of Representatives. Congress passes laws. Small states liked the Senate because each state, large or small, got two senators. In the House, a state's population determines the number of representatives.

(bkgd) Garry Gay/Riser/Getty Images; (c) Architect of the Capitol

The president heads the Executive Branch. The president can sign, veto, and enforce laws. The president also commands the nation's military.

The Judicial Branch is the third branch. The highest court is called the Supreme Court. District, state, and federal courts determine whether a law follows the Constitution.

The Constitution was officially approved in September 1787, but it did not become the law of the nation right away. Why? It had to be ratified, or approved, by nine of the thirteen states.

Some states held out. They felt the Constitution did not give enough power to the people. They wanted to add amendments, or changes, that guaranteed important personal rights such as freedom of speech or religion. James Madison jumped in again. He wrote the Bill of Rights, the first ten amendments to the Constitution. These were added to the Constitution in 1791. Finally, our nation had a plan of government that was approved!

All the People

Our Constitution begins with the words *We the People*. Back in 1791, however, the Constitution gave certain rights, such as voting, only to some people. That has changed over time. Today, our Constitution grants all citizens over the age of 18 the right to vote. Politicians continually revisit this founding document to ensure that all people are treated equally in our democracy.

Make Connections

Why did delegates from the states meet to write a Constitution in 1787? **ESSENTIAL QUESTION**

Why is it important to be an active participant in our democracy? Use details from the selections to explain. **TEXT TO TEXT**

Vincent Ricardel/The Image Bank/Getty Images

Genre • Historical Fiction

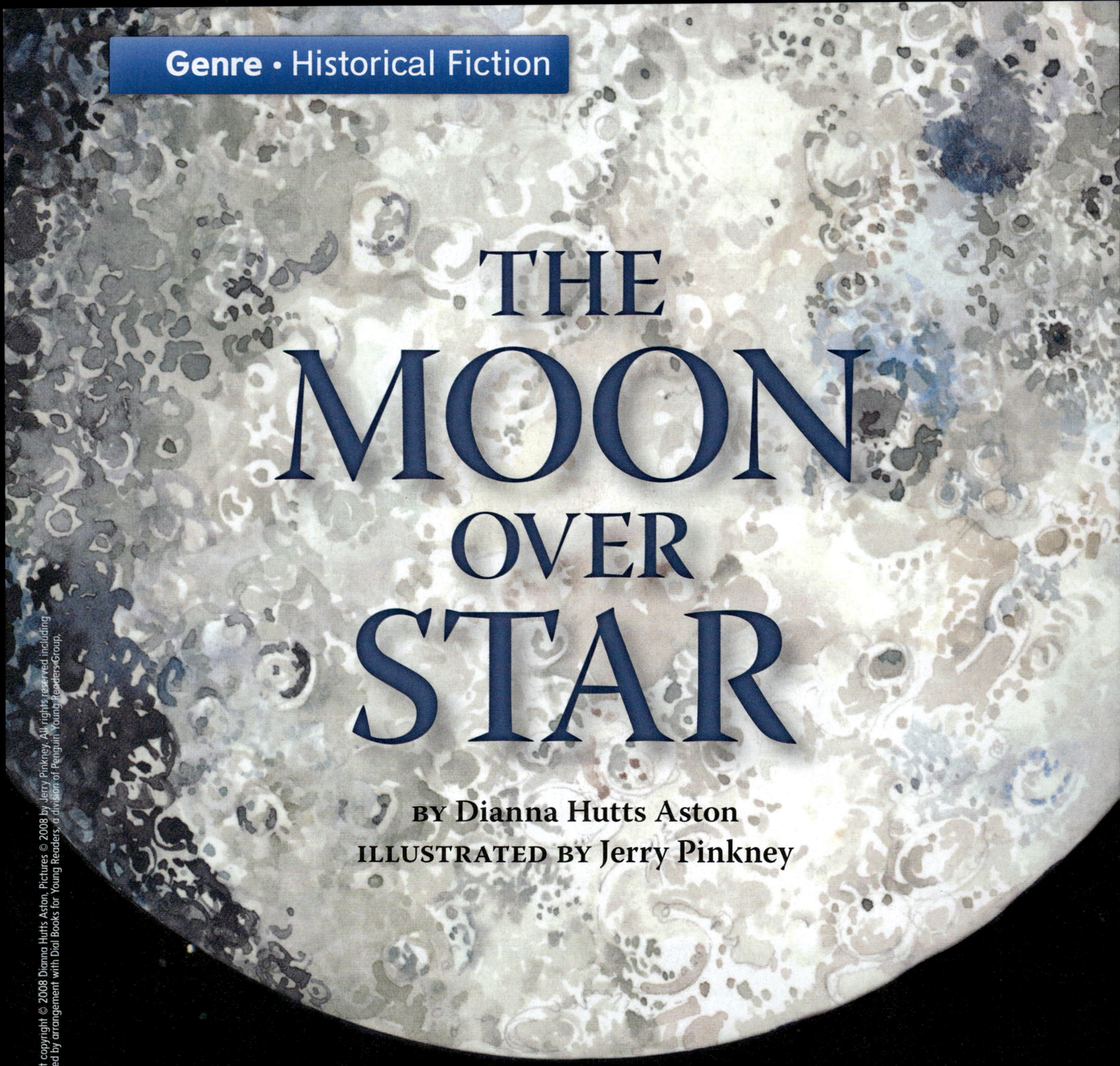

THE MOON OVER STAR

BY Dianna Hutts Aston
ILLUSTRATED BY Jerry Pinkney

Essential Question

How does technology affect your life?

Read to find out how the moon landing affected Mae and her family.

Go Digital!

Once upon a summer's morning, in 1969, Grandpa led the singing in church, the light of Sunday gleaming on his silvery head. Through the open windows our voices sailed over Star, our town. Then we bowed our heads and prayed for the astronauts, Neil Armstrong, Edwin Aldrin, Jr., and Michael Collins. If all went well a spaceship would land on the moon today, and I dreamed that maybe one day, I could go to the moon too.

My gramps thought the space program was a waste of money, but I knew he was praying for them too. I thought about the astronauts' kids and wondered if they were scared—scared but proud. I know I'd be. I slipped my hand into my dad's and whispered so only I could hear, "Please bless the astronauts' children too."

Once upon a summer's noon, my cousins and I **scouted** Gran's watermelon patch for the biggest one. It took three of us to carry it to a tub of ice—three and a half, counting my littlest cousin, Lacey. We decorated the picnic table with pails of wildflowers. Then, our chores done, we built our own spaceship from scraps we found in the barn.

"T minus 15 seconds ... 12, 11, 10, 9 ..." As the oldest grandchild, I got to be launch controller and Commander Armstrong. "Ignition sequence start ... 6, 5, 4, 3, 2, 1, 0. Liftoff, we have liftoff!"

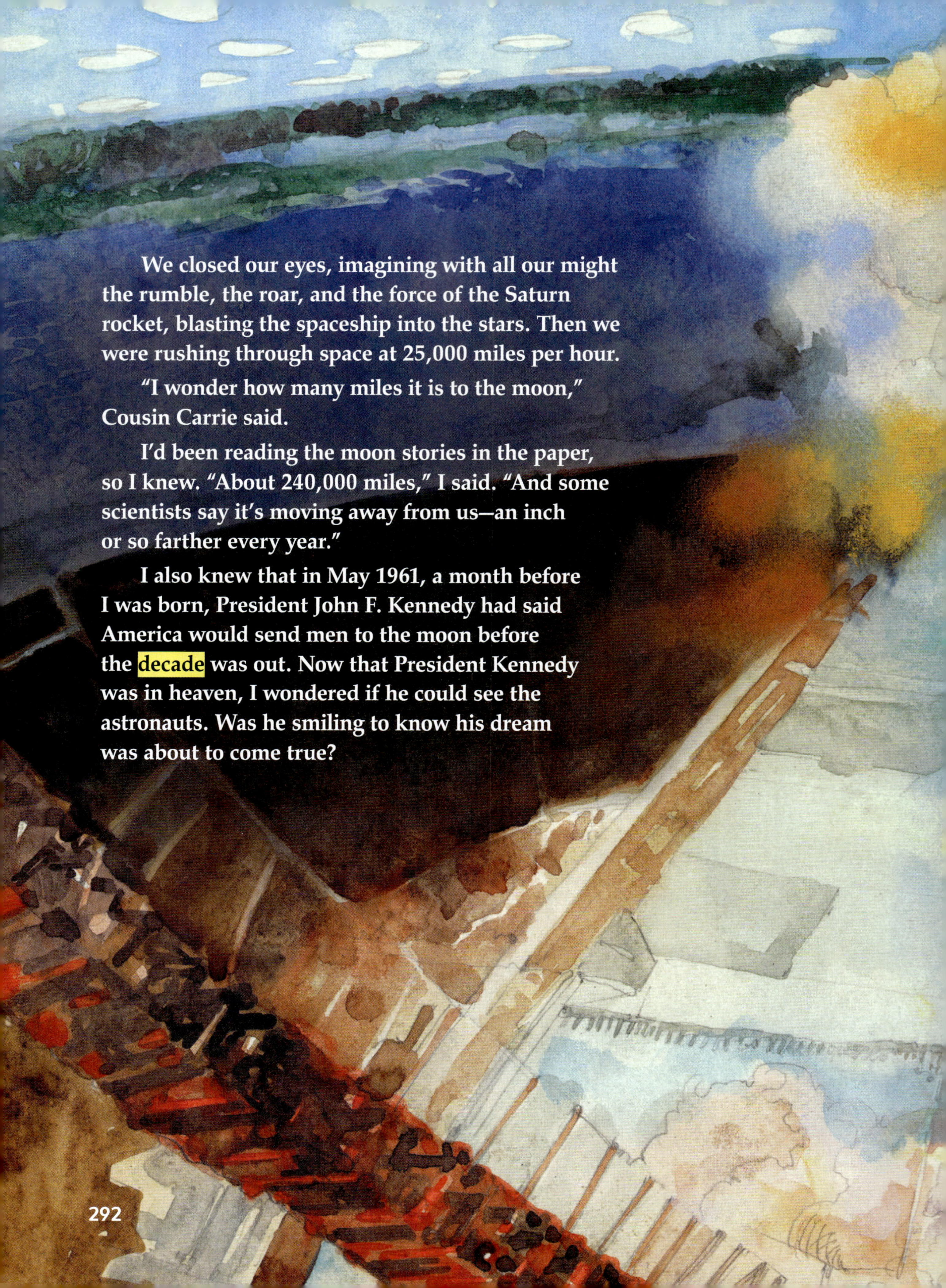

We closed our eyes, imagining with all our might the rumble, the roar, and the force of the Saturn rocket, blasting the spaceship into the stars. Then we were rushing through space at 25,000 miles per hour.

"I wonder how many miles it is to the moon," Cousin Carrie said.

I'd been reading the moon stories in the paper, so I knew. "About 240,000 miles," I said. "And some scientists say it's moving away from us—an inch or so farther every year."

I also knew that in May 1961, a month before I was born, President John F. Kennedy had said America would send men to the moon before the decade was out. Now that President Kennedy was in heaven, I wondered if he could see the astronauts. Was he smiling to know his dream was about to come true?

That afternoon, we were helping Gramps with the tractor when Gran hollered, "Come quick! They're landing!"

Gramps kept right on **tinkering** with the engine. The rest of us ran pell-mell for the house and **squirmed** around the television screen as it glowed with equal parts of moon and the spaceship called *Eagle*.

We heard the voice of Commander Armstrong **directing** the landing. "Forward ... forward," he said.

Then the newsman we all knew, Walter Cronkite, exclaimed, "Man on the moon!"

For a split second we were silent—the whole universe must have been—as we waited ... waited ... waited to hear the voice of an astronaut 240,000 miles away.

And then: "Houston, Tranquility Base here," Commander Armstrong said. "The *Eagle* has landed."

Boy, did we cheer, all of the cousins and even the grown-ups—all except Gramps.

I remembered something he'd once said: "Why spend all that money to go to the moon when there's so many folks in need right here on Earth?"

"Because we can!" I'd almost shouted, but caught myself.

I began to wonder then what Gramps's dreams had been. From the time he was little, he had worked the farm, doing the same jobs, day to day, season to season.

When the crickets began to sing, Gramps took out his pipe. I pulled off his dirt-caked boots for him and stomped around the porch.

"Gramps, will you watch it with me tonight ... the moon walk?"

"I'm mighty worn out today," he said, "but maybe."

Suddenly, I could see how tired he was. Lifetime-tired. There were deep lines in his face—a farmer's face, an old farmer's face.

"All right, Gramps," I said. "It's okay."

Once upon a summer's night in 1969, we spread blankets and folding chairs on the edge of the yard, where the buffalo grass grew thick and soft. The cornstalks whispered while we gazed at the pearly slice of moon, and the stars, gleaming like spilled sugar. What were the astronauts seeing, right at this very second? Could they see beyond the moon, to Mars or Neptune or Jupiter? We passed around a bowl of popcorn. What I could see above me, and what I could see in my imagination, were better than any picture show.

Later on that summer's night, in 1969, the television screen flashed with words that gave me goose bumps: LIVE FROM THE SURFACE OF THE MOON.

And Mr. Cronkite said, "... Neil Armstrong, thirty-eight-year-old American, standing on the surface of the moon on this July twentieth, nineteen hundred and sixty-nine!"

I didn't know it then, but there were 600 million people the world over watching with me, and listening, when Commander Armstrong said, "That's one small step for man, one giant leap for mankind." All of us—from New York to Tokyo to Paris to Cairo ... to Star—and maybe even President Kennedy too—all of us watched it together, the astronauts bounding across the moon like ghosts on a trampoline.

I felt a hand on my shoulder. "I reckon that's something to remember," Gramps said quietly.

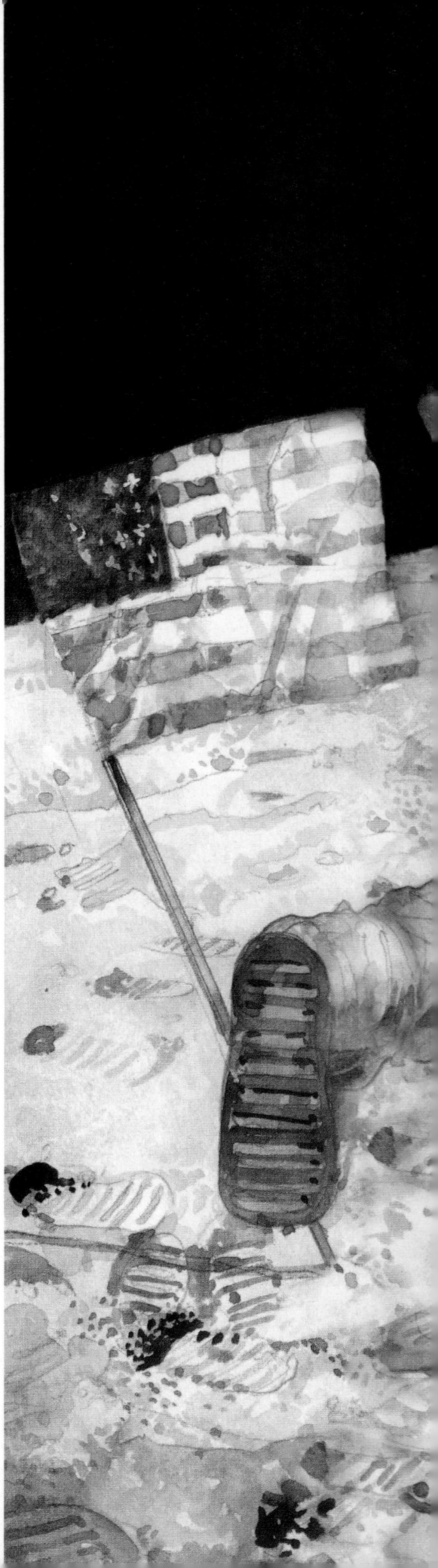

Later, when it was as quiet as the world ever gets, Gramps and I stood together under the moon. "What's mankind?" I asked him.

He puffed on his pipe. "It's all of us," he finally said. "All of us who've ever lived, all of us still to come."

I put my hand in his. "Just think, Gramps: If they could go to the moon, maybe one day I could too!"

"Great days," he said, "an astronaut in the family. Who'd a thought."

I smiled in the dark. My gramps was proud of me.

"First airplane I ever saw ... I was your age ... was right over yonder," Gramps said, nodding toward the cornfield. "That was something to see, oh boy ... something to see."

A sigh in Gramps's voice made my heart squeeze.

"Keep on dreaming, Mae," he said. "Just remember, we're here now together on the prettiest star in the heavens."

Gramps had looked to the moon all of his life. It told him when to plant and when to harvest. And once upon a summer's night, it told me to dream.

ABOUT THE AUTHOR AND ILLUSTRATOR

Dianna Hutts Aston was five years old when astronauts landed on the moon. She grew up in Houston, Texas, home of the Johnson Space Center. Today, Dianna's nonprofit organization gives hot air balloon rides to Mexican children in orphanages and rural villages. To her, an important part of writing is "thinking and dreaming."

Growing up, **Jerry Pinkney** used artistic skills to overcome a reading problem. He turned the words into pictures in his imagination to understand a story. Jerry has illustrated more than 100 children's books and novels. He has also created paintings for the NASA Art Collection at the Kennedy Space Center.

Author's Purpose

Why does the author use the phrase "Once upon a summer's morning . . . noon . . . night" at different points in the story?

(t) Renee Edy; (b) Thomas Kristich

Respond to the Text

Summarize

Summarize the sequence of events in *The Moon Over Star*. Think about how the moon landing affects Mae as she tells her story. Information from your Character Perspective Chart may help you.

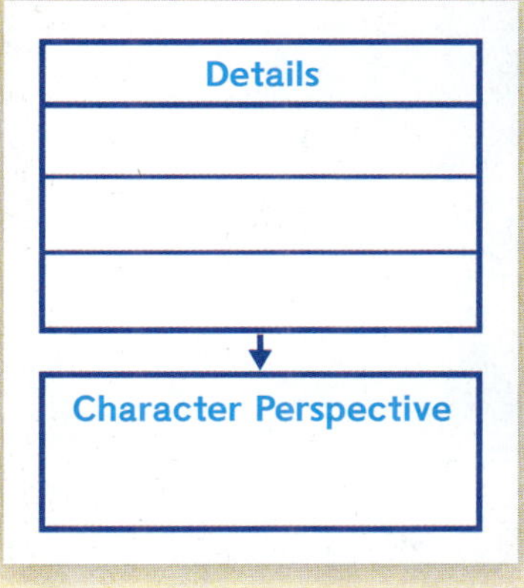

Write

What can readers learn through Mae's experience with the moon landing? Use these sentence starters to help organize your text evidence.

The story takes place . . .
Readers learn that . . .
Another example is . . .
Mae learns that . . .

Make Connections

What does the moon landing mean to Mae and her family? **ESSENTIAL QUESTION**

Which invention or technology has had the biggest impact on our world since the moon landing? **TEXT TO WORLD**

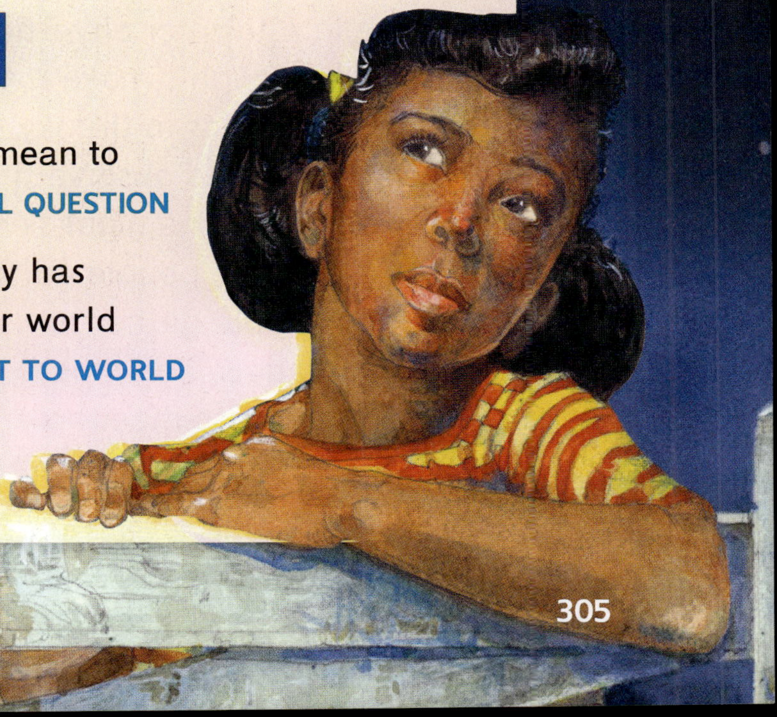

Genre • Expository

Compare Texts

Read how people are coming together to learn about astronomy.

Star Parties

Look up at the night sky. You probably won't see many stars in the sky if you live in a town or city. The street and building lights make it too difficult to view objects in the sky. So where can you go to observe the **gleaming** wonders of the night sky?

Around the world, people go to star parties. People gather to observe stars, planets, and much more. It is a fun way to meet new people and learn about the universe.

Larry Landolfi/Science Source

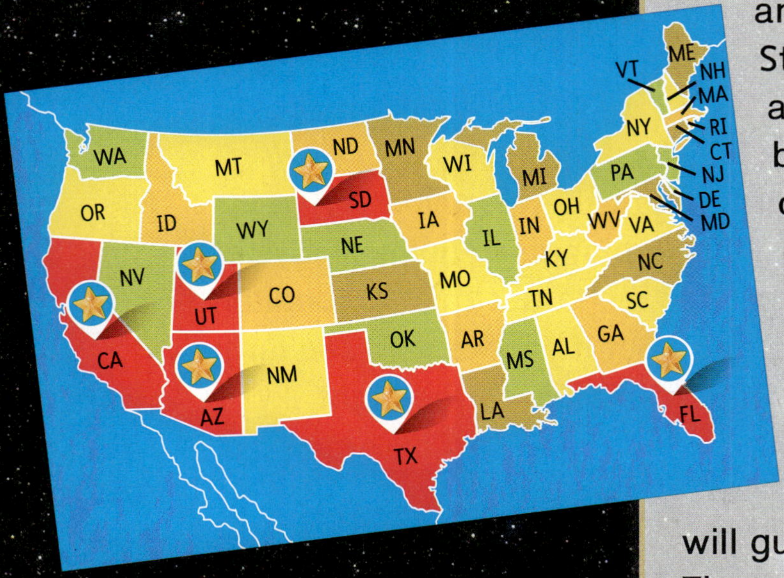

There are star parties in many states. The map shows some of those states.

Find a Star Party

For **decades,** many national parks and observatories in the United States have held star parties. These are great locations for star parties because they can provide total darkness. Many astronomy clubs give star parties, too. All you need is a location with dark night skies and telescopes.

National parks in every part of our country offer star parties. Park rangers and astronomers will guide you through the night sky. They will point out and explain the different objects in the sky. There may be sights that are impossible to see where you live. For example, on a moonless night, Bryce Canyon, Utah, is so dark that the Milky Way covers the sky like a huge silver rainbow. Go to the National Park Service website to find the nearest star party in your area.

The McDonald Observatory

Observatories have powerful **technology** that astronomers use to do their research. The McDonald Observatory in Texas is located in the Davis Mountains. At the observatory, star parties are held at a telescope park. The park has dome structures with different sized telescopes. One dome has a 24-inch telescope that can be operated by a robot in a remote location—now that's great **engineering**!

The McDonald Observatory hosts many star parties.

If you plan to go to a star party, look up the moon phase for that date. When the Moon lights up the sky, you may not be able to see some objects clearly. But you will get great views of the Moon!

What to See

During different times of the year, you will get good views of some of the planets in our solar system. Many star gazers look for the largest planet, Jupiter, with its moons and rings. But if you want to see larger and brighter rings, look for Saturn in the night sky.

Phases of the Moon

As the Moon orbits Earth, it follows a regular pattern. The pattern repeats every 29 or 30 days. People on Earth see different parts of the Moon as it orbits Earth. The different patterns are called moon phases. The beginning phase is the new moon phase. In the new moon phase, the Moon is between Earth and the Sun. You will not see the Moon in the sky. After a few days, a thin sliver of the Moon appears. Each night, the Moon looks larger. In a week, the Moon looks like a half circle. A week later, a full Moon lights up the sky. The diagram at right shows the different moon phases.

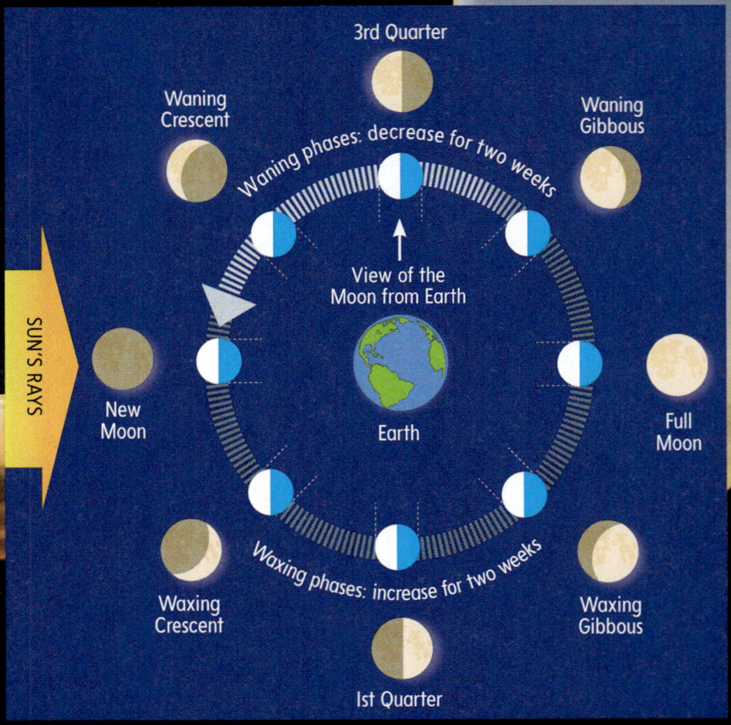

The Moon does not have a light source. When we see the Moon in the night sky, the Sun is shining on it. The Sun's light is reflecting off the Moon's surface.

There are also numerous constellations. A constellation is a group of stars that form a pattern or image. For example, Orion the Hunter is a constellation that the ancient Greeks thought looked like a hunter with a sword attached to its belt.

At a star party you may get a chance to make a wish under a shooting star, or a meteor. Meteors are not really stars. They are bits of rocks. But they appear in the sky as beautiful streaks of light. When there are many shooting stars in the sky, it is called a meteor shower.

No matter what time of year you go to a star party, you will not be disappointed. There is always something fascinating to see in the night sky.

Moon Clock Activity

1. Draw a clock face with numbers 1 to 12.
2. Next to numbers 12, 3, 6, 9 draw circles to represent the Moon.
3. Label Number 12 as New Moon, Number 3 as First Quarter, Number 6 as Full Moon, and Number 9 as Last Quarter.
4. Shade in the circles for each moon phase.
5. Observe and record the dates for each phase on the clock.

Make Connections

What technology do people use to observe objects in the night sky? **ESSENTIAL QUESTION**

Would Mae from *The Moon Over Star* go to a star party? Why or why not? **TEXT TO TEXT**

Genre • Poetry

Swimming to the Rock

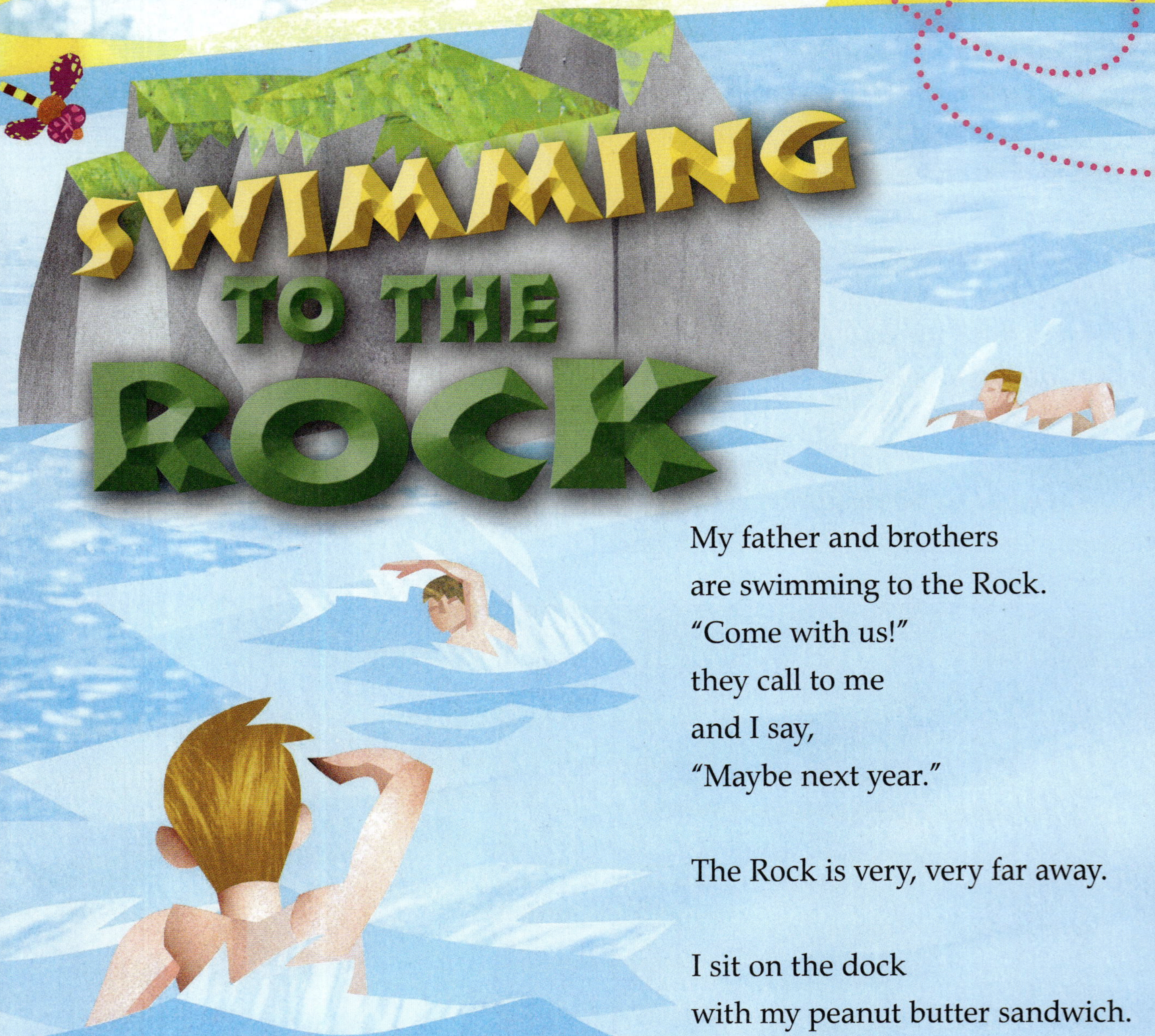

My father and brothers
are swimming to the Rock.
"Come with us!"
they call to me
and I say,
"Maybe next year."

The Rock is very, very far away.

I sit on the dock
with my peanut butter sandwich.
I watch them
dive into the water
and swim the distance
their kicks and
splashes and elbows
getting smaller and smaller
as they near the Rock.

Essential Question

How do writers look at success in different ways?

Read how two poets describe accomplishments.

Go Digital!

It takes them a long, long time.

They arrive and pull themselves to stand
and wave their arms in the air.
I can't see it but I know their hands are in fists.
I can't hear it but I know they are cheering.
Even the loons call to celebrate their arrival!

I sit on my dock
dangling my feet in the water
counting dragonflies.

My father and brothers
come closer
and from the water
lift their faces with
wild wet smiles.
And I think

This year!

– *Mary Atkinson*

The Moondust Footprint

For Joshua Katz
Woodstock, Vermont, July 20, 1969

We'd been watching, watching, watching
all day long into the night:
Mission Control in Houston,
Apollo astronauts in flight.
A new chapter of history
was about to open soon.
The Apollo slowed...then quickened,
speeding closer to the moon.

The others went to bed,
but not Aunt Mary and me.
We kept watching, watching, watching
each slow stage on the TV:
the hovering Landing Module
the Sea of Tranquility,
and the astronaut, Neil Armstrong,
moving oh so carefully...
I was holding my breath
—Aunt Mary said she'd held hers, too—
until we saw the moondust footprint
made by Armstrong's ribbed left shoe!

That footprint marked a moment—
an awesome human victory.
We were watching history happen,
my aunt Mary...and me.

– *Bobbi Katz*

Respond to the Text

Summarize

Use important details from "Swimming to the Rock" to summarize what happens in the poem. Information from your Theme Chart may help you.

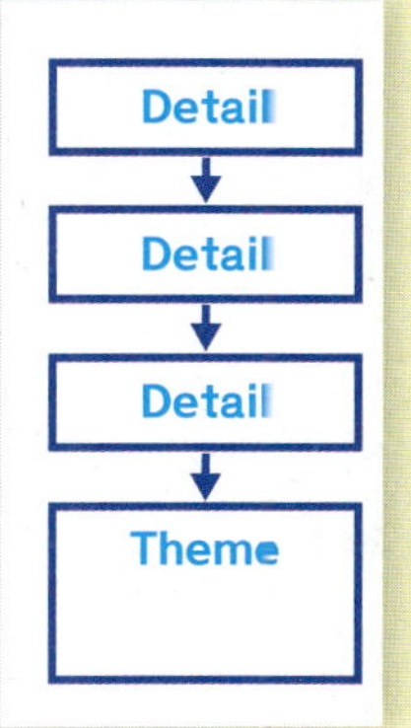

Write

What can readers learn about success from "Swimming to the Rock" and "The Moondust Footprint?" Use these sentence starters to help organize your text evidence.

> In "Swimming to the Rock" the speaker. . .
> In "The Moondust Footprint" the speaker feels . . . because . . .
> This tells me that success can be . . .

Make Connections

What does accomplishment mean to each of the poets? **ESSENTIAL QUESTION**

These poems treat the idea of success differently—it is personal for one poet and universal for the other. What are other achievements, large or small, that poets might use as examples of success? **TEXT TO WORLD**

Genre • Poetry

Compare Texts

Read how two poets describe moments of triumph.

Genius

"Sis! Wake up!" I whisper
in the middle of the night.

Urgently, I shake her
till she switches on the light.

The spiral notebook in my hand
provides her quick relief.

It tells her there's no danger
of a break-in by a thief.

"Okay,"she says, then, props herself
up vertically in bed.

She nods for me to read my work.
I cough, then forge ahead.

The last verse of my poem leaves
her silent as a mouse.

I worry till she says, "We have
a genius in the house."

– *Nikki Grimes*

WINNER

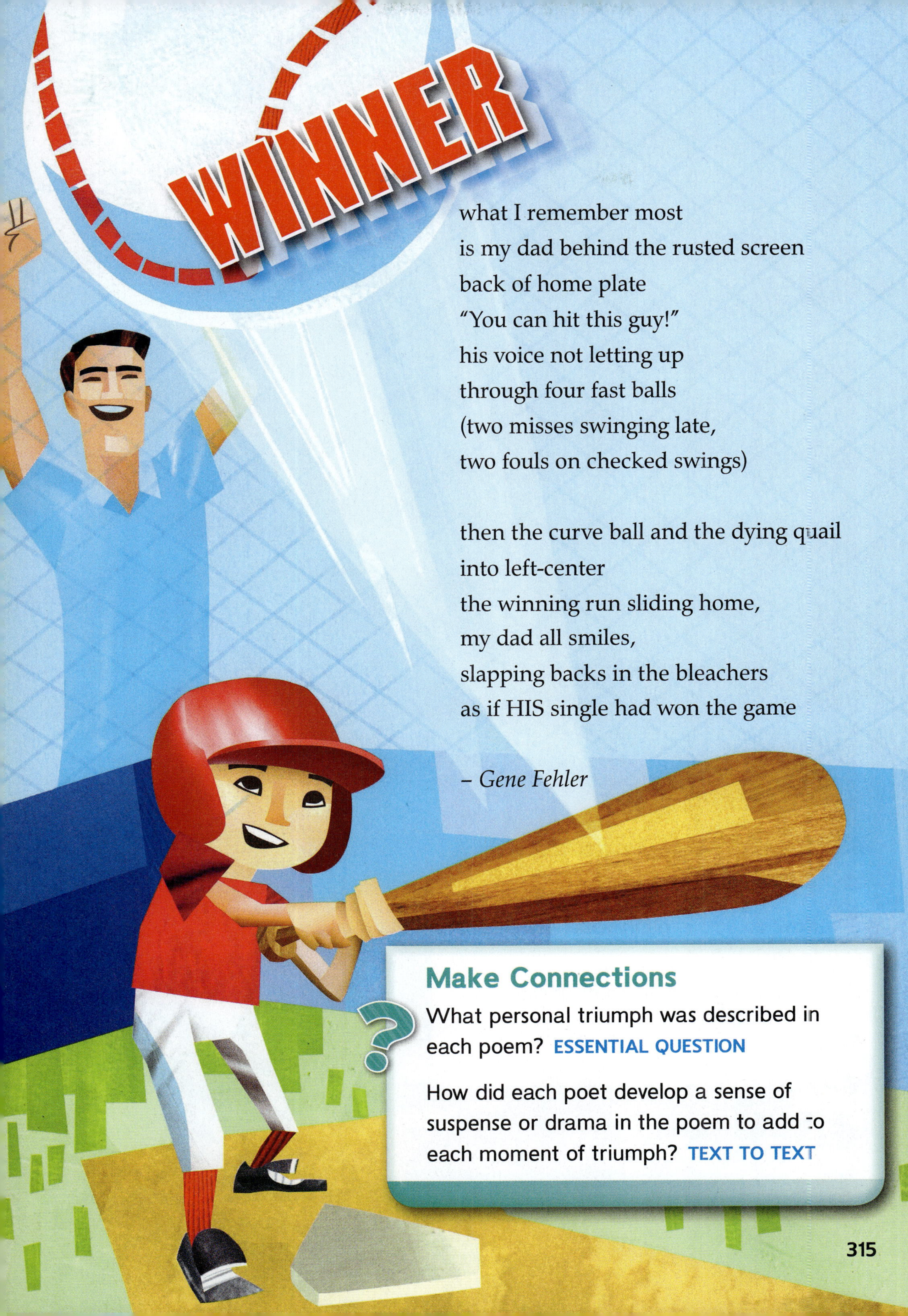

what I remember most
is my dad behind the rusted screen
back of home plate
"You can hit this guy!"
his voice not letting up
through four fast balls
(two misses swinging late,
two fouls on checked swings)

then the curve ball and the dying quail
into left-center
the winning run sliding home,
my dad all smiles,
slapping backs in the bleachers
as if HIS single had won the game

– *Gene Fehler*

Make Connections

What personal triumph was described in each poem? **ESSENTIAL QUESTION**

How did each poet develop a sense of suspense or drama in the poem to add to each moment of triumph? **TEXT TO TEXT**

Genre • Expository Text

Why Does the MOON Change Shape?

BY Melissa Stewart

Essential Question

How do you explain what you see in the sky?

Read about the different phases of the moon.

Go Digital!

The Mysterious Moon

For as long as people have lived on Earth, they have asked questions about the bright lights that fill the nighttime sky. What causes them? How far away are they? Why do they move from night to night?

(bkgd) 4 Girls 1 Boy/Shutterstock.com

For thousands of years, the Moon has been the most mysterious nighttime object of all. It is the largest object in the night sky, and it is the brightest. What amazed ancient people the most is how the Moon's shape is constantly changing. Sometimes it looks like a full bright circle. Other times, only a tiny **sliver** appears.

It did not take ancient people long to realize that the Moon's changes, or **phases**, follow a regular pattern. The Moon's phases repeat themselves every twenty-nine or thirty days. If you watch the Moon every night for about a month, you can see all its phases.

At the beginning of each cycle, people on Earth cannot see the Moon at all. After a few days, a tiny sliver of light appears in the nighttime sky. Each night, the Moon looks a little larger. After a week, it looks like half of a circle. And about a week after that, a full round disk brightens the night sky.

But then the Moon starts to shrink. Each night it gets a bit smaller. After about a week, the Moon looks like half of a circle. And a week after that, the Moon disappears completely. But a few days later, a tiny sliver of light returns.

This 600-year-old drawing shows two European astronomers studying the Moon and recording their observations in a notebook.

This **series** of photos shows what the Moon looks like during each night of its cycle. You can see one half of the Moon lit up on Day 7, a Full Moon on Day 14, and the other half of the Moon lit up on Day 21.

(bkgd) Shigemi Numazawa/Atlas Photo Bank/Photo Researchers, Inc.

Our Place in Space

Earth is one of eight planets in our solar system. The other planets are Mercury, Venus, Mars, Jupiter, Saturn, Uranus, and Neptune.

All eight planets orbit, or move around, a star called the Sun. A year is the amount of time it takes a planet to circle the Sun once. Earth completes the trip in about 365 days, so an Earth year is 365 days long. That is the amount of time between your last birthday and your next birthday.

Mercury is the closest planet to the Sun. It makes one full orbit in just eighty-eight days, so a year on Mercury is much shorter than a year on Earth. Neptune is the farthest planet from the Sun. It takes Neptune 165 Earth years to circle the Sun. That is a really long time to wait between birthdays!

Each planet in our solar system follows a specific path as it orbits the Sun.

Asteroids are small, rocky objects that orbit the Sun.

Planets are not the only objects that orbit the Sun. Thousands of smaller, rocky chunks called asteroids and dwarf planets do, too. Most asteroids follow paths located between Mars and Jupiter. Dwarf planets, such as Pluto, are larger than asteroids. Their orbits are located beyond Neptune. Comets are small icy objects that orbit the Sun. Their orbital paths around the Sun are long and thin, like a cucumber.

Planets, asteroids, dwarf planets, and comets do not fly off into space because the Sun's gravity is always tugging on these smaller objects. Their forward movement is perfectly balanced with the pull of the Sun's gravity.

The Moon in Motion

The Sun is not the only object in our solar system with enough gravitational pull to attract smaller bodies. Six planets—Earth, Mars, Jupiter, Saturn, Uranus, and Neptune—have smaller objects orbiting them. So do a few asteroids and dwarf planets. These smaller objects are moons.

Scientists have identified at least sixty moons circling Jupiter. Saturn probably has even more. But Mars has just two moons, and Earth has only one.

In this image of Earth and the Moon, you can see part of the far side of the Moon, the half of the Moon that never faces Earth.

Earth's Moon is closer to Earth than any other object in space. Still, it took Apollo astronauts traveling at rocket speed about four days to reach the Moon in the late 1960s and early 1970s. The Moon is about 238,860 miles (384,400 kilometers) from Earth. That is almost one hundred times farther than the distance between New York, New York, and Los Angeles, California.

It takes the Moon about twenty-seven days to complete one full orbit around Earth. That means it circles our planet about twelve times each year.

As the Moon orbits Earth, it also **rotates**, or spins like a top. Earth rotates too. Our planet takes about twenty-four hours—or one full day—to complete one rotation. The Moon spins much more slowly. It rotates just once during each twenty-seven day orbit.

As Earth spins, different areas of the planet face the Sun. It is daytime in the places that are facing the Sun. That is why days are bright and sunny. It is nighttime on the part of Earth facing away from the Sun. That is why it is dark at night.

The amount of time it takes the Moon to rotate is the same as the time the Moon takes to orbit Earth, so people on Earth always see the same side of the Moon. Scientists call the side we see the near side. When the near side of the Moon is lit up by the Sun, we see a full, bright circle. When the far side of the Moon is fully lit up by the Sun, we cannot see the Moon at all.

A total of six Apollo spacecraft carried people to the Moon. The astronauts returned with photos, rock samples, and amazing stories of what they saw as they cruised around in lunar rovers.

(b) NASA/Corbis Historical/Getty Images

This x-ray image of the Sun shows some of the fiery gases it sends out into space.

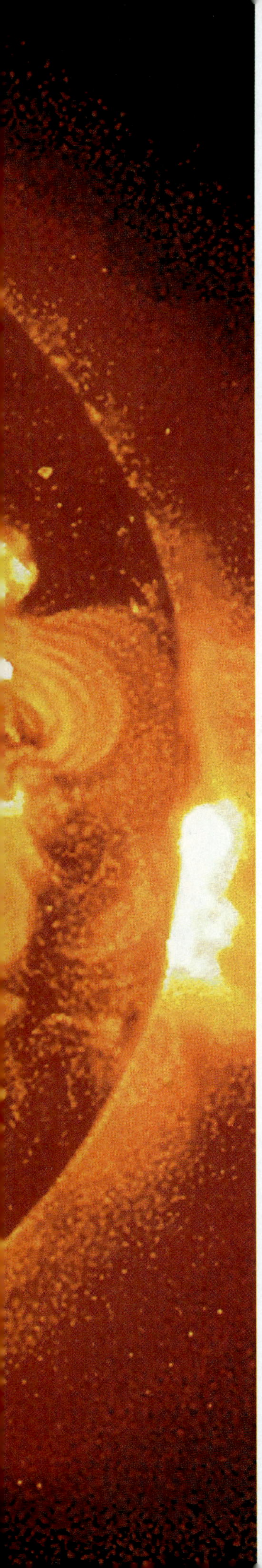

Let There Be Light

The Sun is a star—a giant ball of boiling gases. The temperature at the center of the Sun is 27 million degrees Fahrenheit (15 million degrees Celsius). The gases inside the Sun are so hot that it glows. The Sun is not the biggest star in the Universe, but it looks the brightest in the sky to us because it is the closest.

During some parts of the year, we can see Venus, Mars, Jupiter, and Saturn as bright, steadily shining dots of light in the night sky. But these planets do not produce their own light. The light we see when we look at them comes from the Sun. As the Sun's rays hit a planet, some of the light bounces off the planet's surfaces and travels back into space. When some of that reflected light reaches our eyes, the planet seems to glow. The Moon reflects the Sun's light, too.

We know from astronauts and space vehicles visiting the Moon that it is made of solid rock. There is no source of light on the Moon. We can only see the Moon when the Sun is shining on it, and then that light is reflected off the Moon's surface and into our eyes. The Moon is much smaller than Venus, Mars, Jupiter, and Saturn, but it looks bigger and brighter to us because it is much closer to Earth than those planets are.

Why Does the Moon Change Shape?

During any twenty-nine or thirty day period, the Moon's appearance seems to gradually change and then return to its original shape. But the Moon is not really changing at all. What you are seeing is the Moon being lit up by the Sun's rays in different ways on different days. What causes these differences? Changes in the positions of the Moon and Earth.

The Moon's light comes from the Sun. It looks different to us on different days because the Moon and Earth are always moving.

(bkgd) Antonio M. Rosario/Iconica/Getty Images

This Crescent Moon appeared 5 days after the New Moon.

In the first phase of the Moon, called the New Moon, the giant ball of rock is not visible on Earth at all. That is because the Moon is in between the Sun and Earth. The far side of the Moon is being lit up by the Sun, but the near side is not.

As the Moon orbits our planet, more and more of the near side is lit up by the Sun's rays. After a few days, you can see a C-shaped sliver called a Crescent Moon. Some people think this phase of the Moon is shaped like a **crescent** roll.

Close to one week after you see the New Moon, the Sun lights up about half of the near side of the Moon. This phase is called the First Quarter Moon because the Moon is now one-quarter, or 25 percent, of the way through its full cycle.

A few days later, the Moon will have traveled far enough in its orbit for you to see a shape that has curved humps on both sides. This phase is called the Gibbous Moon because *gibbous* is the Latin word for *humped*.

Around two weeks after you see the New Moon, the Sun shines directly on the near side of the Moon. The entire Full Moon is lit up.

As the Moon continues to orbit around Earth, the Moon begins to disappear. After a few days, you will see another Gibbous Moon in the sky.

Close to three weeks after you saw the New Moon, the Sun lights up only about half of the near side of the Moon. This phase is called the Last Quarter Moon because the Moon is now just one-quarter, or 25 percent, away from completing its full cycle.

A few days later, all but a tiny sliver of the Crescent Moon will have disappeared. Most of the Sun's rays are now falling on the far side of the Moon.

In just a few more days, the Moon will disappear completely. The Moon has returned to its original position in its orbital path. The far side of the Moon is fully lit up by the Sun, but the near side is in complete darkness.

The Moon has cycled through its phases for years, and it will continue to do so as long as our planet and its mysterious moon exist.

This stunning Full Moon appeared over gigantic rock formations called buttes in Monument Valley, which is located in Utah and Arizona.

(bkgd) Imagebroker/Alamy

This Last Quarter Moon appeared about three weeks after the New Moon.

About the Author

Melissa Stewart believes in the power of nature. She thinks that every part of nature has a story to tell— and Melissa is listening!

Melissa fell in love with nature as a child while walking through the woods with her father. Today, she writes science books about what she loves. Melissa enjoys writing children's books because kids are so curious. Some of her best books have grown out of her own wonderings.

When Melissa isn't writing, she likes to be outside. She also speaks about science at schools, and she teaches writing courses. Melissa has advice for kids everywhere: Go out and explore!

Author's Purpose

Why does the author include photographs with captions in *Why Does the Moon Change Shape?*

(t) Melissa Stewart; (c) Shigemi Numazawa/Atlas Photo Bank/ Photo Researchers, Inc.; (bkgd) Astrofoto/Photolibrary

Respond to the Text

Summarize

Use relevant details from *Why Does the Moon Change Shape?* to summarize what you learned about the phases of the Moon. Information from your Cause and Effect Chart may help you.

Cause	→	Effect
	→	
	→	
	→	
	→	

Write

How does Melissa Stewart help you understand how the Moon changes? Use these sentence starters to help organize your text evidence.

> Melissa Stewart uses text features to . . .
> She also uses cause and effect to explain . . .
> This helps me understand . . .

Make Connections

Why does the Moon have different phases? **ESSENTIAL QUESTION**

Why have people all over the world been fascinated by what they see in the sky? Explain your response. **TEXT TO WORLD**

Genre • Myth

Compare Texts

Read two myths that seek to explain what people see in the sky.

HOW IT CAME TO BE

The following two myths originated thousands of years ago, during a time when people did not yet enjoy all the benefits of modern science. ***Astronomers*** *with* ***telescopes*** *did not exist to answer questions about the universe. Instead, people told stories to explain what they saw in the sky above.*

WHY THE SUN TRAVELS ACROSS THE SKY

A retelling of a Greek myth

Helios, the Titan god of the sun, brings light to the earth. He dwells in a golden palace in the east on the river Okeanos. Each morning, Helios follows his sister Eos, the goddess of the Dawn, across the sky. He drives a shining chariot, drawn by four noble steeds, upward through the clouds. The chariot moves higher as rays of brilliant light pour forth from Helios's crown. Slowly, the steeds climb with a single purpose. Hours later, they finally reach the highest point of the sky.

Gerardo Suzan

Pausing only briefly to rest, Helios then begins the long and difficult journey downward. He travels toward his western palace. The path is steep and treacherous. Helios must master his steeds so that they do not fall headlong into the earth. If his chariot happened to drop too low in the sky, it would scorch the land and all its people.

After many hours, Helios arrives safely at the gates of his western palace. As darkness overtakes the earth, he begins his journey back to the east. Instead of traveling across the sky, he and his steeds sail in a golden boat from the gods along the river Okeanos. He returns to his eastern palace to repeat his journey across the sky.

Helios will continue to take this journey for as long as there are days and nights. His shining light warms us each day as the sun travels tirelessly across the sky.

WHY THERE IS THUNDER AND LIGHTNING

A retelling of a Norse myth

Thor, the mighty Norse god of thunder and lightning, is both large and powerful. With his long hair, flowing beard, and quick temper, he often intimidates other gods. Despite his fierce appearance, he is considerably popular. Thor is admired for his ability to protect both gods and humans against evil. Among the Norse gods, he is the strongest of all.

Thor lives with other warrior gods in Asgard, one of the nine worlds located at the highest level of the Norse universe. Odin, Thor's father, rules Asgard. Odin is a great warrior who is often associated with a quest for wisdom. Still, he is not nearly as popular as his son.

Three treasures help Thor emerge victorious time and time again. One is a belt that increases his strength. Another is a pair of iron-clad gloves. The third treasure is his greatest—a mighty war hammer. This hammer helps Thor protect Asgard from all enemies. When Thor throws his hammer, it magically returns to him like a boomerang.

During thunderstorms, Thor is said to be riding through the heavens in his mighty chariot, pulled by a pair of enormous goats. The sound of the chariot wheels creates a thunderous rumbling that shakes the world. Lightning flashes across the sky whenever Thor throws his magical hammer.

The experience of thunder and lightning can be frightening and oddly reassuring at the same time. It reminds us that Thor is a fierce and all-powerful warrior but one who will always be able to protect us from harm.

Make Connections

How do the myths of Helios and Thor help to explain what people see in the sky? Compare and contrast the myths. **ESSENTIAL QUESTION**

Contrast how ancient people understood their world and how modern people understand the world today. Explain using examples from the selections. **TEXT TO TEXT**

Genre • Fantasy

by
Mark Teague

Essential Question

Why do people run for public office?

Read why LaRue thinks he should run for mayor.

Go Digital!

The Snort City Register/Gazette

September 30

Bugwort Launches Campaign for Mayor

Former Pumpkinville police chief Hugo Bugwort announced yesterday that he will run for mayor of Snort City. Calling himself the "Law and Order" candidate, Bugwort, who spoke to a cheering crowd in Gruber Park, is widely considered a shoo-in for the job. "Snort City is a disgrace!" he said, to polite applause. "We need to be more like Pumpkinville. That means no more sloppiness, no more silliness, and no more foolish behavior." The speech was interrupted when several dogs in the back of the crowd overturned a hot-dog cart. Injured in the fracas was Gertrude LaRue of Second Avenue. The dogs were not identified.

Dogs Disrupt Rally

October 1

Dear Mrs. LaRue,

How sorry I am to hear about your injuries! Who knew that hot-dog carts were so unstable? I was simply trying to get a better view of Chief Bugwort when it collapsed. Heaven knows what those other dogs were doing. I must admit that they created an unfortunate impression of delinquency. Anyway, I'm shocked to hear that you'll be confined to the hospital for so long.

No doubt you are worried about me. So am I! But Mrs. Hibbins has promised to serve my meals, and somehow I will persevere.

With Deepest Sympathy,

Ike

October 2

Dear Mrs. LaRue,

Thank you for your concern. Yes, this will be a difficult time for me, stuck here all alone while you recuperate in your pleasant hospital bed. But please do not worry. I have become friendly with some of the dogs I met the other day in the park. We have decided to form a social club, which will perform various services to the community. Spending time with Fifi, Buck, and Chewy should help ease the pain of your absence. Plus, think of all the good deeds we will be doing!

Virtuously Yours,
Ike

The Snort City Register / Gazette

October 6

Wild Dogs Rampage!

Game Disrupted

Unruly dogs plagued Snort City again yesterday, as one of the animals broke up a double play and ran away with the baseball during a Snort City Rabbits game at Morley Field. The episode capped a week of problems that began on Tuesday when a pack of the rambunctious creatures broke up the annual Fishin' Derby on Blat Lake. Apparently the dogs first rolled in, then ate, the catch. The following day a group of dogs snuck into a "Mr. Ding-a-Ling" truck outside Gruber Park and made off with two gallons of rocky road ice cream. None of the dogs have been apprehended, though ice-cream vendor Eugene Phelps describes the leader as a "scruffy black-and-white fellow."

Dear Mrs. LaRue, October 7

Please do not worry about me. I will not starve or die of loneliness, probably.

Yes, I read the newspaper accounts regarding "dog problems." Frankly, I find them ridiculous. Can this cheerful and spirited behavior really be a problem? Where is the harm? And yet, with such lurid reporting, some weak-minded individuals might come to believe that dogs represent a menace to our community.

Hope you are feeling better,
Ike

BUTCHER
OP
WE
SUPPORT
BUGWORT
VOTE
BUGWORT

The Snort City Register/Gazette

October 8

Bugwort Calls for Canine Crackdown

Calling dogs "a menace to our community," mayoral candidate Hugo Bugwort yesterday announced his plans to crack down on the beasts. "We can no longer **tolerate** this sort of behavior," he said, citing recent dog-related problems. Mr. Bugwort proposes not only a leash law and a curfew, but a complete ban on the animals in most public places. "This town is literally going to the dogs," said Bugwort. "I **intend** to stop it."

In related news, a dog reportedly snuck into Branmeier's Butcher Shop on Second Avenue and made off with a string of beef sausages.

October 9

Dear Mrs. LaRue,

I must say I have become alarmed by the ravings of this man Bugwort. Imagine if he actually were elected to our city's highest office! The idea is unthinkable. I must figure out some way to stop this impending disaster!

Your Worried Dog,

Ike

The Snort City Register / Gazette

October 10

Letters to the Editor:

As a longtime resident, I must decry the wave of anti-dog hysteria sweeping over our city. Can we so quickly forget the loyalty of Man's Best Friend? Who **accompanies** our firefighters and police on their perilous rounds? Who rescues the **weary** traveler stuck high in the Alps? Who serves the blind (and the deaf, too, most likely)? Dogs, that's who!

Signed,
A Concerned Citizen

VOTE
IKE LARUE
SNORT
"PROTECT AND SERVE"

October 11

Dear Mrs. LaRue,

How I envy you the safety of your hospital bed! Here in the outside world, things have become perilous indeed—at least for dogs! The awful Bugwort continues his scurrilous attacks. Yesterday he referred to dogs as "gangs of hooligans." He must be stopped. Therefore I have decided to "throw my hat into the ring." This afternoon I will announce my candidacy. Doubtless the public response will be **overwhelming**.

Your Next Mayor,

Ike

October 12

Dear Mrs. LaRue,

My first day on the campaign trail was fabulous! Everywhere huge crowds turned out to cheer my message of dog-friendliness. My chums from the social club have agreed to help. Of course we will do our best to keep this **campaign** positive, though I can't speak for my **opponent**, who appears to be vicious and unstable, if not insane.

Honestly Yours,

Ike

Dear Mrs. LaRue, October 13

In my appearances I have been pointing out that if dogs are banned from places like Gruber Park, cats will run wild. Not a pleasant thought! The campaign continues to gather steam. I think we have Bugwort on the ropes.

Politically Yours,
Ike

P.S. I hope you don't mind, but I have been using the apartment as campaign headquarters.

The Snort City Register/Gazette

October 14

Bugwort Challenged by Mystery Candidate!

A mysterious new candidate has emerged to challenge Hugo Bugwort in his run for mayor. Supporters of Ike LaRue describe him as "dog-friendly." Opponents point out that he is, in fact, a dog. Either way, the furry LaRue has begun to wage a fierce campaign against Bugwort, who promises to virtually ban all dogs from Snort City. Surprisingly, LaRue's message has begun to catch on. "We didn't anticipate this," admits Bugwort campaign manager, Walt Smiley, referring to the dogs. "It turns out some folks are really fond of the little devils."

"I'm not worried," said Bugwort. "Tomorrow is my big rally in Gruber Park. I'll deal with these dog-lovers then."

October 15

Dear Mrs. LaRue,

My supporters and I have decided to confront Chief Bugwort at today's rally. We will be out in force, and though we will conduct ourselves in a dignified manner, I am sure that the results will be interesting.

Hope you are well,

Ike

P.S. Nothing will distract me from this important cause.

The Snort City Register / Gazette

October 16

LaRue Rescues Bugwort!

Dog Called Hero

Hugo Bugwort was rushed to Memorial Hospital yesterday after collapsing onstage during a rally in Gruber Park. Apparently he grew dizzy while trying to shout down hecklers. Among his rescuers was his opponent, local dog Ike LaRue. "When the Chief collapsed we rushed him to the nearest vehicle, a Mr. Ding-a-Ling truck," explained campaign manager, Walt Smiley. "For some reason the dog was already inside. But give him credit —he really did his best to help."

"LaRue saved me," said Bugwort. "All the way to the hospital he fed me cool, delicious rocky road ice cream. By the time I got here I was feeling much better." The rescue puts a new twist on an already unusual campaign. "I have completely changed my mind about dogs," said Bugwort. "In fact, I would be honored if Ike would serve with me as Assistant Mayor, to make sure that the interests of dogs are represented in a Bugwort administration." LaRue, who departed in the Mr. Ding-a-Ling truck, could not be reached for comment.

Dear Mrs. LaRue, October 16

It turns out that Chief Bugwort is not such a bad fellow after all. In fact, he's swell! Anyway, politics are not for me. I would rather make friends than engage in this constant bickering. And since all I ever wanted was to make this a great city for EVERYONE, I have decided to wrap up my campaign and accept the Chief's offer to serve as Assistant Mayor.

I'm so glad that you are feeling better and will be able to attend my swearing-in ceremony.

Your Loyal Dog,
Ike

The Snort City Register/Gazette

November 3

Bugwort Sworn In!

LaRue Joins Former Adversary

Promising to have the most dog-friendly administration ever, new mayor Hugo Bugwort was sworn in yesterday during a ceremony in Gruber Park. At his side was Assistant Mayor Ike LaRue, whom many credit with his success. "This is a great day for everyone in Snort City!" proclaimed Bugwort, to loud cheers from the audience. The speech was interrupted when several dogs in the back of the crowd overturned a hot-dog cart. Bugwort promised to look into the matter.

"It certainly is worrisome," he said. "Who knew those carts were so unstable?"

GOING
TO THE
DOGS

About Mark Teague

Mark Teague is an author and illustrator of many children's books. He often writes stories about activities that some kids try to avoid–things like getting a haircut, doing homework, and cleaning one's room. Mark adds his own quirky sense of humor to his stories. Many of the ideas for his books come from things he did as a child. The character Ike LaRue was inspired by two dogs he and his brother had. Mark uses these childhood inspirations to create new stories in upstate New York. His daughter loves to watch him paint the illustrations for his books.

Author's Purpose

Why does Mark Teague use both black-and-white and color illustrations in *LaRue for Mayor*?

Respond to the Text

Summarize

Summarize *LaRue for Mayor*. Include the most important events from the story. Information from your Character Perspective Chart may help you.

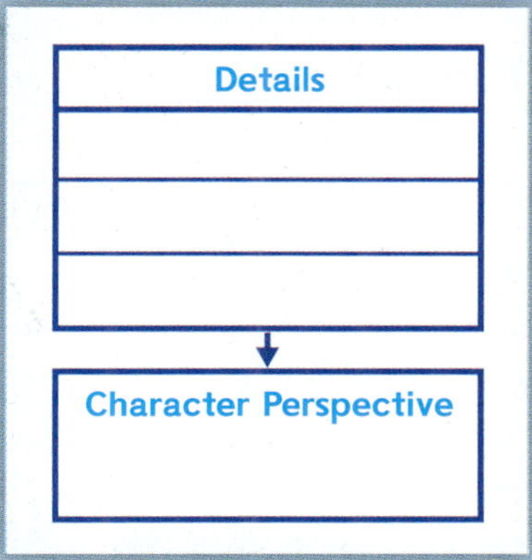

Write

How does the author use letters and newspaper articles to develop the characters of Ike and Bugwort? Use these sentence starters to help organize your text evidence.

The author uses letters to . . .
The newspaper articles help me . . .
The author develops the characters by . . .

Make Connections

Why does Ike run for mayor? ESSENTIAL QUESTION

Bugwort and Ike have very different qualities, yet the people of Snort City like them both as candidates. What qualities are most important in someone running for public office? TEXT TO WORLD

Genre • Expository Text

Compare Texts

Read about the duties and accomplishments of state and local officials.

Bringing Government Home

Understanding State and Local Government

What do you think of when you picture the United States government? Do you see the White House or perhaps the President? These images are accurate yet incomplete. There are also many U.S. leaders at the state and local levels—in the counties, cities, and neighborhoods where we live.

National, state, and local governments share the same basic structure. The executive, legislative, and judicial branches make up the three branches of government. Each branch of government has specific duties and powers. These powers differ in national and state governments.

Just a Few National Powers Versus State Powers

National Leaders Can ...

- Print money
- Declare war
- Enforce the U.S. Constitution

State Leaders Can ...

- Issue licenses
- Provide for public health and safety
- Amend state constitutions

The Executive Branch

The President is the leader of the national executive branch. Similarly, a **governor** heads up each state executive branch. The governor makes important decisions about the state. Each state has its own structure and set of officials who are below the governor.

Mayor Mick Cornett

At the local level, a city mayor might head up the executive branch. One example of a successful mayor is Mick Cornett of Oklahoma City. Every day, mayors such as Cornett oversee city departments, such as police, schools, and transportation. They also work with others to try to improve their city. Mayor Cornett launched a **campaign** against obesity in Oklahoma City. Cornett added sidewalks, bike paths, and walking trails. He also created a 70-acre park to promote walking and exercise. Thanks to Cornett's efforts, the people of Oklahoma City have lost over 600,000 pounds.

(cl) Jim Beckel/Daily Oklahoman/AP Photo;
(cr) Courtesy of Mayor Mick Cornett;
(cb) Image Source/Getty Images

The Legislative Branch

State legislatures also have strong leaders called senators and representatives. These members try to improve their state by passing new laws. Senator Anthony C. Hill worked hard for the state of Florida. He helped to create and pass new laws. As a legislator, Hill worked to pass important civil rights legislation. He also improved African American voter turnout in Florida elections. In addition, Hill helped to increase the state's minimum wage and reduce class sizes in schools.

Senator Anthony C. Hill

Local legislators can create similar results in their counties, cities, and towns. They may pass laws that relate to parks, public transportation, and police departments, to name a few.

The Judicial Branch

The judicial branch makes sure that all these laws are understood. It also ensures that the other two branches adhere to the U.S. Constitution. At the state level, this branch usually includes a Supreme Court and lower-level courts.

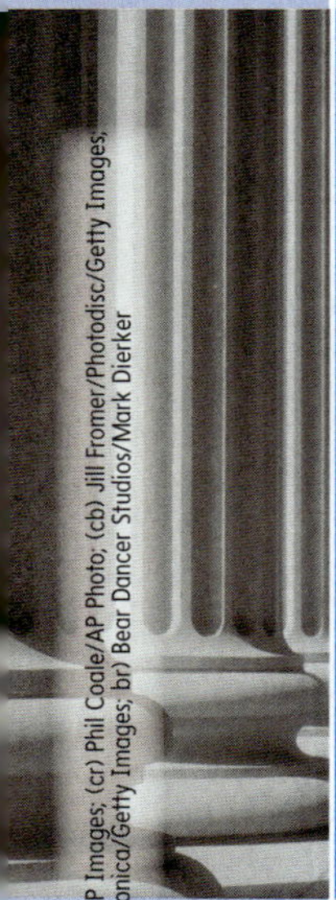

DID YOU KNOW that in addition to the U.S. Constitution, each state has its own constitution and set of laws to follow? The purpose of a state constitution is to outline the structure of the state government.

Many state constitutions are longer than the national one! That is because leaders want to make sure their state is protected. For example, Florida's constitution includes laws that intend to protect the land and animals of the Everglades, an area of natural wetlands in the southern part of the state.

The earliest state constitutions were created hundreds of years ago. Today, state leaders amend, or change, state constitutions to address modern concerns from citizens. South Carolina leaders recently amended their state constitution to include hunting and fishing as a constitutional right for citizens.

County, city, and town courts exist at the local level. Judges may be chosen by public officials. They may also be elected. State and local judges represent a wide range of backgrounds.

Justice Eva Guzman is a good example. A judge for the Supreme Court of Texas, Guzman was the first Hispanic woman to be elected to a state office in Texas. State Supreme Court justices decide if judges in lower courts have made the right decisions based on the state constitution. In addition, Justice Guzman has headed up legal education programs in Texas. She does this so that others can learn about the law.

Justice Eva Guzman

Checks and Balances

The three branches of government help to create balanced national, state, and local governments. Our forefathers created this system to make sure one branch did not become more powerful than the others. Public officials at each level of government are responsible for the laws we vote on and follow. So the next time you think about who makes up our government, keep your local leaders in mind!

Make Connections

What can people achieve in local and state public offices? **ESSENTIAL QUESTION**

Tell why elected leaders are important in our society. **TEXT TO TEXT**

(tl tr) Erich Schlegel/AP Images; (c) Siede Preis/Photodisc/Getty Images; (bl) Joshua Roberts/Bloomberg/Getty Images; (br) Mel Curtis/Photonica/Getty Images; (bkgd) Dennis Flaherty/Photographer's Choice RF/Getty Images

Genre • Expository Text

Essential Question

What can you discover when you look at something closely?

Read about water molecules and how they change.

Go Digital!

A DROP

OF WATER

BY WALTER WICK

MOLECULES IN MOTION

If a drop of water is added to a jar of still water, and if the water in the jar is not stirred, where will the new drop go? Will it stay near the top or sink to the bottom? A simple experiment reveals the answer.

A drop of blue water enters a jar of clear water. It begins to split up. Parts of the drop sink and swirl in different directions. At last, the colored drop breaks into so many parts that it has become part of the whole jar of water.

The molecules in a liquid are moving all the time, pushing and pulling each other, attaching to and breaking away from neighboring molecules. The molecules in the blue drop break apart because they are pushed and pulled all over the jar by other water molecules. The energy that keeps the molecules moving is heat. This heat can come from the sun or the room in which the jar is standing. Without heat, water would not remain a liquid.

ICE

When water cools, it loses energy. The molecules slow down and eventually stop swirling and pushing each other. When water freezes, the molecules lock together, forming a rigid structure. A drop of blue water no longer moves. The water has changed from a liquid to a solid—ice.

Ice is a solid, like metal or rock. But, unlike metal or rock, ice is solid only at temperatures of 32 degrees Fahrenheit (0 degrees Celsius) or colder. At room temperature, ice melts, changing back to a liquid.

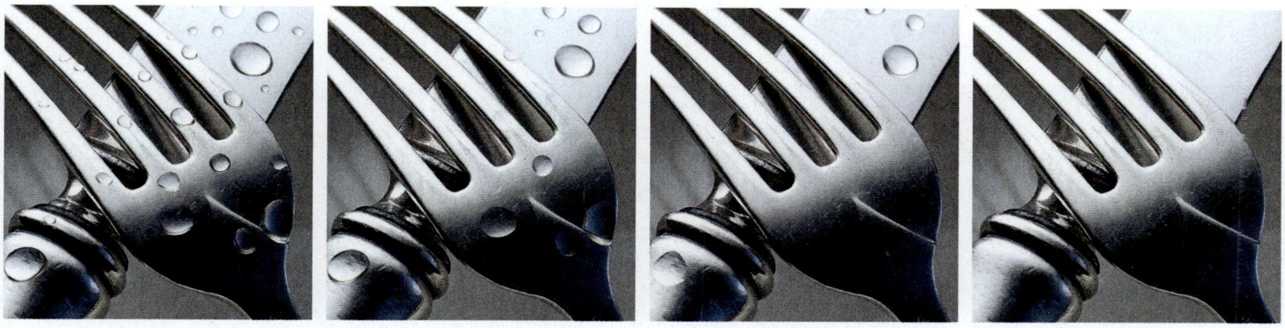

WATER VAPOR

Water always seems to be disappearing: from wet clothes on a line, from puddles on the ground, and from dishes on a draining board. We say it has dried up, but where has the water gone?

Just as water can be a liquid or solid, it can also be a gas. The water from the wet dishes *evaporates.* That is, it turns into a gas called *water vapor.* Molecule by molecule, the water from the drops on the wet dishes drifts invisibly into the air.

Heating water in a kettle speeds evaporation. Heat from the stove makes the water turn to steam, which is extremely hot water vapor. When the steam hits the cooler air, tiny droplets form, and we see a cloud just beyond the kettle's spout. Almost immediately, the droplets evaporate and change back to invisible vapor. Then the water molecules **mingle** with other molecules that make up air.

CONDENSATION

The air around us always contains some water vapor. Water molecules move rapidly through the air and hit everything in their paths. The molecules bounce off most warm surfaces, but stick to surfaces that are cold. In these photographs, molecules of water vapor stick to the coldest part of the glass. Gradually, droplets form on the glass as the molecules accumulate. Water vapor changes from a gas to a liquid; that is, it *condenses.*

EVAPORATION VERSUS CONDENSATION

In the photographs above, why do the water drops outside this glass disappear, while the drops inside remain?

Outside the glass, the water evaporates and spreads throughout the room as vapor. In time, the drops disappear. Inside the glass, water also evaporates, but the vapor is trapped. The air inside the glass becomes ***humid***, which means that the air is full of water vapor. And that vapor condenses back onto the water drops as quickly as water molecules can evaporate. Therefore, the drops remain.

Remove the glass, and the vapor expands throughout the room. Evaporation continues, but condensation slows down. In time, the uncovered drops will disappear.

HOW CLOUDS FORM

Clouds are made of tiny water droplets, too small to be seen without a microscope. If a cloud droplet is to form, water vapor must first condense on a particle of dust. Carried by wind, these dust particles are often bits of pollen, soot, soil, or salt.

This experiment shows how cloud droplets form. Salt is placed on a jar lid above a dish of water. A glass cover traps the water vapor. In minutes, the vapor condenses on the salt and coats each grain with water. Hours later, the salt **dissolves** in the water drops.

Clouds form when water evaporates from the earth's surface and rises into colder air. There, the vapor condenses on cold, airborne particles. More and more molecules cling to the particles until droplets form. It takes about a million cloud droplets to make one raindrop. Rain does not taste salty or appear **gritty** because the particles that allow clouds to form are usually too small to be noticed in raindrops.

SNOWFLAKES

This snowflake is shown 60 times its actual size. The angles between the six major branches are repeated over and over again in many of the smaller details of this amazing structure. How can such an intricate object form in the sky?

Cloud droplets form when water vapor condenses on particles. But in very cold air, water molecules that **cling** to particles form tiny ice crystals. As more water molecules from the air freeze onto the crystal, they join at angles that allow a six-sided structure to form. If the crystal grows large enough, it will fall to the ground as a snowflake.

Clouds that produce snow often contain both ice crystals *and* liquid droplets. At the center of this snowflake is a cloud droplet that froze, allowing the snowflake to form around it. Scattered throughout are other cloud droplets that have frozen onto the snowflake as it fell through the cloud.

Sometimes snow mixes with pellets of sleet, which are frozen raindrops like the ones shown below. By contrast, snowflakes are ice crystals that form when water vapor changes directly from a gas to a solid.

Sleet, 15 times actual size

ENDLESS VARIETY

Many ice crystals grow into shapes that are just tiny slivers, rods, or clumps of ice. Of these, the underlying six-sided structure may not always be visible. But when weather conditions are just right, the crystals will grow into an astonishing variety of elaborate six-sided designs.

All the snowflakes on these two pages were photographed on the same day. All share the same angles, but vary in design. One has six branches of unequal length, giving the appearance of a three-sided snowflake. Another snowflake has only four branches. Apparently, two of its branches didn't grow. Odd variations like these are **typical**. Because different conditions of humidity, wind, and temperature affected the growth of each snowflake as it fell, each design holds secrets of its unique journey to earth.

When a snowflake melts, its intricate design is lost forever in a drop of water. But a snowflake can vanish in another way. It can change directly from ice to vapor. The sequence below shows a single snowflake as it gradually disappears.

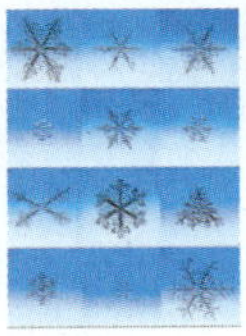

Snowflakes, actual size

FROST AND DEW

On some days, when the air is humid, a sudden drop in temperature during the night will cause water vapor to condense on cold surfaces. By morning, the landscape is covered in sparkling drops of water—dew. If temperatures fall below freezing, the cold-weather relative of dew appears—frost.

On windows, frost forms along tiny scratches and other imperfections in the glass. As with snowflakes, frost is the result of water vapor changing from a gas to a solid. That's why the angular structure of ice crystals is evident in the fern-like patterns of frost.

When dew forms, a short walk through the grass will soak your feet. On spider webs, dewdrops appear like glistening pearls. In the photograph above, we can see how water reflects and bends light; an upside-down landscape appears in each drop of water.

WATER AND LIGHT

If you look carefully at this beam of light, you'll see the mysterious way in which light interacts with water.

Some of the light is reflected, which means that it bounces off the surface of the water. But some of the light passes into the water. As the light enters the water, molecules bend the light, or *refract* it. The bent rays of white light are transformed into all the colors of the rainbow.

How is this possible? White light is made up of waves of many different sizes, or *wavelengths*. The shortest wavelength, which we see as violet, bends the most. Red, the longest wavelength, bends the least. All the other colors fall in between.

Sun shining on spray from a garden hose creates a rainbow. The spray produces drops of water that bend the light and flash bright colors when seen from the correct angle. Natural rainbows work exactly the same way. The sun must be behind you and low in the sky. The arc of the rainbow is caused by the sun shining on billions of spherical raindrops that fill the sky.

THE WATER CYCLE

The sun's heat and the earth's gravity keep water in constant motion. Water evaporates from puddles, ponds, lakes, and oceans; from plants and trees; and even from your skin. Water vapor moves invisibly through the air, but it is always ready to condense on a cool blade of grass or the surface of a pond. Massive clouds form as vapor condenses on tiny particles of dust in the air. Then, and only then, can water fall from the sky as rain, replenishing lakes, rivers, and oceans. Hard to predict, impossible to control, water cycles around the earth.

And water is precious. Without it, not a single living thing could survive. No plants would grow, not even one blade of grass. No animals would roam the earth, not even a spider. But somewhere in the world right now, snow drifts on a mountaintop and rain falls in a valley. And all around us, we are reminded of the never ending journey of a drop of water.

Photo courtesy of NASA

About Walter Wick

Walter Wick is a children's author and photographer. He is best known for the I Spy book series, which he created with author Jean Marzollo.

Walter says he tries to "make the experience of looking at my creations as exciting to others as it is to me." As a result, his photos usually end up fresh and different. Walter spends a lot of time setting up photos that have many parts. His very detailed photos serve to introduce kids to complicated things, such as water molecules!

The photos in Walter's science books explain topics in unexpected, unusual ways. Most readers would agree that in Walter's books, the photos matter at least as much as the words.

AUTHOR'S PURPOSE

How do Walter Wick's highly technical photos help you understand difficult concepts?

Walter Wick

Respond to the Text

Summarize

Use the most important information from *A Drop of Water* to summarize the selection. Details from your Chronology Chart may help you.

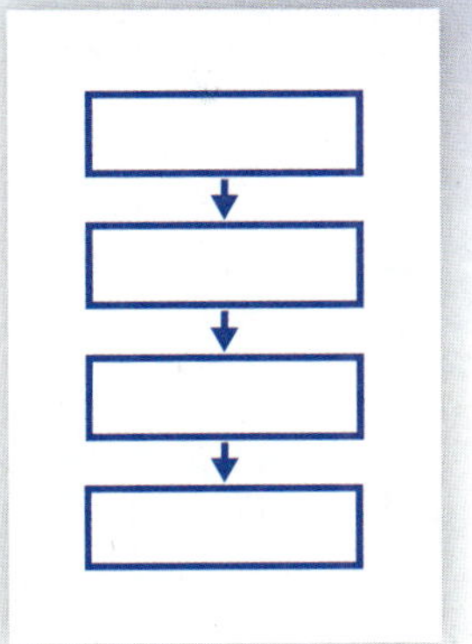

Write

Why does the author begin and end the selection with a drop of water? Use these sentence starters to organize your text evidence.

> The author begins and ends the selection with a drop of water because . . .
> The author explains the water cycle because . . .

Make Connections

What are some of the various ways that water molecules can change? **ESSENTIAL QUESTION**

How can viewing things up close change the way people think about the world? **TEXT TO WORLD**

Genre • Fantasy

Compare Texts

Read about two girls who gain a new perspective as they attempt to save their classmates.

The Incredible Shrinking Potion

It began as a simple science project.

It was only one week ago that Isabel, Mariela, and Hector were working on a shrinking potion that would amaze everyone at the science fair. Mariela and Isabel had perfected the potion, but it was Hector who had created the antidote. Since his discovery, Hector had become less interested in winning the science fair prize and more interested in how this experiment could increase his popularity. His short stature made him practically invisible to everyone at Washington Elementary School.

That wasn't the case anymore—now the entire class was looking up at Hector. He had come to science lab bearing "special" cupcakes, which made it easy for him to shrink the entire class, including his science teacher, Ms. Sampson. Hector smirked as he placed his miniature classmates inside the tank of Rambo, the class pet.

Richard Johnson

Isabel and Mariela overheard the shrinking shrieks of their classmates outside the classroom door. The girls had been late to lab again. Upon peering inside, they quickly realized they had to do something. Mariela saw that Rambo, outfitted with a vest of tiny tubes, was sniffing merrily outside his tank.

"Rambo has the antidote!" Mariela whispered to Isabel. "We will have to shrink ourselves to sneak inside and get the antidote. Then we can help everyone out of the tank!" With shaking hands, Isabel pulled out a vial. The girls took a deep breath and sipped the shrinking potion. The world around them began to grow....

As Isabel and Mariela walked under the classroom door, everything was **magnified** to the extreme. Desks and chairs towered over them—even the complex details of each nut and screw became clear, as if viewed under a **microscope**. The girls made their way to the other side of the lab, dodging mountainous cupcake crumbs and wads of gooey gum.

Next they had to climb up onto the table without being seen. Isabel grabbed onto a wire plugged into an outlet. Hand over hand, she pulled herself forward on the sloped wire until she could see the back of the tank. Then, swinging like an Olympic gymnast, she launched herself onto the table. Isabel stepped along the **gritty** surface, avoiding wide wooden grooves that she had never noticed before. Feeling lighter than air, she realized that gravity worked very differently at her new size.

To Mariela, it seemed a Herculean task to join Isabel on the tabletop. "How did you get up there?" Mariela whispered. "I'll fall if I try to jump!"

Isabel smiled. "Gravity doesn't work the same way when you're small. If you miss, you can walk up the side, like an ant!"

Swinging with sweaty palms, Mariela launched herself with all of her might. The lack of gravity slowed her, and she felt herself starting to float gently down, down, down—just missing the table. Panicking, she lunged forward, using her legs to **cling** to the wooden leg.

"You did it!" shouted Isabel's tiny voice. Her excitement was short-lived as a humongous hamster cornered her and Mariela. Their even bigger problem, Hector, seemed to realize that something was happening behind the tank.

"Quick! Grab the antidote!" said Mariela. Pulling out a bag of sunflower seeds from her pocket, she offered some to Rambo as Isabel unfastened a vial. She nearly dropped it upon hearing giant footsteps heading her way, followed by her teacher's voice.

"You girls are late," Ms. Sampson said as she grasped the vial. Isabel and Mariela breathed a sigh of relief as their teacher took a sip and prepared to put Hector in his place.

Mariela grinnned at Isabel. "Think our science project will be a big hit after all this?" The tiny friends shared a huge laugh.

Make Connections

What do Isabel and Mariela discover after they take the shrinking potion? **ESSENTIAL QUESTION**

How can taking a closer look at things help people understand the world around them? **TEXT TO TEXT**

Richard Johnson

Genre • Realistic Fiction

Essential Question

In what ways do people show they care about each other?

Read how Luisa plans something special for her mother.

Go Digital!

Mama, I'll Give You the World

by Roni Schotter

illustrated by

S. Saelig Gallagher

When Papa was around, Mama loved to dance, but Mama doesn't dance anymore. She works hard every day at Walter's World of Beauty, cutting, coloring, and curling.

After school each afternoon, Luisa's bus drops her at the door to the World. Everyone greets her—Walter, Rupa, Georges, but especially Mama.

Mama smiles and makes a place for Luisa—on a cushion, under the palm tree. "First things first," Mama always says, so there by Walter's Bottles of Beauty, with names that whisper promises—

Raspberry Radiance, Evening Glamour Glow, Sunday Night Soother—Luisa does her schoolwork.

While Mama, like a magician, turns Mrs. Koo's dark hair the color of sunset, Walter, Georges, and Rupa cut and comb. Luisa does a math problem. Then she writes a story for English about a girl with a magic brush that brushes people's cares away.

When she finishes her homework, Luisa takes out her scissors, her glue, and her paper and does what Mama does—cuts and colors and curls—**portraits** of the customers. "Everyone in the world is a flower," her mother always tells her. "Together, they make a **bouquet**." So Luisa cuts slowly, noticing how different each flower is, and how each one comes in a special size and shape.

In between customers, Mama rests in her chair and lets Luisa brush her long, thick curls. Luisa brushes hard, pretending she is the girl in her story, carefully watching her mother's face to see if she can make her smile. Mama hardly ever smiles, but when she does, she is the prettiest flower in the World.

Luisa loves to look at the pictures at her mother's station. One is of Luisa; the other is of Mama long ago—happy and *dancing*—in a large room that looks like a palace, crowded with people and full of lights. Mama says the name of the palace is Roseland, but Luisa doesn't believe her. She thinks her mother has made up the name because she loves flowers.

"Can we go there?" Luisa asks. She imagines the two of them holding hands and dancing at the palace Mama calls Roseland....

But Mama shakes her head, no. She holds the picture in her hands, and her eyes look at something far away and once upon a time—something Luisa can only guess at.

Under the dryers, the ladies loudly whisper their secrets, but Luisa has a secret of her own. Tomorrow is Mama's birthday, and tonight Luisa is going to give her the present she's been planning for such a long time.

For the past few weeks, whenever Mama isn't looking, Luisa has whispered her secret in the ear of each of Mama's favorite customers–

–when she sweeps up snippets of hair for handsome Mr. Anselmo, who always tells Mama, *"Just a little off here and a little off there, please leave it as long as you dare, for you see, don't you know? You can see it is so, that I haven't a lot left to spare."*

–when she helps Mrs. Malloy, bent over and sad as she inches into the World on her walker, but smiling and standing nearly straight an hour later, when, feeling beautiful again, she leaves.

—when she helps Mama brush and braid Hazel Mae Dixon's go-everywhere hair till it looks like neat, shiny rows of licorice.

—when she sprays **fussy** Mrs. Fogelman's hair that refuses to stand up and obey until Mama teases it with a comb so it can't *help* standing up—fluffy and high as a great, gray cloud, just the way Mrs. Fogelman likes it!

—and when she removes the giant pink and purple rollers that turn Mrs. Rodriguez's dark tangles into an ocean of gentle waves.

At six o'clock it's time at last to go home. Luisa exchanges secret winks with Walter, Georges, and Rupa. Then she and Mama hang up their smocks and empty their pockets, heavy with tip money.

It all goes into a special envelope. "First things first," Mama says. She is saving for Luisa—for college. Mama wants Luisa to learn *every*thing.

Outside, the world stretches before them—dark, mysterious, and twinkling with store- and street- and starlight. Luisa and Mama stand together looking at it, feeling oh, so small. Mama's hair **sparkles** in the light. So do her eyes.

"The world is big. So much more for you to know. So much more for you to see. One day, if I can," Mama says, patting the envelope deep in her coat pocket, "I will give the world to you."

No, thinks Luisa. Tonight, if I can, I will give the world to *you*...for your birthday!

At home that evening Luisa asks Mama to try on her prettiest dress—the one with the roses and violets and vines that **encircle** Mama's waist the way Luisa's arms do when they hug. "Please, Mama?" Luisa begs.

"Not now," Mama says. "I'm tired."

"*Pretty* please?" Luisa asks, opening her eyes as wide as Walter's windows and looking at Mama in a way she knows Mama can't refuse.

"Allll right," Mama says, and puts on her dress.

While she does, Luisa pretends to be searching for something. "Mama!" she calls out. "We have to go back to the World! I forgot my book." Luisa hurries and hands Mama her coat.

Mama pushes the coat away. "No," she says. "It can wait until tomorrow."

Luisa is worried. "But Mama," she pleads. "It's for my *book report*. Don't you always tell me 'first things first'?"

Mama sighs and puts on her coat. Luisa tries not to smile.

When they get to the World, it is dark.

Luisa holds her breath as Mama takes out her keys and opens the door.

The moment Mama turns on the light, music fills the World. Surprise!

Luisa's portraits dance along the walls and mirrors. Walter, Rupa, and Georges have filled the room with roses and have hung tiny lights that wink like eyes. All of Mama's favorite customers are there, dressed up, but Mama, smiling, is the prettiest of all.

"Happy birthday!" everyone yells. Then, "Speech!"

Mama blushes. "First things first," she says, and gathers Luisa into her arms.

"For your birthday," Luisa says, "I wanted to turn the World into Roseland."

"You did, Lulu-belle," Mama says. "Thank you.... Thank you all."

"Mama," Luisa asks as the music swells from Walter's boom box, "will you dance with me?"

Mama doesn't move and she doesn't answer. She looks at Walter, Rupa, and Georges smiling at her. She looks at Mrs. Malloy's two old feet tapping beside her walker, like two new feet. She looks at Mrs. Fogelman's great, gray cloud of hair turned golden by the lights and changed into a clear-weather cloud. She looks at Mr. Anselmo and Hazel Mae Dixon and Mrs. Rodriguez and Mrs. Koo all dressed in their finest clothes to honor her. Then she looks deep into Luisa's eyes, and Luisa sees that Mama's eyes are no longer far away. They are near and clear and wet with tears. "Shall we dance?" Mama asks Luisa.

And Mama and Luisa dance! They twirl and whirl and laugh together. Soon everyone is dancing, and the World seems to sparkle and spin faster and faster around them.

Then Mr. Anselmo, with a bow so deep that his bald spot shows (and he doesn't even care!), asks Mama and Luisa to dance with him...and they do!

And the way Mr. Anselmo smiles at Mama and the way she smiles back at him make Luisa think there is no more beautiful place in the world than *this* world—the world they are dancing in now.

About the Author and Illustrator

Unlike Luisa, **Roni Schotter** was extremely shy growing up. She even had difficulty asking the school librarian for help finding books. But like Luisa, Schotter had a great imagination. Thinking up stories made her want to become a writer. She has written more than 30 books for young people.

Like Luisa, **S. Saelig Gallagher** uses her imagination to bring words and ideas to life. As an artist, she imagined the way Luisa changed the salon into Roseland and created paintings to show it. She has illustrated many books for young people, including several books of fairy tales.

Author's Purpose

Why doesn't the author reveal the secret that Luisa whispers to the customers before the end of the story?

Respond to the Text

Summarize

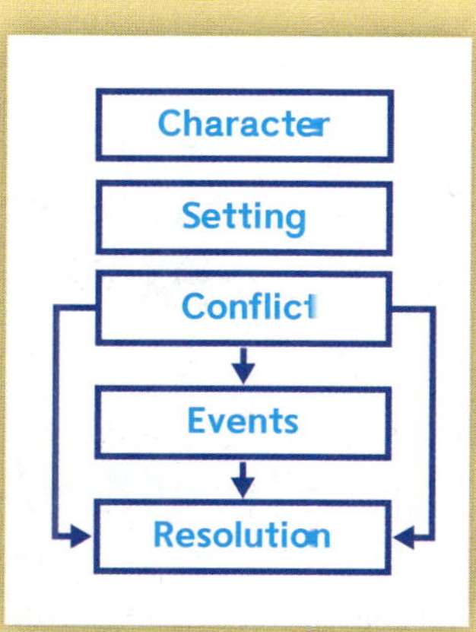

Summarize the most important events in *Mama, I'll Give You the World*. Information from your Plot: Conflict Chart may help you.

Write

Why is *Mama, I'll Give You the World* a good title for this story? Use these sentence starters to organize your text evidence.

Mama, I'll Give You the World is a good title because . . .
An example of this is . . .

Make Connections

Why does Luisa plan something special for her mother? **ESSENTIAL QUESTION**

In what other ways do people show they care about each other? What are some things they do and say? **TEXT TO WORLD**

Genre • Realistic Fiction

Compare Texts

Read how a girl discovers who she really is.

Miami by Way of Fujian

Sometimes, I wonder who I really am.

You're thinking, hey, Mariel, you're a short fifth-grade girl with straight black hair and almond eyes. You live in Miami. I know where my family comes from.

My *abuelos* talk about Cuba: the pristine beaches and smooth jazz bands. So when my mom told me we were going to visit where I came from, for a moment I imagined a village in Cuba.

"No, *mi vida*. We're going to China to see where you were born." Her voice trembled with **emotion** as we got on the plane.

The flight to Hong Kong lasted twenty hours! The city amazed me. How could so many people crowd onto the sidewalks? Many people had black straight hair and almond eyes like mine.

We walked to the markets in Kowloon. At the Temple Street Market, my father bought me a jade coin necklace. I put it on next to the little charm necklace I always wore. My *abuela* had put the charm around my neck when my parents first brought me home.

We ate at a dim sum restaurant. Carts wheeled everywhere. A low buzz and appetizing aromas filled the air.

The next day we took a flight to Fuzhou. After the flight, there was an all-day car ride to the village. Mami smiled while she cried. She was remembering when they had first come to the orphanage to adopt me.

Papi explained, "*Princesa,* we were going crazy because the paperwork took forever. All we had was a little **portrait** of you."

We drove into the mountains toward the orphanage. I thought I might recognize the place—I'd lived there until I was two years old—but nothing looked familiar. Ms. Guo, the director, met us and fussed over me.

"Min Zhi! I wondered if we would ever be reunited."

Glossary

Abuela: grandmother

Abuelos: grandparents

Arroz salteado: fried rice

Bai cai: bok choy, a type of cabbage

Chica China: a Chinese girl

Dim sum: dumplings and other small dishes served from carts

Fujian: location on the southeast coast of mainland China

Kowloon: a dense urban area in Hong Kong

Mi vida: "My life"—a term of endearment

The nursery had white walls, and the floor was covered with soft foam puzzle pieces that looked like giant marshmallows. A row of wheeled bassinets lined a wall, where an older woman rocked a crying baby. When she saw us she spoke excitedly.

Ms. Guo translated. "Xing Hua can't believe how big you are." Ms. Guo led us to a classroom jammed with kids. The teacher wrote on the board in English. After the lesson, the kids raced to the playground for recess. A girl about my age hung back. She was shorter than me and her hair was tied in ponytails.

I asked, "What's your name?"

"Mei Jing."

"Are you the oldest here?"

"Yes, I'm ten years old."

I had a million questions but I didn't want to be pushy. She hesitated, then asked me, "Is your school fun? Do you like it?"

"Sure. What about you?"

"Yes. But I want to go to school in the city, with older children."

I felt bad for Mei Jing. I hoped that one day she would find parents.

After recess the kids went to the garden. Mei Jing showed me how to harvest vegetables for lunch. She taught me how to cook them and what their names were.

Then Ms. Guo gathered us all together. The kids were very curious as she introduced me and my family, in both English and Chinese.

"This is your sister, Min Zhi, and her parents. They came a long way to visit. I hope she will remember us. She will always be welcome to return."

Then Mei Jing raised her hand. "In America, are you happy?"

"Yes, I am really happy."

The next morning before we left, Ms. Guo was waiting to say goodbye. We all hugged. As I was getting into the car, Mei Jing scampered toward us. She handed me a piece of paper. Scrawled on it in English was the recipe for the vegetable dish.

"Cook this and remember me."

I almost cried. I didn't know enough Chinese to **express** all the good things I wished for her. Instead I took off my charm necklace and fastened it around her neck. We quickly hugged and then I left.

Back home, my *abuela* took me to a Chinese market. She liked the *bai cai* I cooked because it tasted great with *arroz salteado*. Now I am practicing Chinese, too—with a boy in my language class at the cultural center.

After the trip I felt different, somehow. Now I know who I really am—a Florida *chica china* by way of Fujian.

Make Connections

How does Mariel's visit to the orphanage change her understanding of herself? **ESSENTIAL QUESTION**

How do unexpected acts of kindness help people understand the world around them? **TEXT TO TEXT**

Genre • Expository Text TIME for KIDS

REDISCOVERING Our Spanish Beginnings

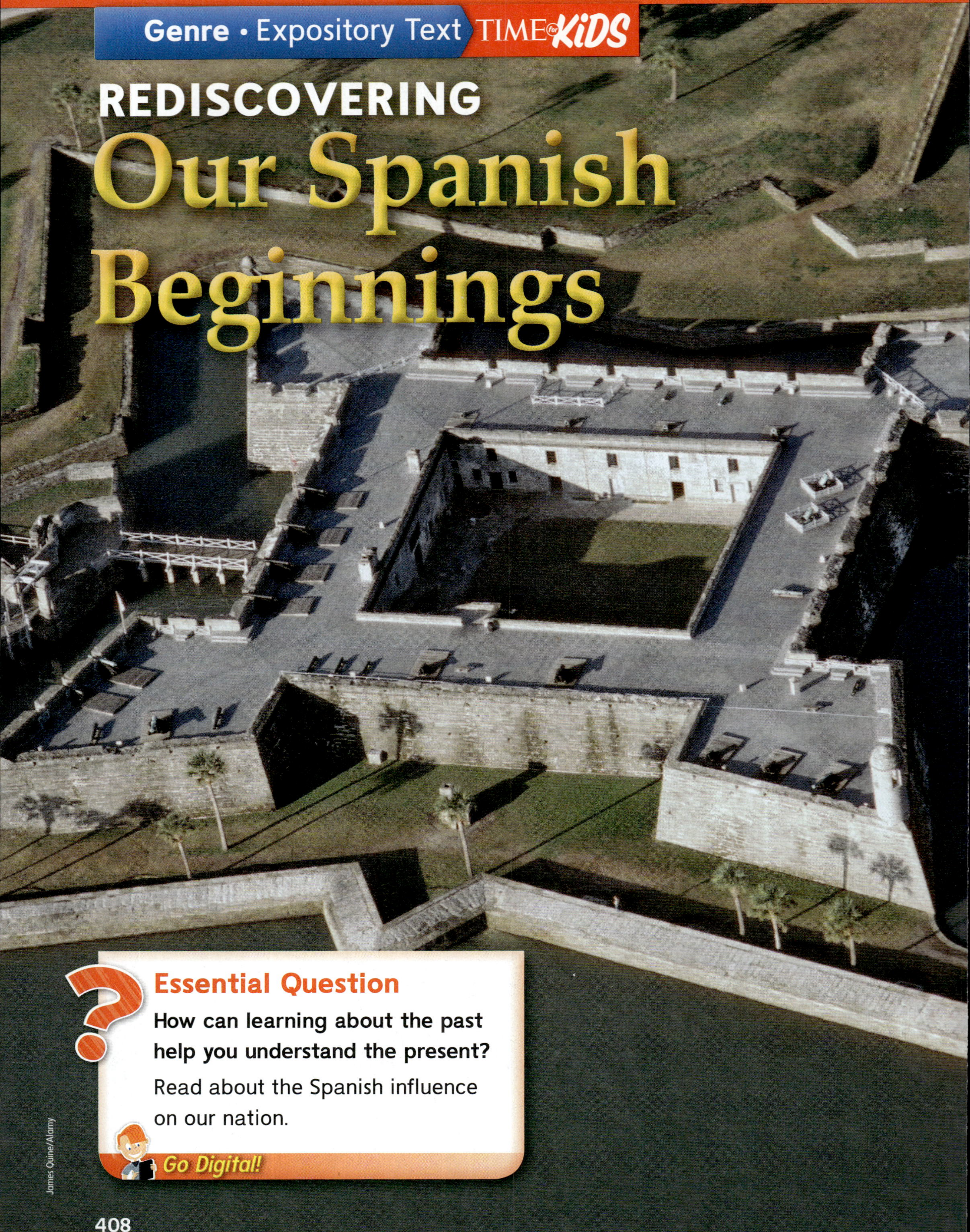

Essential Question

How can learning about the past help you understand the present?

Read about the Spanish influence on our nation.

Go Digital!

James Quine/Alamy

St. Augustine, Florida, is the oldest city founded by Europeans in the United States. Its history begins with the founding of Florida by the Spanish conquistador Juan Ponce de León.

In 1493, Ponce de León began his career as a member of Christopher Columbus's second **expedition**. After serving as governor of the Dominican Republic, Haiti, and then Puerto Rico, he later set out on his own to find the legendary Fountain of Youth. Instead, his expedition in 1513 entered the lands we now call Florida. He claimed the peninsula, home to thousands of Native peoples, for Spain. It was named *La Florida* after a Spanish feast of flowers.

Spain's Foothold

Establishing a colony on *La Florida* was easier said than done. After Ponce de León's arrival, six more expeditions were made to the Spanish-claimed peninsula. Unfortunately, all attempts to settle there failed. Native tribes did not want them there. European crops would not take hold in the soil. This meant that settlers would have to depend on supplies from Spain to survive. Explorers also noted the heat, humidity, frequency of tropical storms, and dangerous animals, as reasons not to settle. Florida was seen as a risk and ignored for many years.

Then in 1564, France successfully established Fort Caroline 35 miles north of where Ponce de León had landed. The Spanish king found this unacceptable. A year later he sent Pedro Menéndez de Avilés, an admiral, to colonize and rule Florida. Menéndez and his soldiers destroyed the French colony. They founded the Spanish settlement St. Augustine on September 8, 1565.

Pedro Menéndez de Avilés founded St. Augustine.

St. Augustine became the main northern outpost of the Spanish empire. It was also the center for Spanish missions in the region. Since it was a target for enemy attack, the settlement was forced to relocate several times over the next six years. The Native people, known as Timucuans, did not welcome Spanish rule. They defended their homes and resisted the Spanish occupation. Before returning to Spain in 1567, Menéndez helped to establish three forts. His nephew returned to govern Florida until 1589.

Before long the English were becoming a threat to Spanish Florida. After Jamestown was settled in 1607, the English continued to colonize up and down the east coast. The Spanish settlers were also under constant attack from pirates and enemy ships. Finally, money from Spain allowed for the building of a massive stone fortress, called the Castillo de San Marcos. This fort remains St. Augustine's most historically significant monument.

A Fearsome Fort

Just as Rome wasn't built in a day, the Castillo (castle) de San Marcos was built over time, between 1672 and 1695. Much of the labor used to build the fort came from enslaved Indians. It was the tenth fort built to protect the city of St. Augustine. The previous nine forts had been made of wood. The Castillo de San Marcos was constructed with a nearly indestructible shell stone, or coquina. Its **tremendous** walls tower 33 feet high and measure 12 feet thick.

Learning About the Past in the Present

St. Augustine has been part of the United States since 1821, when Florida became a U.S. territory. You can still see **permanent** signs of the Spanish **era** in the city. Many streets have Spanish names, and some buildings look like they are from colonial times.

Today, part of the city is like living **archaeology**. Visitors can come to St. Augustine to **uncover evidence** about life in the old days. Many Spanish colonial sites have been restored, and the city's museums **document** its history. Visitors to the Colonial Spanish Quarter learn how Spanish settlers lived centuries ago. Much of the information is based on what archaeologists have uncovered, including buttons, beads, dishes, and tools. More than one million artifacts have been uncovered since the 1930s.

What's in a Name?

Do you speak Spanish? You may, without even knowing it! Over hundreds of years, many Spanish words have entered the English language. In the U.S., many place names come from the Spanish language, including California, Nevada, and Los Angeles.

Other words that come to us from the Spanish settlers include *burrito, cafeteria, canyon, fiesta, mosquito, patio, plaza, rodeo,* and *tango*.

Respond to the Text

1. Use details from the selection to summarize. **SUMMARIZE**
2. What does "Rediscovering Our Spanish Beginnings" help you understand about Florida? **WRITE**
3. Write about the Spanish influence on the United States. **TEXT TO WORLD**

(t) Courtesy of the Center for Disease Control/James Gathany; (b) Amy Sancetta/AP Images

Genre • Informative Article

TIME for KIDS

Compare Texts

Read about two early colonies that vanished.

HISTORY'S Mysteries

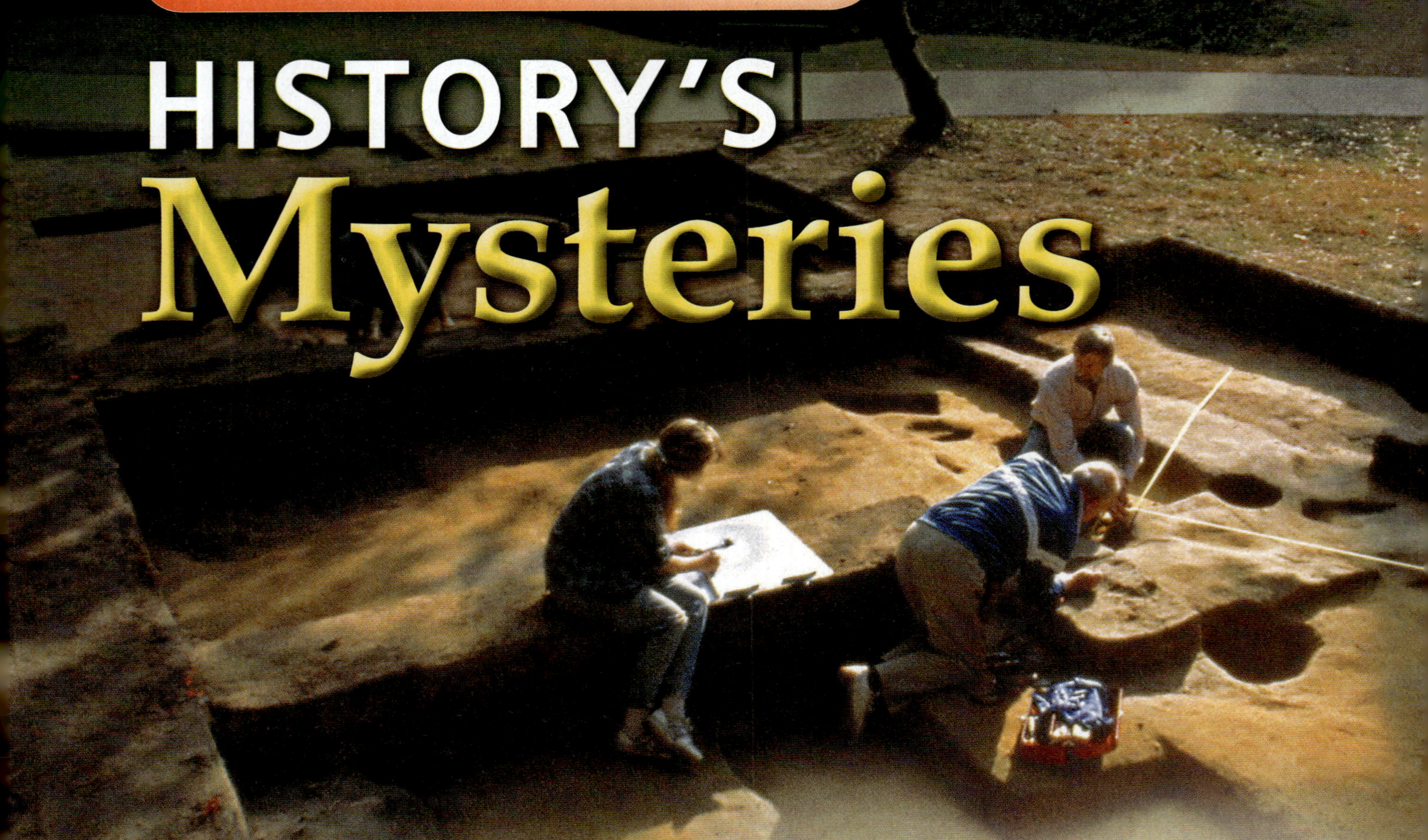

Ira Block/National Geographic/Getty Images

Archaeology, the study of relics, artifacts, and remains, helps us piece together the past. Read on to learn about two of history's mysteries.

Vanished into Thin Air

In 1587, an English colonist named John White and a small crew sailed to England from tiny Roanoke Island, off the coast of North Carolina. They left more than 100 people behind. White returned to Roanoke three years later with supplies. He found nothing but an abandoned fort. On a post was written "Croatan." How did the entire colony vanish without a trace? And what did *Croatan* mean? The mystery remains unsolved.

There are many theories, however. Some historians believe that a Native American tribe killed the colonists. Others think that the settlers abandoned the colony to live with nearby tribes.

Archaeologist Jeffrey Brain (right) and his team of colleagues and volunteers spent ten years digging for clues about the Popham colony. The discovery of a man-made hearth (left) confirmed that the excavation site was once a home.

Disease, drought, or starvation may also have decimated the settlement. Archaeologists found a gold ring, pipes, coins, beads, and bone rings from the Croatan site. While these items serve as evidence of early contact between the native tribes and the first English colony, it's not enough to know for sure what happened to the colonists.

Finding Popham

In 1607, a crew of 125 English colonists set out on an **expedition**. They landed on Maine's coast. They erected a small settlement and named it for its principal backer, Sir John Popham, and his nephew George. But the Popham Colony—England's first attempt at a New England settlement—didn't survive. One year later, the colonists boarded their ship and sailed home.

For centuries, no one knew precisely where the colony had been. Then archaeologist Jeffrey Brain began excavating the area in 1994. After ten years of digging, Brain and his team uncovered traces of the colony's storehouse, a hearth (or floor of a fireplace), and stoneware fragments. Their work has helped unearth clues about the way the colony lived.

Make Connections

What did archaeology reveal about the two early colonies? **ESSENTIAL QUESTION**

How does digging up the past help us understand the present? **TEXT TO TEXT**

Genre • Biography

How Ben Franklin Stole the Lightning

ROSALYN SCHANZER

Essential Question

How can inventions solve problems?

Read about a great inventor who solved problems.

Go Digital!

It's true!

The great Benjamin Franklin really did steal lightning right out of the sky! And then he set out to tame the beast. It goes to figure, though, because he was a man who could do just about anything.

Early to bed and early to rise makes a man healthy, wealthy and wise.
Silence
BENJ. FRANKLIN
SOAP
OINTMENT for the ITCH

Why, Ben Franklin could swim faster, argue better, and write funnier stories than practically anyone in colonial America. He was a musician, a printer, a cartoonist, and a world traveler! What's more, he was a newspaper owner, a shopkeeper, a soldier, and a **politician**. He even helped to write the Declaration of Independence *and* the Constitution of the United States!

Ben was always coming up with newfangled ways to help folks out, too. He was the guy who started the first lending library in America. His post office was the first to deliver mail straight to people's houses.

He also wrote almanacs that gave **hilarious** advice about life and told people when to plant crops, whether there might be an eclipse, and when the tides would be high or low.

And he helped to start a hospital!

A free academy!

A fire department!

In colonial days, fire could break out at any time. And it was lightning that caused some of the worst fires. Whenever thunderstorms were brewing, they would ring the church bells for all they were worth, but it didn't do anybody a lick of good.

Of course, after Ben stole the lightning, there weren't nearly as many fires for firefighters to put out. "Now, why was that?" I hear you ask. "And how did he steal any lightning in the first place?" Well, it's a long story, but before we get to the answer, here's a hint. One of the things Benjamin Franklin liked to do best was to make inventions.

Why, Ben was a born inventor. He loved to swim fast, but he wanted to go even faster. So one day when he was a mere lad of eleven, he got some wood and invented swim paddles for his hands and swim fins for his feet. Ben could go faster, all right, but the wood was pretty heavy, and his wrists got plumb worn out.

That's why his second invention was a better way to go fast. He lay on his back, held on to a kite string, and let his kite pull him lickety-split across a big pond. (You might want to remember later on that Ben always did like kites.)

Ben kept right on inventing better ways to do things for the rest of his life.

Take books, for example. Ben read so many books that some of them sat on shelves way up high near the ceiling. So he invented the library chair. If he pulled up the seat, out popped some stairs to help him reach any books on high shelves. And in case climbing stairs made him **dizzy**, he invented a long wooden arm that could grab his books, too.

He also invented an odometer that told how far he had ridden to deliver the mail. And the first clock with a second hand. And he even thought up daylight saving time. Then he invented bifocals so older folks could see up close and far away without changing glasses.

Everybody and his brother and sister just had to find better ways to heat their houses in wintertime. So Ben came up with a Franklin stove that could warm up cold rooms faster and use a lot less wood than old-fashioned stoves and fireplaces.

People all over Europe and America loved Ben's glass armonica. This instrument could spin wet glass bowls to make music that sounded like it came straight from heaven. Mozart and Beethoven wrote music for it, and it was even played at a royal Italian wedding.

But as popular as warmer stoves and glass armonicas were, they aren't anywhere near as celebrated **nowadays** as the invention Ben made after he stole the lightning.

Another hint about Ben's most famous invention is that it helped make life easier for everyone. His scientific ideas were helpful, too, and were often way ahead of their time. For example, he had a lot of ideas about health. He said that exercise and weight lifting help keep folks fit, but they have to work hard enough to sweat if they want to do any good.

He wrote that breathing fresh air and drinking lots of water are good for you. He was the guy who said "an apple a day keeps the doctor away."

And before anyone ever heard of vitamin C, he wrote that oranges, limes, and grapefruit give people healthy gums and skin. Sailors soon got wind of this idea. They began eating so many limes to stop getting sick from scurvy at sea that they became known as limeys.

Didn't the man ever stop to rest? Even when he was outside, Ben kept right on experimenting.

For instance, he often sailed to England and France to do business for America. As he crossed the Atlantic Ocean, he charted the Gulf Stream by taking its temperature. Once sailors knew the route of this fast, warm "river" in the cold ocean, they could travel between America and Europe in a shorter time than ever before.

He was probably the first person to write weather forecasts, too. Once he chased a roaring whirlwind by riding over the hills and forests of Maryland just to find out how it worked.

Ben had an old scientific trick that he liked to show people every chance he got. He used to store some oil inside a bamboo walking stick, and whenever he poured a few drops onto angry waves in a pond or lake, the water became smooth as glass!

Meanwhile, over in Europe, people called "electricians" had started doing some tricks of their own. One trick was to raise a boy up near the ceiling with a bunch of silk cords, rub his feet with a glass "electric tube," and make sparks shoot out of his hands and face.

Another mean trick made the king of France laugh so hard he could hardly stop. His court electrician had run an electric charge through 180 soldiers of the guard, and they jerked to attention faster than they ever had in their entire lives.

But although people were doing lots of tricks with electricity, nobody had a clue about why or how it worked. So Benjamin Franklin decided to find out. He asked a British friend to send him an electric tube so that he could do some **experiments**.

In one experiment, he made a cork "electric spider" with thread for legs. It kept leaping back and forth between a wire and an electric tube just like it was alive.

Another time he asked a lady and gentleman to stand on some wax. One held an electric tube, the other held a wire, and when they tried to kiss, they got shocked by all the sparks shooting between their lips.

Ben even figured out how to light up a picture of a king in a golden frame. Anyone trying to remove the king's gold paper crown was in for a shock!

Doing all these tricks gave Ben his idea for stealing lightning out of the sky. He believed that lightning was nothing more nor less than pure electricity. Now he set out to prove it.

First he made a silk kite with a wire on top to attract some lightning. Next he added a kite string, tied a key to the bottom, and knotted a silk ribbon below the key. Ben and his son William stood out of the rain inside the doorway of a shed on the side of a field. To keep from getting shocked, Ben held on to the dry silk ribbon. Then he flew his kite straight up toward a big rain cloud.

For the longest time, nothing happened.

Just as Ben and William were about to give up, the hair on that wet kite string began to rise up and stand at attention. Ben put his knuckle near the key, and *YIKES!!!!* Out jumped a bright spark of **genuine** electricity!

Real lightning had traveled all the way down that kite string! Ben had stolen electric fire out of the heavens and proven that he was right.

(Of course, now we know that if the storm had been any stronger, the great inventor would have been toast.)

Finally! Here's the part of the story where Ben's practice from thinking up all those inventions came in so handy. Way back then, you remember, lightning was always setting fire to ships, houses, and church spires. Even the best fire departments couldn't keep entire towns from going up in smoke. So Ben decided to make his most famous invention of all—the lightning rod!

The whole idea was to pull lightning safely out of the sky before it could do any **mischief**. Ben showed people how to put a pointed iron rod on the tip-top of a roof or ship's mast and connect it to a wire leading all the way down under the ground or into water. Now the lightning could follow a safe path without burning up a thing.

This simple but brilliant invention worked beautifully. It saved more lives than anyone can count and made Ben Franklin a great hero.

Scientists from around the world lined up to give Ben medals and awards. But during his long life, he became much more than the master of lightning. Why, when America fought against Great Britain for the right to become a free nation, Ben convinced France to come help win the war, and when it was over, he helped convince Great Britain to sign the peace. He had helped in so many ways that the people of France honored him with a beautiful medallion. It says "He snatched the lightning from heaven and the scepter from tyrants."

And he did.

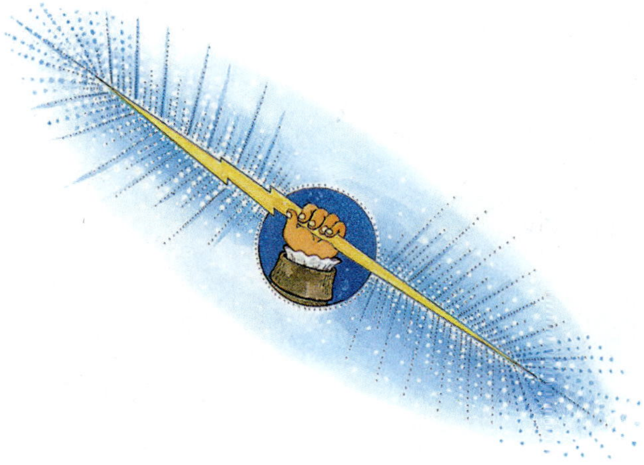

About Rosalyn Schanzer

Just like Ben Franklin, **Rosalyn Schanzer** is a person with many interests. In addition to being an artist, a photographer, and a writer, Schanzer enjoys swimming. Growing up, Schanzer loved to draw pictures. She studied art in college, and her first job was illustrating greeting cards. Then she became an illustrator for children's books and magazines. Her interest in famous people and events in history led her to take on the challenge of becoming a writer. Now, she follows her interests by illustrating the books she writes.

Author's Purpose

Ben Franklin's invention of the lightning rod was the main focus of this selection. Why did the author choose to point out many of Franklin's other inventions?

Respond to the Text

Summarize

Summarize *How Ben Franklin Stole the Lightning*. Information from your Problem and Solution Chart may help you.

Problem	Solution

Write

Think about how Rosalyn Schanzer talks about Benjamin Franklin's accomplishments. How does she help you understand that Ben Franklin was a great problem-solver? Use these sentence starters to organize your text evidence.

Rosalyn Schanzer introduces Ben Franklin by . . .
Then she describes how . . .
Finally, she shows that . . .

Make Connections

How did the invention of the lightning rod solve a problem? **ESSENTIAL QUESTION**

Think about some modern inventions. Describe an invention that solves a problem in our world today. **TEXT TO WORLD**

Genre • Expository Text

Compare Texts

Read about the different kinds of energy.

Energy is Everywhere!

Thunder and lightning forewarn of an impending storm. Massive gray clouds roll in, hovering over the neighborhood. A heavy rain falls from the sky, flooding the streets. High winds push and pull at the trees. A large branch snaps off and falls onto the power lines below. Suddenly, we cannot turn on lights, cook, watch TV, use computers, or do many of the daily tasks we take for granted. Electricity—the particles of energy that traveled down Ben Franklin's kite string during his most famous experiment—is essential to our lives.

(bkgd) qingyi/iStock/Getty Images

Nowadays we depend on electricity in ways that people in the past could never have imagined. We also understand more about it. Or do we? Did you know that the first step in understanding electricity is understanding energy? And did you know that energy is everywhere?

Kinds of Energy

Scientists define energy as the ability to apply force. So, energy is used when someone or something flies, falls, runs, beeps, moves, or cooks. But energy is not always that obvious because there are many different kinds. Chemical energy is stored in things such as petroleum, coal, wood—even food. Mechanical energy is stored in objects under tension such as springs on trampolines. Mechanical energy may also be energy in motion, such as the energy of wind blowing down branches during a storm.

The sun is a source of light energy. Sunlight makes life possible. Plants transform the sun's light energy into chemical energy, or food. You can think about it this way—when you eat oatmeal for breakfast and then run to the bus stop, your motion energy is a result of sunlight helping oat plants to grow.

Another kind of energy is thermal energy, or heat. Wood burned in a stove or fireplace changes the chemical energy in the wood into thermal energy.

Energy also lies in sound. Sound energy occurs when air particles move and vibrate. When you pluck guitar strings, the mechanical energy of your fingers and the vibrating strings is transformed into sound energy.

Sunlight and sound are just two of the many different kinds of energy.

Electrical Energy

Electrical energy is an energy carrier. That means it is created from certain forms of energy and can then produce other forms of energy. For example, when you dry your hair after a shower, you plug in a hair dryer and turn it on. That may seem simple, but many things happen before your hair dries. First, the electricity for the hair dryer comes from a power plant, which is the energy source. This energy source transforms the chemical energy of oil, coal, or natural gas into electric charges. These electric charges, or electricity, then follow wires to the socket and into your hair dryer, creating a current. So when you flip a switch to turn the hair dryer on, that action provides a path for the electrical current. It also transforms electrical energy into thermal and mechanical energy—the heat and blowing air.

Power Is Enlightening

Learning about electricity is important. Learning to control electricity puts it to work. By creating a simple circuit, you can get a better sense of how electrical energy works.

Energy is all around you! The next time a storm knocks out the power to your home, explain to your family what happened as you sit with them by candlelight.

This hair dryer blows heat and air because it is plugged into an energy source. When the hair dryer is turned on, a path is created, allowing electricity to travel from the power plant into your home.

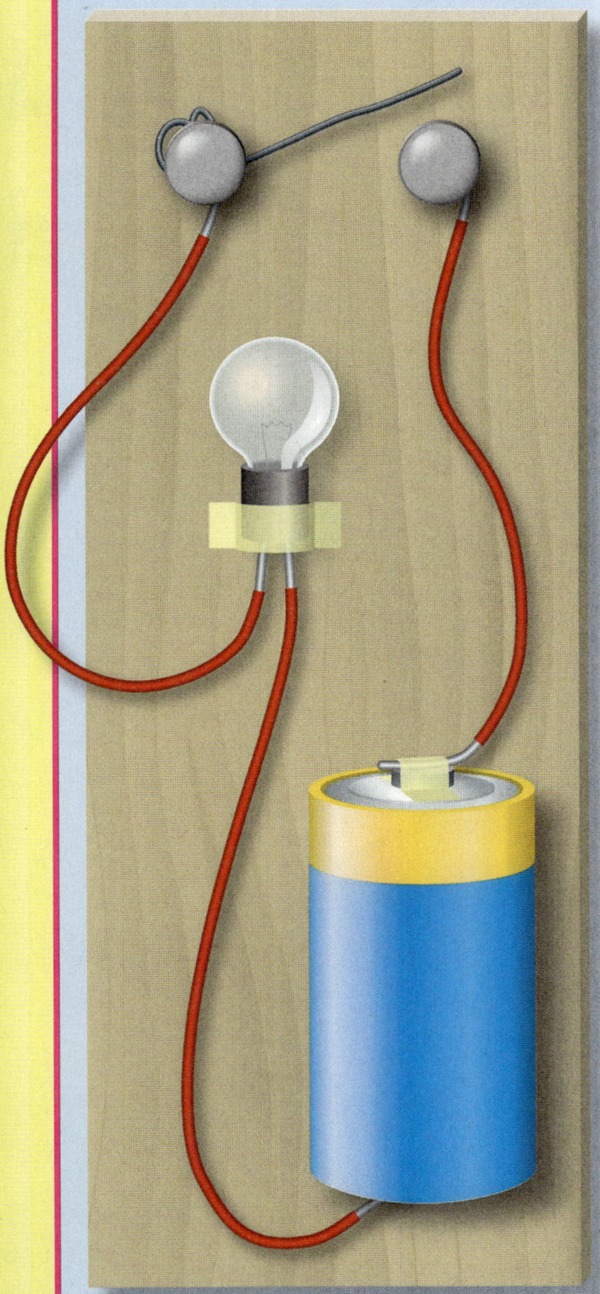

Make a Circuit

See for yourself how energy is transformed by building a simple electrical circuit. A battery stores chemical energy. Follow the **procedure** to transform chemical energy into electrical energy and then light energy. Remember to use only the provided battery. Do not use wall sockets. Have an adult supervise the experiment.

What You Need

- A flashlight bulb
- A battery (size D)
- Three 6-inch pieces of stripped wire
- Tape
- A straightened paper clip
- Two thumbtacks
- A block of wood

What You Do

- Push one thumbtack into the wood.
- Wrap one end of the paper clip around the second thumbtack and push it into the wood. Make sure the straightened end of the paper clip can touch the first thumbtack. That's the switch.
- Connect one wire to each thumbtack.
- Tape the bulb to one of the wires.
- Connect the remaining wire to the bulb with tape.
- Place the battery in between the two wires and use tape to connect one to either end of the battery.

When you connect the paper clip with the thumbtack, you complete the electrical circuit. The bulb will light.

Make Connections

Explain how "energy is everywhere." **ESSENTIAL QUESTION**

Why are inventions important? **TEXT TO TEXT**

Neil Stewart

Genre • Tall Tale

Essential Question

What are some reasons people moved west?

Read about a family's journey west with fruit.

Go Digital!

APPLES TO OREGON

Being the (Slightly) True Narrative of How a Brave Pioneer Father Brought Apples, Peaches, Pears, Plums, Grapes, and Cherries (and Children) Across the Plains

BY DEBORAH HOPKINSON

ILLUSTRATED BY NANCY CARPENTER

My daddy loved growin' apples. And when he got ready to pull up roots and leave Iowa for Oregon, he couldn't bear to leave his apple trees behind.

So Daddy built two of the biggest boxes you could ever hope to see. He set them into a sturdy wagon and shoveled in good, wormy dirt. Then he filled every inch with little plants and trees. Hundreds of them!

Daddy was ready for the most daring adventure in the history of fruit.

"Apples, ho!" he cried.

Along with apples, my daddy took peaches, pears, plums, grapes, and cherries.

Oh, and by the way, he took us along too.

We all had lots to do on the journey. Each morning I helped Momma bake biscuits, while Daddy prepared for another long day on the trail. At night Momma and I tucked in the little ones, then Daddy fiddled lullabies under the stars. Why, I can still hear him crooning to the Gravensteins,

"Hush, little babies, don't you cry
Momma's gonna bake you in an apple pie.
If that apple pie ain't sweet,
Daddy's gonna munch you for his own special treat."

We rolled along just fine till we came to the Platte River. It was wider than Texas, thicker than Momma's muskrat stew, and muddier than a cowboy's toenails. Just looking at it made my insides **shrivel**.

The riverbank was crowded with folks in prairie schooners trying to get up the nerve to cross.

When they saw us and all our little fruit trees fluttering in the breeze, they burst out laughing.

"Those leaves will be brown as dirt before you hit the plains," declared one old geezer.

"Plains?" **scoffed** someone else. "That nursery wagon won't make it halfway across the river."

But Daddy didn't let their talk worry him. He just looked me square in the eye and said, "Delicious, I'm gonna need your help."

Right then and there we built a raft for his tiny trees, then Daddy loaded me and my little sisters and brothers onto the edges.

"Now, make sure my precious plants don't **topple** into the water," Daddy warned.

Well, we hadn't gone far when that muddy drink started to pull us down.

"The peaches are plummeting!" my sisters shouted.

"The plums are **plunging**!" boomed my brothers.

"Don't let my babies go belly-up!" howled Daddy.

I had to think quick. "We're too heavy. If we don't go faster, we'll sink. We gotta take our shoes off and kick!"

And so we kicked.

'Course we'd all been raised on apples, and everyone knows young 'uns raised on apples are strong, mighty strong. Before you could say "Johnny Appleseed," we'd kicked ourselves clear to the other shore.

But no sooner had we got every last tree loaded back in the wagon than I spied a foul-looking bunch of clouds stomping round the sun just fit to be tied.

The wind began to throw around everything that wasn't lashed down—our boots, baby Albert's diapers, every pot and pan Momma had, even our own little wagon.

Next, hailstones big as plums came hurtling out of the sky.

"Guard the grapes! Protect the peaches!" Daddy howled.

So we all started tearing off our clothes and holding them over Daddy's darlings. Bonnets, petticoats, trousers, hats—even Daddy's drawers!

Whew! At last the storm passed and Daddy's dainties were safe.

After all that excitement it felt good to hit the trail again. But before long we came to an endless sandy desert. Now remember, us young 'uns didn't have our wagon or our boots. In no time our feet were redder than the poison apple the old witch gave to Snow White.

"Delicious, this is our toughest challenge," said Daddy, wiping his brow as I followed him on tippy toes. "We got to find a water hole or my babies are done for."

Sure enough, by noon the fruit trees began to droop. By three their itty-bitty tender leaves were getting crispy. By nightfall Daddy was crying, a handful of dead branches pressed against his heart.

I couldn't bear to see my daddy suffer. So early next morning I took off to look for water. But although I searched and searched, I couldn't even find a splash or a puddle.

After a while I got so tuckered out, I plopped down under an old sagebrush.

"Ouch!" I yelled, landing on something hard. But when I saw what it was, I whooped for joy. My very own boot! What's more, it still had some water in it from all those melted hailstones.

That was our lucky day, let me tell you. We found every one of Momma's pots and pans spread out across the sand. They all had a few drops of water in them too. Just enough to get Daddy's trees to the next water hole before they all keeled over.

My, that first sip of water sure tasted good, even if I did have to wait my turn behind some Baldwin apples.

Oh, and I'm pleased to say our wagon and all the boots turned up too.

All except one.

I reckon that nasty wind blew my left boot clear to the other side of the moon. And if it should happen to drop out of the sky on your head one of these days, I'd sure appreciate your sending it along to me.

Well, we kept on going, past Courthouse Rock and Chimney Rock and Independence Rock and lots of other rocks that didn't have names. We climbed up rocks and down rocks. And at last we reached the Columbia River.

"Just a hundred miles to go," declared Daddy.

But time was running out. Our little trees had almost drowned in the river, got pounded by hailstones, and got withered by drought. How much more could they take?

And now we were set for a showdown with the most ornery varmint of all: Jack Frost.

Oh, I'd already spied him sneaking around our campsite, brushing the cottonwoods with his cold white tongue. But I wasn't about to let him get close to my daddy's apples.

So that night I made a big fire and sat by it, waiting for Jack Frost to show himself. Sure enough, as soon as the moon came up I spotted that ole good-for-nothing slinking across the meadow, heading straight for the Sweet Junes.

I got ready to fight. Jack Frost came at me, turning the ground so cold my toes went numb. But I didn't give up.

I grabbed a flaming stick and threw it right at him. Before you could say "Peter Piper picked a peck of pretty pippins," that low-down scoundrel was hightailing it out of there, heading straight for Walla Walla, Washington.

“I’m mighty grateful, Delicious,” said Daddy as he scrutinized his sweeties the next morning. “Thanks to you, even the Sweets stayed snug.”

“We were nice and cozy too,” added Momma, checking the children.

Sure enough, all Daddy's trees survived, just as if they'd come across the plains in a swanky carriage. We floated them on boats down the mighty Columbia to a pretty place near Portland.

Then we planted them in that sweet Oregon dirt at last.

Gold was discovered in California not long after, and thousands of people rushed there to seek their fortunes.

But not us. We already had our fortune. Those apples, peaches, pears, plums, grapes, and cherries made us richer than any **prospector**.

We were happier, too. After all, apples taste a whole lot better than gold.

As for my daddy, he was always sweet as a peach. He and Momma lived happily to a ripe old age.

Daddy never forgot my brave deeds on the trail. Why, as soon as he sold his first bushel of apples, he bought me the prettiest pair of boots you ever saw.

"Delicious," said Daddy, "you'll always be the apple of my eye."

ABOUT THE AUTHOR AND ILLUSTRATOR

Deborah Hopkinson has brought history to life with dozens of books for kids. She particularly enjoys writing historical fiction about people who have done great things but are less well-known. She also visits schools to talk about why history is important. Deborah lives near Portland, Oregon with her husband and two children.

Nancy Carpenter loves to illustrate books for kids. She particularly likes to draw spunky characters who act on their own (and sometimes get into trouble), rather than characters who just do what they are told. Nancy believes that these characters—like Delicious in *Apples to Oregon*—represent how kids are in real life.

AUTHOR'S PURPOSE

Why did the author choose to tell this story from Delicious's point of view?

Respond to the Text

Summarize

Use important details to summarize *Apples to Oregon* and describe the journey west for Delicious and her family. Include information from your Cause and Effect Chart.

Cause → Effect
→
→
→
→

Write

Think about how the author tells you about the characters and setting. How does the author show that the family's trip to Oregon was successful? Use these sentence starters to organize your text evidence.

> The author tells me about Delicious and her family by using . . .
> Through descriptive details, I learned . . .
> The illustrations help me understand . . .

Make Connections

Why do Delicious and her family make the journey west despite the obstacles? **ESSENTIAL QUESTION**

Like Delicious, many Americans traveled west in the 1800s. What are some reasons why people would choose to make such a difficult journey? **TEXT TO WORLD**

Genre • Expository Text

Compare Texts

Read how people came west to find gold.

GO FOR THE GOLD!

One January day in 1848, a worker named James Marshall spotted some shiny bits in the gravel of the American River at Coloma, California. He showed them to his boss, the owner of Sutter's Mill Lumber Company. When tests proved that it was gold, Sutter tried to keep the discovery secret. But news spread. His workers left the lumber mill, squatters took his land, and his business failed.

Why is gold valuable? It's beautiful, rare, useful, and durable, and it doesn't rust or tarnish. Gold can be cast, carved, pressed, rolled, polished, and hammered thinner than any other metal. Most important, though, people worldwide believe it has value.

Gold Rush miners were also called **prospectors, gold-seekers, Argonauts** (after the gold-seekers of Greek mythology), or **forty-niners** (after the year 1849).

A mining operation in 1852 on the American River near Sacramento, California

Forty-niners panning for gold in California

By 1849, California's population exploded with gold-seekers. Some newcomers came overland from the East Coast in wagon trains. Others braved long sea voyages around Cape Horn or via Panama to reach San Francisco.

Mining gold was backbreaking, dirty, dangerous, and sometimes violent. Some miners worked by hand. They used picks, shovels, and pans to sift gold-bearing sand and gravel from rivers and streams. Hard-rock rock mining required machinery, high-pressure hoses, and water to crush and move huge quantities of rock. Deep holes scarred valuable farmland.

Miners "staked a claim" to specific land where they looked for gold. But claim jumpers frequently took over other miners' claims. And thieves stole their finds. Some miners camped inside their hillside tunnels to protect their claims.

Miners took their gold dust, flakes, and nuggets to people called assayers. They weighed and tested it for purity. Some who thought they had gold learned it was worthless iron pyrite.

Miners needed tools, food, and clothing to survive. Storekeepers gladly provided supplies at sky-high prices. They demanded payment in gold. Many businessmen became far richer than even the luckiest miners. Peddler Levi Strauss is a good example. He sold tent canvas. But then he made more money selling rugged denim work overalls. He later founded a company that manufactured blue jeans. (And you know what they're called today!)

Miners and the equipment they used in 1852 to look for gold

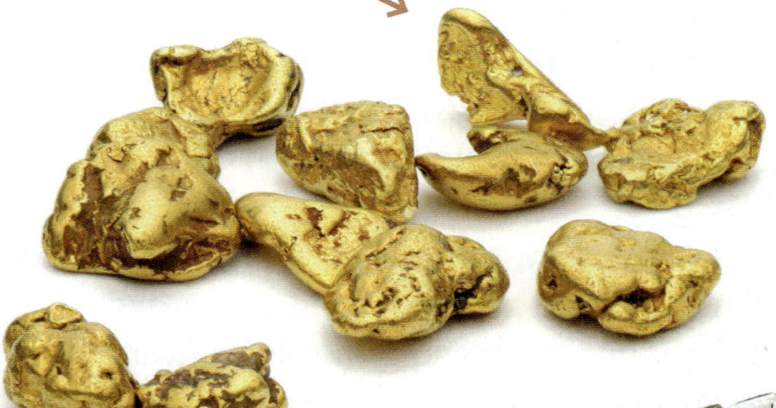

A California Gold Rush town in 1853. There is a business district, houses, and barns.

Machinery and lumber suppliers did well, too. Two men who exchanged miners' gold for dollars established what is today one of America's largest banks. Sea and land transportation improved. **Settlements** became towns. Hotels, entertainment halls, and gambling houses flourished.

Not everything was "golden," however. As veins of gold-bearing rock played out, many miners ended up penniless and left.

The Gold Rush lasted only a few years, but it changed California from frontier territory to a prosperous statehood. In September 1850, California became the thirty-first state in the United States. Today, abandoned mine tunnels and rock and gravel piles left from dredging are silent reminders of this history-making period.

Make Connections

How did the discovery of gold impact the number of people who moved west in the 19th century? **ESSENTIAL QUESTION**

What are some of the different ways people made their living when they moved west? **TEXT TO TEXT**

Genre • Narrative Nonfiction

Essential Question

How have our energy resources changed over the years?

Read how a community came to use renewable energy resources.

Go Digital!

Energy Island

How One Community Harnessed the Wind and Changed Their World

by ALLAN DRUMMOND

Welcome to Energy Island! The real name of our island is Samsø, but we like to call it "Energy Island."

Not too long ago we were just ordinary people living on an ordinary island in the middle of Denmark. In many ways, Samsø was—and still is—not very different from where you live. We have lots of fields and farms, where farmers raise cows and sheep, and grow crops like potatoes, peas, corn, and strawberries. And there is a harbor where the ferry and fishing boats come in.

Our little home has recently become quite famous, and scientists travel from all over the world just to talk to us and learn about what we've done. Why is that? Well, it's an interesting story...

Let's go! Hold on to your hats!

Our island is in the middle of Denmark...and it's in the middle of the sea. That's why it's always very windy here! Oops!

In the summer we have fun at the beach. And in the winter we play games inside. We have villages and schools. Kids play soccer, and grownups go the grocery store. It's very ordinary here–apart from the wind.

The way we used to use energy was very ordinary, too. On dark winter nights we switched on lots of lights, and turned up our heaters to keep warm. We used hot water without even thinking. Our oil arrived by tanker ship and truck, and we used it to fill up our cars and our heating systems. And our electricity came from the mainland by cable under the sea.

A few years ago, most of us didn't think much about where our energy came from, or how it was made. That was before our island won a very unusual competition. The Danish Ministry of Environment and Energy chose Samsø as the ideal place in Denmark to become independent of nonrenewable energy.

A teacher named Søren Hermansen was selected to lead the energy independence project. He was a very ordinary person, too...

Renewable Energy

Renewable energy comes from resources that will never run out, or that can be replaced. For example, wind is a renewable resource, since the wind will always blow. Windmills were invented to catch that energy.

Rivers keep flowing all year, so they are also a source of renewable energy. People have been using dams, water mills, and other means of harnessing water power for thousands of years.

Sunlight, which can be **converted** into solar power, is another example of a renewable resource, and so are the plants and trees that can be harvested and converted into *biofuels* and then replanted.

Scientists are even figuring out how to create energy from burning garbage and human sewage!

Okay, he did play bass guitar in a band. But his favorite subject was environmental studies. And he was very excited about energy independence. "Tell me, class, what are some ways we could make our own energy, right here on the island?"

"Imagine if we really could make enough energy from the sun, and our crops, and even our own legs, to power up the whole island! Then we wouldn't need the oil tankers to come here. We wouldn't have to worry about all the world's oil running out. And we wouldn't need electricity to be sent from the mainland. Renewable resources are so much cleaner. And think of the money we'd save! We just need to think big."

"But do you think we can really create that much energy ourselves?" asked Naja. "From just the sun, our crops, and our legs?"

"Well, you know," said Kathrine, "if there's one thing our island has plenty of, it's wind! Maybe we should start with wind energy."

"That's a wonderful idea!" said Mr. Hermansen. "Who's with me?"

"Hold on to your hats!" we all said.

The Problem of Nonrenewable Energy

Coal, oil, and natural gas are amazing sources of energy. They have helped create the modern world we live in—full of cars, plastic, and electricity. But that progress has come at a price, and that price is CO_2.

Carbon dioxide—CO_2—is a gas produced as waste when fossil fuels are burned for energy. CO_2 does occur naturally—in fact, you make some every time you breathe! But when we produce very large amounts of CO_2, as we do when we use fossil fuels, it can become a serious problem for the world.

When gases such as water vapor, methane, ozone, and carbon dioxide are released into the Earth's atmosphere, they trap heat. When heat is trapped inside the atmosphere, this is called the *greenhouse effect*. When the average temperature of the planet increases over time due to the greenhouse effect, it is called *global warming*. *Global warming* is a type of *climate change*.

We kids were very excited about all the new ideas. But as for the grownups...Well, it took them a while to catch on.

"It will cost millions!" said Jørgen Tranberg. "All these cows keep me busy enough already!"

"Heat from the sun?" said Peter Poulen. "Why would we bother with that? As long as I can keep my house warm and watch TV, I'm happy. I don't need change."

"Bicycles?" said Mogens Mahler. "No way. I love my truck!"

"Why us?" said Dorthe Knudsen. "Let some other island take on the challenge."

"Renewable energy?" said Jens Hansen. "I'm too old for all that."

"Samsø is just an ordinary place," said Ole Jørgensen. "What difference can we make to the world?"

"Energy independence? In your dreams!" said Petra Petersen.

Global Warming

Global warming can have serious **consequences** for all living things. Scientists predict that in the coming years summers will become hotter, winters will become colder, and storms will be fiercer.

Many scientists also believe that global warming is causing the ice caps at the North and South poles to slowly melt away, which changes the level of water in the ocean and affects animals like polar bears and penguins, not to mention people living on coastlines all over the world.

That's one of the reasons why scientists are making such an effort to use less and less nonrenewable energy. One way to do this is to use more renewable energy, which usually releases less CO_2.

But scientists can't do it alone! Today we should all be thinking about the problem of nonrenewable energy, just like the islanders of Samsø.

But Søren Hermansen wouldn't give up. He called lots of local meetings. "There's energy all around us!" he told the islanders. "We just need to work together and think big to make the best use of it."

He talked to everyone...The soccer team. The farmers at the market. All the teachers. The police. The fishermen. The harbormaster. The lighthouse keeper. The dentist.

This went on for several years. People listened, and lots of them even agreed with what Søren Hermansen was saying, but nothing happened. Was anyone willing to make a change?

Then one day, the electrician Brian Kjær called Søren Hermansen. “I’m thinking small,” he said. “I’d like to put up a secondhand wind turbine next to my house.”

Jørgen Tranberg was thinking big. “I want a huge wind turbine. I’ll invest my money and then sell the electricity it makes.”

Mr. Hermansen was excited. Two renewable energy projects had begun. One very small...and one very big!

Brian Kjær called on his family and friends to help him put up his wind turbine...while it took a big ship, some giant trucks, and two enormous cranes to build Jørgen Tranberg's! The project on Samsø had begun, but we were still using a lot of nonrenewable energy. It looked like we might never achieve our dream. Until one dark winter night...

Sleet and snow blasted across the island. Suddenly, all the electricity on the entire island went out! Everything was dark.

Everything, that is, except Brian Kjær's house. "Free electricity!" shouted Mr. Kjær. "My turbine works! Tonight I'm energy-independent!" Sure enough, the blades on Mr. Kjær's new turbine were whooshing and whirring in the wind! "Hold on to your hats!" cried Søren Hermansen.

News travels fast on a small island like Samsø.

After that night, everyone was asking how they could make energy of their own.

Suddenly, Søren Hermansen was busier than ever, helping people start new energy projects. The whole island got to work. Some people had big ideas. Some people had small ones. But all of them were important in working toward our goal.

The Holm family **installed** solar panels on their farm. Today their sheep are munching grass while the panels soak up energy from the sun. Ingvar Jørgensen built a biomass furnace. It burns straw instead of oil, and now heats his house and his neighbors' houses, too. In fact, biomass is so big on Samsø that whole villages are now heated by burning wood and straw grown on the island. Erik Andersen makes tractor fuel oil from his canola crop. And Brian Kjær's wife, Betina, whizzes around in an electric car. Their windmill powers the batteries.

Today we even have electric bicycles, charged by the power of the wind. Every one of us has an energy independence story. And that's why people all over the world want to hear the latest news from Energy Island.

Let's see if Jørgen Tranberg will take us up the ladder to the very top of his fantastic wind turbine, so we can see what Samsø looks like today.

Wind Energy

Windmills were first invented over 1,000 years ago in the land that is now Iran. Back then the windmills were used to grind corn and pump water. It's a strange **coincidence** that today Iran is a place where huge amounts of oil—a fossil fuel—are drilled from the ground and shipped all over the world.

Windmills are still used in the modern world, and they can do lots more than grind corn. The wind turbine, a modern type of windmill, actually makes electric power.

When wind blows across a wind turbine's blade, the blade turns and causes the main shaft to spin a generator, which makes electric power. The more wind there is outside, the faster the blades turn, and the more energy the turbine makes.

Before a turbine is built, scientists take measurements to discover which places are the windiest. Today there are turbines on hills, on top of city buildings, and even in the ocean! The electricity that is created by wind turbines can be used to power a single home or building, or it can be connected to an energy grid where the electricity is shared by a whole community.

As you can see, there's plenty going on! Now we have lots of wind turbines. Down there is Samsø's brand-new learning center, the Energy Academy, where kids and grownups from all over the world come to learn about what we've achieved, and to talk about new ideas for creating, sharing, and saving energy. Guess who the director of the academy is. An extraordinary teacher named Søren Hermansen.

Energy in the World

The more fossil fuel a country uses, the more CO_2 it produces. The United States produces nearly six billion metric tons of CO_2 per year. That weighs more than eight hundred million elephants!

As countries across the world become more developed and use more energy, they produce ever-increasing amounts of CO_2. Global warming is becoming a more frightening prospect every single day.

But there is good news. In this modern world we are able to share ideas and work together much more easily than ever before. Scientists are working on **incredible** new ways to use renewable resources and to save energy.

Some places are windy, some are sunny, some are hot, and some are cold. Each country or community must look at what special resources it has available, so as not to be dependent on nonrenewable resources in the future.

The Samsø Energy Academy is a place where people of all ages can share ideas about energy and how it is made and used.

Things have certainly changed on our little island in the past few years. We no longer need the oil tankers to bring us oil. And we don't need electricity from the mainland. In fact, on very windy days we have so much power that we send our own electricity back through the cable under the sea for other people in Denmark to use! Samsø may be a small island, but we have made a difference in the world—reducing our carbon emissions by 140 percent in just ten years. And we did it by working together.

Saving Energy

One thing that will take a lot of pressure off our need for energy, both renewable and nonrenewable, is simply making an effort to save energy.

We waste huge amounts of power to keep warm in the winter and cool in the summer. Badly designed doors, windows, and walls mean our heating and cooling systems work harder than they should, and produce too much CO_2. Building more **efficient** heaters and coolers, along with more efficiently designed buildings, would greatly help us cut down on the problems of global warming.

We can also save fuel by building new cars, trucks, and machines that waste less energy. Taking a bus or a train is another great way to cut down on energy use. And riding your bike is even better! To save energy, we need to think about how we use it every day.

So that's how we got the name Energy Island! And what can you do to make a difference on *your* island? What's that? You say you don't live on an island? Well, maybe you *think* you don't live on an island, but actually you *do*. We all do. We're all islanders on the biggest island of them all—planet Earth. So it's up to us to figure out how to save it.

There's renewable energy all around us. We just need to work together to make the best use of it. Hold on to your hats!

About Allan Drummond

If there is one thing that Allan Drummond has a surplus of, it's energy. He is an illustrator, a designer, a writer, and, like Søren Hermansen in *Energy Island*, a teacher. Drummond grew up in the United Kingdom and studied art in London. Before becoming an illustrator, he worked as a newspaper journalist. His murals are seen every day by commuters in the Holborn subway station in London. Drummond also designed the Royal Mail's special millennium stamp. Today he teaches college students in Georgia about children's book illustration. Drummond has written and illustrated more than 25 books for young people, including *Solar City*, which tells about a community powered by sunlight.

Author's Purpose

Why does the author use sidebars throughout *Energy Island*?

Respond to the Text

Summarize

Use the most important information from *Energy Island* to summarize how a community harnessed the power of the wind. Information from your Central Idea and Relevant Details Chart may help you.

Central Idea
Detail
Detail
Detail

Write

At the end of *Energy Island,* Allan Drummond reminds readers that renewable energy is all around us. He says that we just need to work together to make the best use of it. Do you agree or disagree? Explain your response. Use these sentence starters to organize your text evidence.

I agree/disagree with the author because . . .
The people of Samsø . . .
Another reason I think . . . is . . .

Make Connections

How did Samsø's residents come to use renewable energy resources?
ESSENTIAL QUESTION

Talk about some places around the world that could become energy-independent by using available renewable resources.
TEXT TO WORLD

Genre • Myth

Compare Texts

Read about the role of resources in Greek mythology.

Of Fire and Water

*In ancient times people used myths to explain our world. The following myths give us a glimpse into how the ancient Greeks viewed two vital **renewable** resources, fire and water.*

The Gift of Fire

Long ago, trouble arose on Mount Olympus, where the Greek gods lived. Zeus, the ruler of the gods, became enraged with Prometheus, a Titan. After creating humans out of clay, Prometheus provided them with three gifts that Zeus wanted to reserve only for the gods: knowledge, bestowed on Prometheus by Athena; the ability to stand upright; and the potential to be noble. With these gifts humans could outsmart animals and could hunt for food, clothing, and shelter. To appease the angry Zeus, humans offered him abundant sacrifices. They kept little for themselves.

Lisa Desimini; (t) Photodisc/Getty Images; (b) Medioimages/Photodisc/Getty images

Prometheus thought this was wrong. He tricked Zeus into choosing a cleverly disguised sacrificial dish rather than a richer dish for his offering. The dish Zeus chose looked delicious on the outside, but within it consisted entirely of fat and bones. When Zeus realized the trick, he took fire away from humans.

Prometheus pleaded with Zeus to change his mind, but Zeus forbade him to bring fire to humans. Prometheus watched his creations eat raw meat and shiver in the cold and dark. Finally, he went to Athena for help, and she led Prometheus to a hidden entrance to Mount Olympus where he could capture fire for humans.

As the chariot of the sun god Helios passed by, Prometheus stole a spark and hid it inside a fennel stalk. He snuck away and gave people fire.

Fury **consumed** Zeus when he learned what Prometheus had done. Zeus ordered the Titan to be chained to a rock. Each day, an eagle pecked at Prometheus's liver. Each night, the liver grew back. For generations Prometheus suffered. At last, the hero Heracles freed him from this torment by shooting a poisoned arrow at the eagle.

From then on, as a reminder of his punishment, Zeus made Prometheus wear around his finger a piece of the rock to which he had been chained. Ever since, humans have worn rings as a symbol of their gratitude for the gift of fire.

Water vs. Wisdom

While Zeus ruled the world from high on Mount Olympus, his brother Poseidon ruled the seas. Athena had upset Zeus, her father, by helping Prometheus. Now she dared to contest with her uncle, Poseidon, about who would rule over the acropolis of Attica.

Attica's king, Cecrops, was half-man and half-serpent. He agreed to judge the contest between Athena, goddess of wisdom, and Poseidon, god of the waters. The winner would be honored with temples and would have the city named after him or her. Each was asked to offer one special gift that would serve the people of the city.

Poseidon was the first to offer a gift. Raising his trident high over his head, he struck the rocky hill with a powerful blow. Cecrops watched in amazement as the hole filled with water. In the hot, dry land of Greece, water was a precious resource.

The people of Attica were impressed. They seemed ready to rule in favor of Poseidon until Athena told Cecrops to taste the water. A servant brought a cup to the king, who drank it and spit it out. It was salt water! There was no use for that in Attica.

Lisa Desimini

Then, Athena came forward with the branch of a tree that no human had seen before. She planted the branch in the ground, and an olive tree sprang up in its place. The king nodded, pleased. His people now had a source of food, wood, and oil. The leaves of the tree suggested a peaceful world.

Cecrops selected Athena as the main goddess of the city and named it Athens in her honor. Poseidon was outraged that his gift had not been accepted. As he returned to the sea, he cursed Athens and promised that the city would never have enough water. From that time on, drought has troubled Athens, the capital of Greece.

Make Connections

What role do fire and water play in these two myths? **ESSENTIAL QUESTION**

How has our understanding of resources changed since ancient times? **TEXT TO TEXT**

Photodisc/Getty Images

Genre • Historical Fiction

THE GAME OF SILENCE

by Louise Erdrich
illustrated by Joel Spector

Essential Question

How do traditions connect people?

Read how Omakayas learns that her way of life could change.

Go Digital!

Glossary of Ojibwe Words

asineeg (ah-sin-ig): a pile of stones

eya' (ey-ah): yes

gego (GAY-go): stop that!

makakoon (mah-kah-koon): containers made of birchbark

makazinan (MAH-kah-zin-ahn): footwear usually made of moose hide or deerskin, often trimmed with beads or fur

In 1850, nine-year-old Omakayas, an Ojibwe girl, realizes her family's life near Lake Superior is about to change. After being forced off their land, her cousins, "the raggedy ones," have arrived, exhausted and starving. While the adults discuss serious matters in the lodge, Omakayas and the other children in her tribe must play a "game of silence."

Words. Words. Words. Pressing up from her stomach, trembling on her lips. Words buzzing in her throat like caught bees. Banging in her head. Harsh words. Angry words. Sounds boiling up in her like sap. Wild things she couldn't let out.

Yow! A kick from her brother almost caused Omakayas to blurt an exclamation.

Joel Spector

No! Omakayas sealed her lips together in a firm line and glared at her brother with all of the force pent up inside. If the fire from her eyes could scorch him, Pinch would be the first to yell out. Then he would lose the game of silence. But Pinch was used to receiving furious looks from his family. He knew just how to respond. First he looked innocently at Omakayas (as though he was *ever* innocent!). He pretended he was unaware of the raging energy stuffed up inside of his sister. Then, as Omakayas bored her eyes at him with increasing **intensity**, he lolled out his tongue and twisted his face into a deranged and awful mask. His features shifted into one ugly and absurd face after the next until suddenly Omakayas just about...almost... laughed. Just in time, she clapped her hand to her mouth. Closed her eyes. Concentrated. Yes. Eya'. She would be a stone. Asineeg. A pile of stones. Each one harder and quieter than the next. She would be silent and more silent yet. And in spite of her annoying brother, she would win. She kept her eyes closed, put her forehead on her knees. Thought stone, stone, stone. Asin. Asin. Filled her mind with the sound of falling rain, which was easy. Outside, it was not just raining but *pouring* down a drenching, cold, miserable, early summer shower.

The rain had lasted for days, since the raggedy ones arrived. That was another thing. Besides Pinch, Omakayas couldn't stand rain anymore. The water made mush of tender new ground around her family's birchbark house. Droplets hissed through the roof vent into the fire, driving stinging smoke into her eyes. Everyone around her was affected. Nokomis's old bones ached and she creaked like a tree every time she moved. The watery wind sent coughs racking through her mother's chest. It was too wet to play outside, and cold when it should have been warm. Worst of all, Omakayas was stuck with Pinch.

He nudged her. Omakayas almost slugged him in return, but controlled herself. She'd had enough of him to last her whole life! She opened her eyes a fraction, then her eyes went wide in shock. Somehow, Pinch had got hold of her beloved doll, and he was making it teeter on the cliff of his knees. Omakayas bit her lip so hard it hurt. Pinch walked her doll to the edge of his knees, then teasingly back. If only Mama was here! If only she would return! Nokomis concentrated on her work so hard it was impossible to distract her.

Omakayas pretended to shut her eyes again, but cleverly watched until just the right moment to snatch back her doll. She sighed as though she was falling asleep and then, with a flash, she grabbed. Taken by surprise, Pinch couldn't react quickly enough to hold on, and Omakayas triumphantly clutched her doll. She stuck it down the neck of her dress. There! Safe! Inside, she laughed, but she didn't make a single sound; not a chirp, not so much as a mouse's squeak.

She was going to win the game of silence, she just knew it. Pinch was now poking little twigs into the fire in the center fire pit, watching them burn. Omakayas tried not to notice him, but his head was so big and fuzzy. Pinch's hair sprang out with its own energy. Crafty eyes in his tough, round face calculated his sister's **endurance**. He was surely cooking up some mischief. Sure enough, Pinch drew the burning wand from the fire and laid it innocently next to her ankle—as though she didn't know that it would scorch her if she moved the slightest inch! And make her cry out, first, and instantly lose the game! She kicked it back at him.

"Gego, Pinch," she nearly warned, but bit her lip.

"Eah, eah, eah," he mouthed the taunt, making an impossibly **irritating** face that almost broke Omakayas's discipline.

Luckily, just at the second that Omakayas decided to **forfeit** the game and to smash her little brother over the head with the big tin soup ladle, the visitors arrived.

"They are here," said their grandmother. "You can quit the game until after we eat."

Joel Spector

"Aaaagh!" Omakayas exploded with such a wild sound of rage that Nokomis jumped. Pinch **retreated**, unnerved by how sorely he'd tested his sister. Omakayas breathed out in relief. These visitors were her friends and cousins—Twilight, Little Bee, and Two Strike Girl. They had brought the boy she called, in her mind, the Angry One. Her cousins were her favorite friends, the ones she counted on. Twilight was much like her name, quiet and thoughtful. Little Bee was funny and bold. Two Strike was tough and she could do anything a boy could do, usually better. Since her mother had died, she was wilder than ever. Even her father had not been able to handle Two Strike, and had left her with Auntie Muskrat. But Auntie Muskrat had had no success in taming Two Strike. Sometimes she was so fierce that she outdid everyone—it was a challenge to play with her. The girls had learned to sew and bead together, gathered berries, and helped their mothers clean fish. They also learned early on how to tan hides, a task that Omakayas **despised**. And now too, her sister, Angeline, was home. Omakayas grinned with satisfaction. Pinch was delightfully outnumbered by girls and would pout, creeping to Mama's side when she arrived, and turning into a baby, hoping to be pampered with tidbits of meat and maple sugar.

Joel Spector

Now everyone—the children and their parents—squeezed into the lodge. They had made the lodge extra big that summer, for visitors. For the first time, it was packed entirely full, but there was enough room for everyone. Even the Angry One found a space to sit. He glared from a little spot against the wall. Together, they ate rich venison soup from the shallow birchbark makakoon they'd brought along with them. Two other men squeezed in, important men. Old Tallow entered, huge and rangy and smelling of wolf. She settled herself while outside her ferocious dogs stood guard, unmoving and alert even in the pelting rain. Each of Old Tallow's feet seemed to take up as much space as a small child, but Omakayas didn't mind. Warily, but completely, she loved the fierce old woman.

Each visitor brought a gift for the pile that the children who won the game of silence would choose from that night. For it was an important night. With the raggedy ones came serious doings. Difficult questions and impossible news. Great attention was needed. The grown-ups needed to council, think, absorb the facts, without having to shush small children. The children could tell how important the meeting was from the degree to which their silence was required. The pile of treats was the best ever.

There was a bag of marbles, some of actual glass, not just clay. A pair of narrow makazinan that Omakayas thought just might fit her. One doll, elaborately dressed in a tiny set of britches and a leather coat. A sharp knife. A deer knuckle game. Two duck's bills of maple sugar tied together with split jack-pine root. Six red ribbons. A little roll of flowered cloth. Eight tiny bells. One small bow, and six arrows tipped with real brass points cut from a trade kettle. The arrows were fletched with the sharp black and yellow feathers of a bird that the island where they lived was named for—the golden-breasted woodpecker. Old Tallow must have brought them. What treasures! The children examined them breathlessly, each picking out one particular prize they meant to win.

Little Bee, of course, wanted the doll. Two Strike Girl, the bow and arrows. Pinch coveted the knife, but he was torn by greed for the maple sugar and the need for marbles to replace those he'd lost. The Angry One did not deign to move from his spot or look at the gifts. No doubt he'd have no problem winning the game! As for Twilight, quiet and serene, she had no trouble playing the game and she would be content with anything. Omakayas wanted the ribbons, the bells, and the marbles, too, but she settled on the makazinan because she had watched her grandmother make them so carefully. They were fancy, with velvet ankle cuffs, the tops beaded with flowers and little white sparkling vines. Worth her silence!

Joel Spector

Now the grown-ups were ready to start talking. Nokomis sang the song of the game of silence four times, nearly catching Pinch at the end. Then she turned away from them too, absorbed in the talk.

Omakayas looked longingly at Twilight, and her cousin made a sad and frustrated face. With her favorite cousin so close and her annoying brother so near, it was difficult to play. If only they could talk! At first, the girls communicated by mouthing words and moving their eyes, but the temptation to laugh was too great. They turned away from each other unwillingly. Omakayas listened to the rain, a solid drumming and hissing. Then she listened to the fire crackling and sighing. She watched the beautiful and changing glow of the coals. At some point, Omakayas couldn't tell exactly when, her attention was caught by something her father said. And then she noticed that her cousin Twilight was also listening to the grown-ups' conversation. Soon, they all couldn't help but listen. They leaned forward, straining to hear every sound, almost forgetting to breathe.

That night, for the first time, everybody got their prizes. Nobody lost the game of silence. For that night they knew the threat of a much bigger loss. They would all fear to lose something huge, something so important that they never even knew that they had it in the first place. Who questions the earth, the ground beneath your feet? They had always accepted it—always here, always solid.

That something was home.

ABOUT THE AUTHOR AND ILLUSTRATOR

Louise Erdrich thinks of herself as a storyteller. That's because she grew up listening to many stories about her heritage and later writing about them. Louise is of Chippewa descent on her mother's side, and her grandfather was a tribal chieftain. Louise has said, "People in [Native American] families make everything into a story."

Louise grew up in North Dakota, an ancestral homeland of the Ojibwe. She has written poetry, novels for adults, and many books for kids. Most of her writing focuses on the history and culture of Native Americans.

Joel Spector moved to the United States from Havana, Cuba when he was twelve years old. He began his art career in fashion illustration but soon moved on to books, newspapers, and advertising. Now an award-winning artist, Joel Spector is known for his beautiful murals and portraits, which have been featured in magazines and museums.

AUTHOR'S PURPOSE

Why does the author include words from the Ojibwe language within the story?

(t) Ulf Andersen/Getty Images Entertainment/Getty Images; (b) Joel Spector

Respond to the Text

Summarize

Summarize *The Game of Silence* using only the most important story details. Information from your Theme Chart may help you.

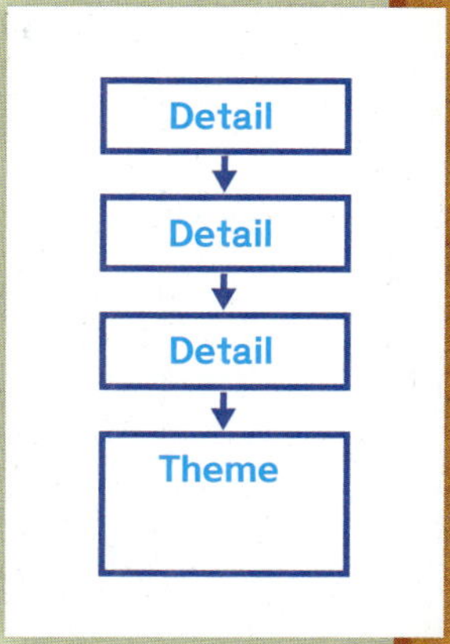

Write

What can readers learn from Omakayas and her experiences during the game of silence? Use these sentence starters to organize text evidence.

During the game of silence, Omakayas . . .
This shows . . .
Readers can learn . . .

Make Connections

How might life change for Omakayas and her family? **ESSENTIAL QUESTION**

The game of silence is a family tradition for Omakayas and her brother. What other family traditions exist around the world? How do these traditions bring people together? **TEXT TO WORLD**

Genre • Expository Text

Compare Texts

Read how Native Americans have fought to keep their traditions alive.

Kevin Cruff/The Image Bank/Getty Images

Native Americans: Yesterday and Today

Native Americans of Long Ago

Long before you lived in your town, Native Americans farmed, hunted, and fished there. Their ancestors had developed technologies suited to the environment to build homes, farm, and harvest resources.

Yet those ways of life changed once Europeans arrived. Scholars believe thousands, perhaps millions, of Native Americans died from diseases brought by white settlers in the 1500s. As the United States expanded, wars between the European immigrants and tribes erupted. Of the Native Americans who survived, many retreated from their lands. Many others were forced westward by white settlers and soldiers. The Indian Removal Act of 1830 forced many tribes west of the Mississippi River. The government and the states claimed 25 million acres of Indian land.

Native American groups in all regions had to cope with loss. While adapting to new environments, tribes struggled to maintain traditions.

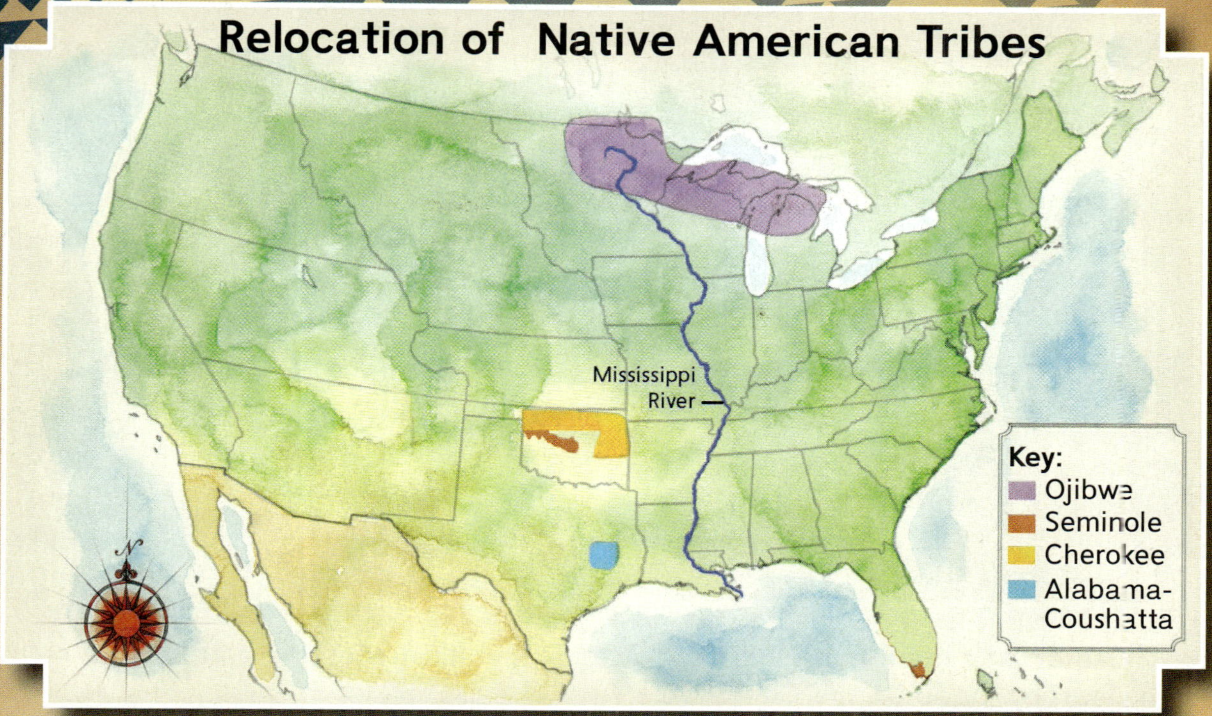

The map above shows where the Ojibwe, Seminole, Cherokee, and Alabama-Coushatta tribes were relocated in the mid-1800s.

North: The Ojibwe

The lands of the Ojibwe, also called Anishinabek, spread across what are now the states of Michigan, Wisconsin, Minnesota, and North Dakota. This group built shelters, called wigwams, from bark. They used the bark from birch trees to make canoes. They hunted wildlife and raised corn and squash. One of the main foods of the Ojibwe was wild rice, a grain that grows on the lakes in northern regions. As settlers pushed into the northern United States, the Ojibwe were forced from their traditional lands onto restricted reservations in those four states.

South: The Seminole

The Seminole settled in what is now central Florida in the 1700s—on land controlled by Spain. They built cabins and wore clothes like those of the white settlers. Many raised horses and cattle.

After the United States gained control of Florida in the 1830s, Seminoles were forced to relocate to Indian territory. Wars broke out between the Seminoles and the United States Army. Many Seminoles hid out in the swamps of Florida and never moved. There they hunted, trapped, and fished.

(t) Steve Stankiewicz

An artist's depiction of "The Trail of Tears" illustrates the painful journey made by the Cherokee.

East: The Cherokee

The Cherokee people lived on lands that are now the southeastern states from North Carolina to Georgia. In the 1800s, a Cherokee leader, Sequoyah, invented a written alphabet for the Cherokee language.

When gold was discovered on Cherokee lands, white settlers wanted the lands. They also wanted the land to grow cotton. This led to the forced removal of the Cherokee from their homeland by the United States government. More than 4,000 Cherokee died on the way to Oklahoma. This event is commonly known as "The Trail of Tears." To the Cherokee, it is called "The Trail Where They Cried."

West: The Alabama-Coushatta

The Alabama and Coushatta were separate nations originally from Alabama. In 1763, Europeans forced them off their land in Alabama to Louisiana and then to southeast Texas. Both nations participated in the Mexican War, helping Texas in its war for independence. When Texas joined the Union in 1845, the nations petitioned for their own land. Finally, in 1854 the Alabama were given land. The Coushatta did not get its own land. In 1859, the Alabama agreed to share the land with them.

Native Americans Today

These days, Native people lead different lives from those of their ancestors. Some groups living on reservations face poverty; others have thrived economically. Some of the wild rice that we buy today comes from the Ojibwe reservation. The Alabama-Coushattas host over 200,000 people a year at their campgrounds. The Cherokee of Oklahoma have built hotels, hospitals, and entertainment centers. Tourism is an important source of income for the Seminole.

Despite what they have endured, Native Americans today maintain ways to **honor** their culture and history. Among some tribes, gatherings such as powwows or feast days allow them to celebrate ancient traditions. Sharing stories with each new generation helps keep the Native American past alive in the present and builds for the future.

Modern Native American children participate in a powwow to honor their tribe's history.

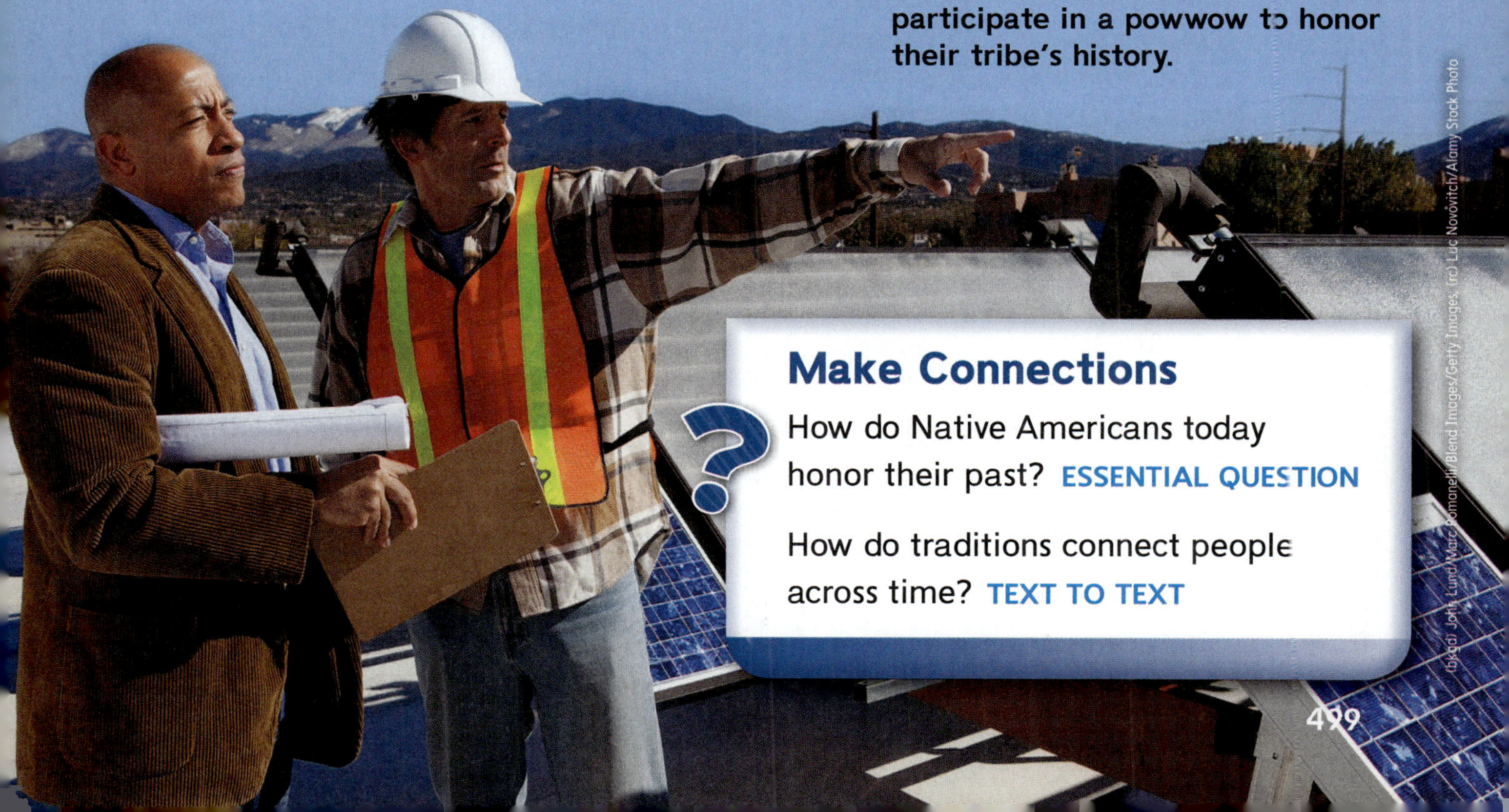

Today, Native Americans work in all different professions.

Make Connections

How do Native Americans today honor their past? **ESSENTIAL QUESTION**

How do traditions connect people across time? **TEXT TO TEXT**

Genre • Poetry

the drum

daddy says the world is
a drum tight and hard
and i told him
i'm gonna beat
out my own rhythm

—Nikki Giovanni

Essential Question

What shapes a person's identity?

Read how poets capture experiences that change people.

Go Digital!

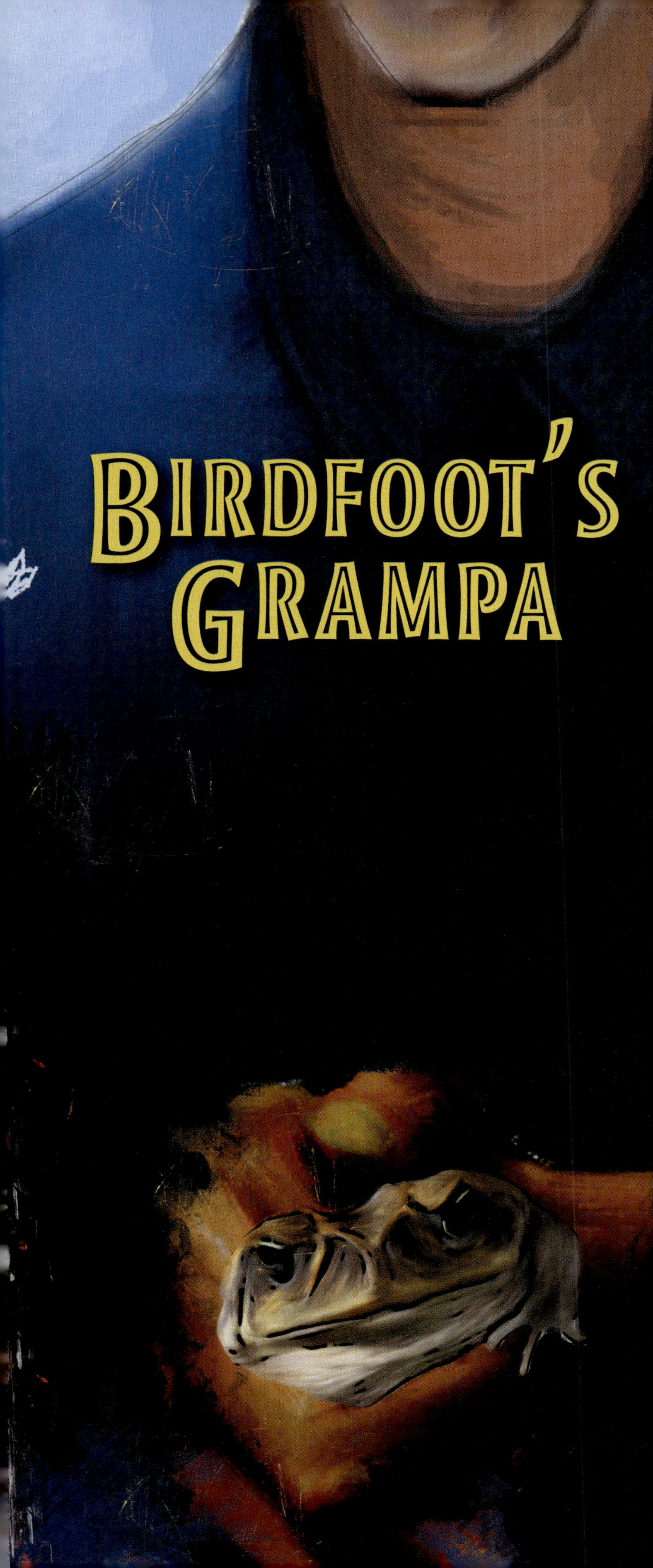

Birdfoot's Grampa

The old man
must have stopped our car
two dozen times to climb out
and gather into his hands
the small toads blinded
by our lights and leaping,
live drops of rain.

The rain was falling,
a mist about his white hair
and I kept saying
you can't save them all,
accept it, get back in
we've got places to go.

But, leathery hands full
of wet brown life,
knee deep in the summer
roadside grass,
he just smiled and said
they have places to go to
too.

—Joseph Bruchac

From My Chinatown

Twelve hours every day
the needle on her sewing machine
gobbles up the fabric,
turning miles of cloth
into pants and jackets, skirts and dresses.
After supper I sit beside my mother,
listening to the hum of the motor,
the soft chatter
of the hungry needle.

Sometimes I fall asleep beside her,
the sound of her work
a lullaby.

—Kam Mak

Respond to the Text

Summarize

Use important details in the excerpt from "My Chinatown" to summarize what happens in the poem. Information from your Theme Chart may help you.

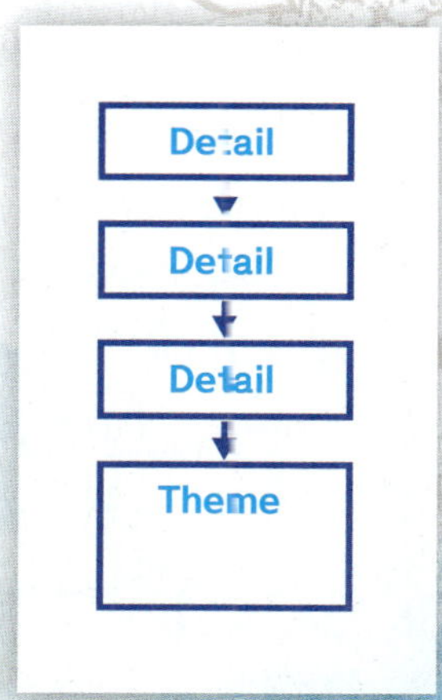

Write

How are the speakers in the poems affected by their families? Use these sentence starters to organize text evidence.

The speakers in the poems are all . . .
In "The Drum," the speaker's father . . .
In "Birdfoot's Grampa," the speaker learns . . .
The speaker in "My Chinatown" feels . . .

Make Connections

How do experiences shape a person's identity? **ESSENTIAL QUESTION**

What are some other customs or traditions that might shape a person's identity? **TEXT TO WORLD**

Genre • Poetry

Compare Texts

Read how roots and family influence a person's identity.

Growing Up

When I grow up,
I want to be a doctor.

M'ija, you will patch scraped knees
and wipe away children's tears.

But what if I become an architect?

M'ija, you will build beautiful houses
where children will sing and play.

And what if I become a teacher?

M'ija, you will teach
your students to read every day.

But what if I become a famous chef?

M'ija, your arroz con pollo
will be eaten with gozo.

And Mami, what if I want to be like you someday?

M'ija, why do you want to be like me?

Oh Mami, because you care for people, our house
is built on love,
you are wise, and your spicy stew tastes delicious.

—Liz Ann Báez Aguilar

MY PEOPLE

The night is beautiful,
So the faces of my people.

The stars are beautiful,
So the eyes of my people.

Beautiful, also, is the sun.
Beautiful, also, are the souls of my people.

—Langston Hughes

Make Connections

What are some ways that family impacts a person's identity? **ESSENTIAL QUESTION**

Why are a person's roots important? **TEXT TO TEXT**

Genre • Expository Text

The Big Picture of Economic$

by David A. Adler

Fuse/Corbis/Getty Images

Essential Question

What has been the role of money over time?

Read how many of our everyday choices are determined by economics.

Go Digital!

Money Matters

What is **economics**? It's the study of how people decide what to make and sell. It's also the study of why people buy some things and not others and of how items reach the **marketplace**—the place where people shop. The marketplace might be a corner grocery store, a large shopping mall, or a site on the Internet.

Now, put your hand in your pocket and take out a nickel, a quarter, or a dollar bill. It may be difficult to imagine, but there was a time before there was money. There was a time before people studied economics.

Thousands of years ago there was no money. People were self-sufficient, so they gathered and hunted for whatever food they needed, made their own tools, and built their own homes.

(tl) Eric Larsen; (tr) Georgios Kollidas/Alamy; (cb) Ben Molyneux/Alamy; United States coin images from the United States Mint

Some people were good hunters, and others were better at making baskets and clubs, so people traded. A hunter might trade an animal skin for some berries. But how many berries is an animal skin worth and what would the hunter do with all those berries?

People needed money—something that everyone would be willing to take in a trade and that could also be used to get the things they needed. People found that precious metals such as gold and silver made good money. Pieces of gold and silver came in all sizes, and you could weigh a piece to know how much it was worth. Then coins were made. Coins didn't have to be weighed because people knew each coin's weight and how much it was worth.

A pocketful of coins is heavy, so paper money was invented. The first paper money was a printed promise that could be exchanged for gold or silver coins. Today few countries make gold and silver coins, but paper money has value because you can use it to buy gold or silver. You can use it to buy bread, shoes, and other things, too.

This ancient Chinese note is from the Ming Dynasty in the 14th century.

You can learn a lot about economics at a restaurant

In a restaurant you'll see a menu with lots of things for sale. Each item has a price, which helps you decide what to buy.

You may not be sure whether you want a hamburger or a tuna sandwich. If you're really not sure, you might buy the one that costs less. Of course, the greater the difference in the prices, the greater the chance you'll buy what's cheaper. If a hamburger costs a dollar and a tuna sandwich costs ten dollars, it's likely you'll buy the hamburger.

Price might even convince people to buy something they didn't really want. Suppose you are in a restaurant and you are hungry for a tuna sandwich. You see the prices on the menu and realize that if you buy a hamburger instead of a tuna sandwich you'll have money left to buy a salad and pudding. Price might convince you to buy a hamburger instead of a tuna sandwich.

Eric Larsen

Now suppose you are walking past a restaurant. You aren't really hungry, but you see a sign in the window that says a hamburger costs just one dollar. At that price you might decide to buy one.

Of course, a high price would have the opposite effect. It might convince you not to buy something you really want. Suppose you are in a restaurant and you're really hungry for a tuna sandwich. You see that a tuna sandwich costs ten dollars, and you really want a tuna sandwich and not a hamburger. At ten dollars for a tuna sandwich you might decide to leave the restaurant and go to a grocery store where you can buy a can of tuna fish and some bread and make your own sandwich.

Price might help someone decide what to make and sell

Suppose you and your friends are walking through town and are suddenly thirsty. You search and find there's a scarcity of places in your neighborhood to buy a drink. Scarcity leads to opportunity and you decide to start your own business, to become an **entrepreneur**. You will set up a table in front of your house and sell drinks. Now you must decide what to sell—hot tea or ice cold lemonade. It's a hot summer day, and lots of people would be willing to pay a dollar for a small cup of cold lemonade. Few people would be willing to pay even a dime for a cup of hot tea. You'll probably decide it's to your benefit to make and sell lemonade. It's to your benefit to make what people are anxious to buy.

Before you set up your business you'll have to **invest** in lemons, sugar, and paper cups. You'll have to spend money even before your very first **transaction**, your very first sale. You'll spend time making the drinks, and that time is a cost, too. It's your opportunity cost. During the time you're making lemonade you've lost the opportunity to be doing something else.

The lemonade you make is your **merchandise**. It's your supply. The people who come to buy it are the demand.

Eric Larsen

The Laws of Supply and Demand

According to one old proverb, "The worth of a thing is what it will bring." The value of your merchandise is determined by how much you can get for it on the open market, and that is determined by the laws of supply and demand. If you expect lots of thirsty people to pass your lemonade stand, you might make lots of lemonade, and if you did, you'd have lots of supply. If few people come by, you would have very little demand. What would you do? You might be anxious to sell the drinks and decide to lower the price. Lowering the price will probably increase the demand.

Few people might be willing to pay two dollars for a cup of lemonade. More people might buy some for just a dollar a cup, and lots of people might buy lemonade at just fifty cents a cup. The lower the price, the greater the demand will be, and if the price of your lemonade is low enough, someone who planned to buy only one cup might buy a second and even a third cup. Someone who isn't even thirsty might buy a drink.

If you only bought a few lemons and made just a small pitcher of lemonade you would have very little supply. What if there's lots of demand, lots of people who are thirsty and want to buy a drink? Perhaps at one dollar a cup you could quickly sell all the drinks, but you might want to raise the price. At two dollars a cup your supply won't sell as quickly, but you'll make much more money on each cup you sell.

In a country with a free market, such as the United States, people can charge whatever they want for the things they sell. In a free market—as supply goes up, prices go down, and as supply goes down, prices go up. In a free market—as demand goes up, prices go up, and as demand goes down, prices go down. Those are the laws of supply and demand.

What's the best price for lemonade? The best price is low enough for people to want to buy some and high enough for you and perhaps others to want to make and sell it.

The higher the price of your merchandise, the lower the demand.

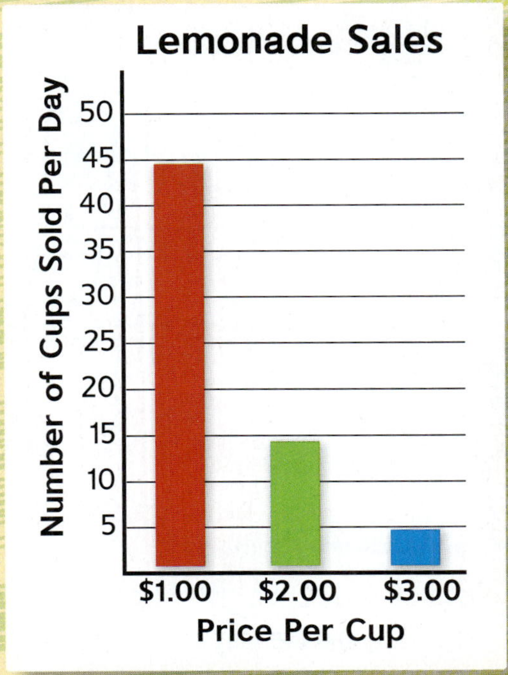

Eric Larsen

The Global Marketplace

In the United States people in one state buy products made in other states—even in other countries—and we sell things to people in other states and countries. The world we live in is truly a **global** marketplace.

The pen you use to write your homework may have been made in China, and the sneakers you wear to school every day may have been made in Japan. The peach you ate for lunch may have been grown in Brazil.

Foreign trade is the exchange of goods and services between people here and in other countries. Of course, when we sell our products to people in other countries we might not be paid in dollars.

In the United States we use dollars and cents to buy things, but people in other countries use different **currency**, different money. In Mexico people use pesos and centavos. In Europe they use euros. In Russia they use rubles and kopeks, in China yuan, in Brazil reals and centavos, in Japan yen, and in India rupees.

Because we live in a global marketplace, the things we eat, wear, and use may come from many different places.

Eric Larsen

It is said that "Money is power." This tells us a lot about our global marketplace. Around the world, the richest countries are also the most powerful. But how did they get this way? The answer is economics. Understanding how our global marketplace works explains why so many people study economics. Economics helps us understand how people live, how they sell, buy, and trade things, how they decide what to grow on their land and what to produce in their factories.

Many of the things we, our families, and our friends do—from buying a hamburger to taking a vacation to trading video games—are determined by economics. Many of the choices you make today and in the future—even what to buy in a restaurant—will be determined by economics.

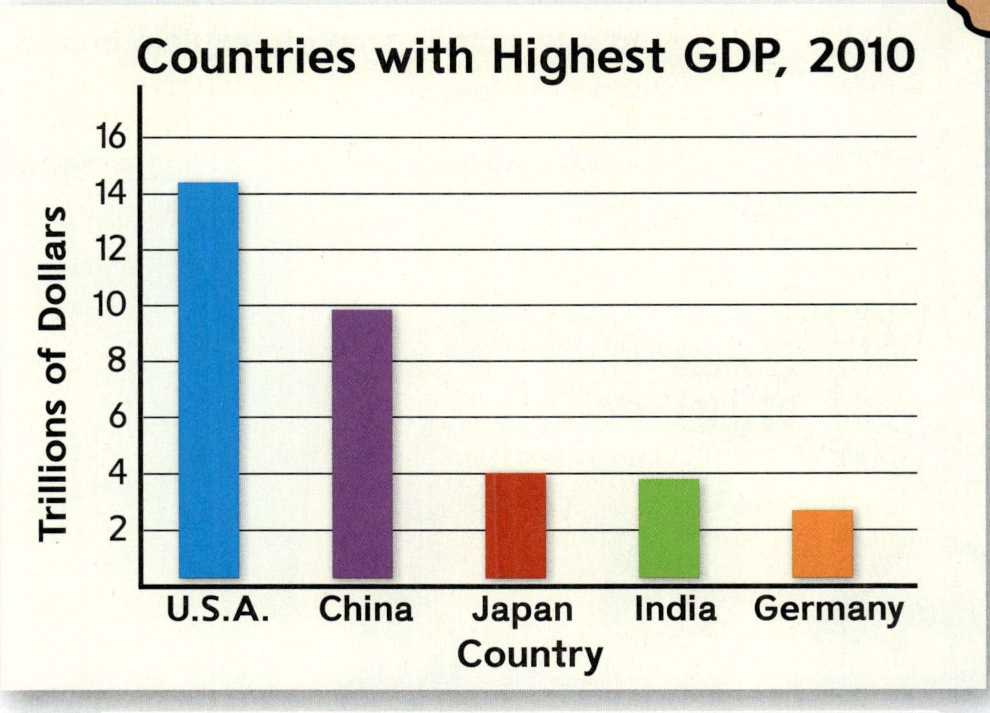

The overall value of a country's total goods and services is its GDP, or "Gross Domestic Product." It is usually calculated annually.

About the Author

David A. Adler got the big picture on economics in college—it was his major! After graduation, he taught mathematics for nine years in the New York City school system. During that time, he earned a little money on the side drawing and selling cartoons. His first book, *A Little at a Time,* was inspired by his three-year-old nephew's questions. Since then, he has published more than 200 books, including the popular Cam Jansen series. If David is inspired or fascinated by something, it's likely to become his next writing project!

Author's Purpose

Why does the author use a restaurant menu and a lemonade stand to explain important economic ideas?

(t) David Adler; (b) Ben Molyneux/Alamy; United States coin images from the United States Mint

Respond to the Text

Summarize

Summarize *The Big Picture of Economics.* Use information from your Central Idea and Relevant Details Chart to help you.

Central Idea
Detail
Detail
Detail

Write

How do the text features help you understand how the role of money has changed over time? Use these sentence starters to organize text evidence.

> The author uses illustrations and captions to help me understand that . . .
> He also uses text features to show . . .
> This helps me see how the role of money has changed because . . .

Make Connections

How does economics affect everyday choices? **ESSENTIAL QUESTION**

Why is money important to people? **TEXT TO WORLD**

Georgios Kollidas/Alamy

Genre • Folktale

Compare Texts

Read how a poor miller becomes wealthy.

The Miller's Good Luck

Libor and Vidal, two wealthy friends, had an ongoing argument. Did wealth come mainly from good luck or hard work?

"Luck is most important," declared Libor. He had become a wealthy **entrepreneur** after winning money in a contest.

"No, work hard and plan ahead—that's the way to wealth," Vidal replied. "'No pain, no gain' is what I always say." He had toiled, saved, and invested wisely, and now owned a vast farm.

The friends decided to test their beliefs. One day, on the way to the marketplace to sell **merchandise**, they encountered Pedro, a poor miller who barely earned enough money grinding grain to feed his family. They gave Pedro 100 pesos to use as he pleased.

Pedro immediately bought meat for his family, but on his way home, a hawk swooped down to steal the meat. Pedro clutched the food, and the hawk flew off with a bag containing the remainder of the money.

Erin Eitter Kono

Two weeks later, the men visited Pedro's mill and refused to believe what had happened. Libor handed Pedro a heavy piece of lead. Laughing cruelly, he said, "Here, take this worthless lead weight; no one will steal it."

Discouraged, Pedro gave the lead weight to a fisherman, who in exchange gave Pedro the first fish he caught. When Pedro's wife cut open the fish to clean it, she found a diamond in its stomach, which Pedro sold for a large sum. He used the money to expand his mill. Working harder than ever, he soon found himself milling grain for all the farmers in the area.

One year later, Libor and Vidal saw how prosperous Pedro had become. When the miller told them about the diamond, Libor nodded. "You became wealthy through luck."

"But if I hadn't worked every day from dawn until dusk, I could have lost everything," said Pedro.

Vidal nodded. "Yes, wealth results from hard work and planning."

In the end, the two men could never agree about the true key to wealth.

Make Connections

How does Pedro become wealthy? **ESSENTIAL QUESTION**

Why does money matter? **TEXT TO TEXT**

Genre • Historical Fiction

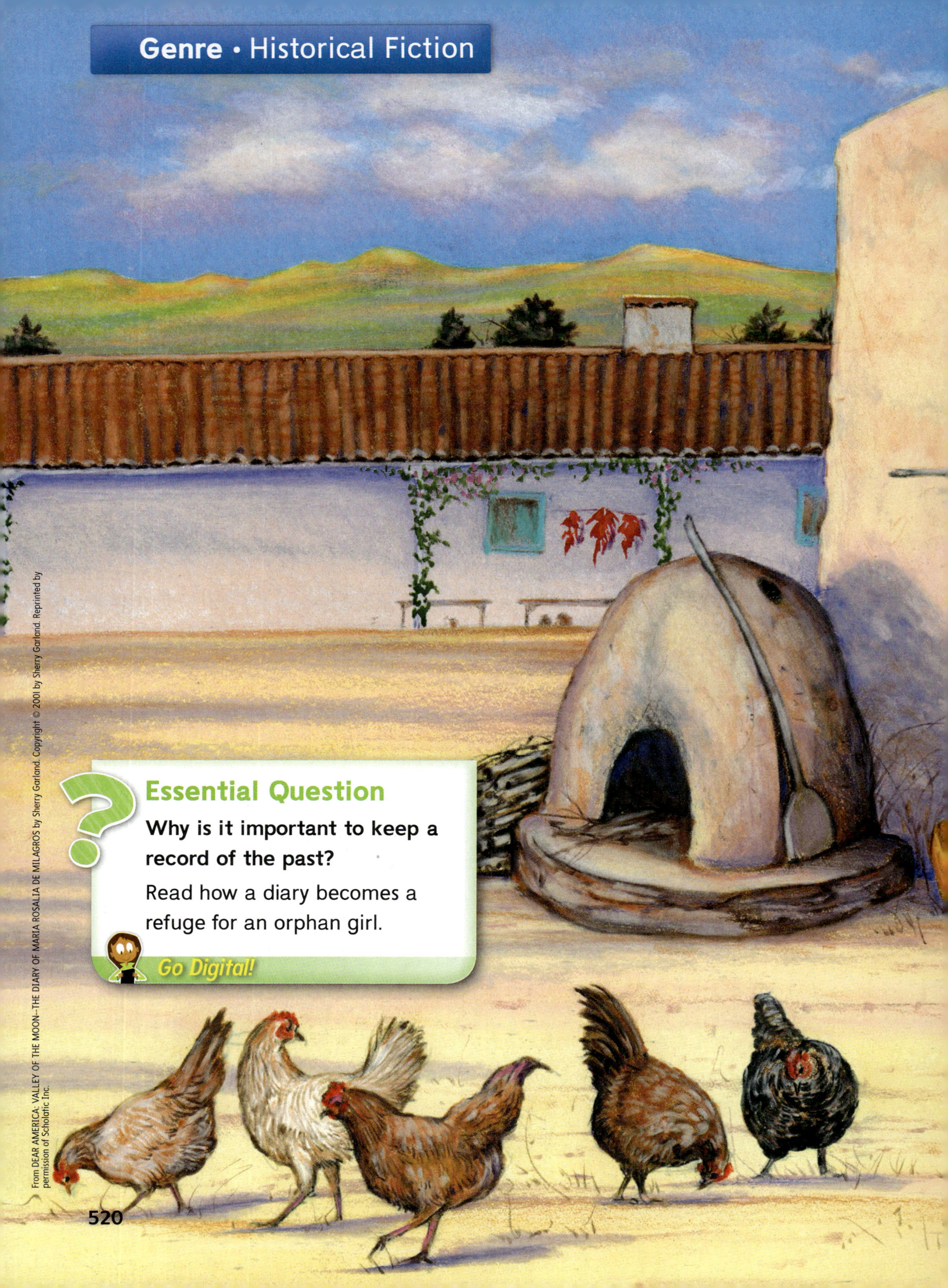

Essential Question

Why is it important to keep a record of the past?

Read how a diary becomes a refuge for an orphan girl.

Go Digital!

Valley of the Moon

by Sherry Garland
illustrated by Kristina Rodanas

Orphaned at an early age, María Rosalia and her younger brother, Domingo, were raised by Padre Ygnacio at the Mission Rafael in Alta California. Now the children have become servants at the Medina Rancho. Taught to read and write by Padre Ygnacio, María Rosalia has recently started keeping a diary about her life at the rancho.

October 10, 1845

Tonight I begin my first diary. The Medina family is asleep, and all is quiet throughout the rancho. Only the wind racing around the corners of the adobe house and the distant yelp of coyotes break the night silence. I am snuggled in a corner of the kitchen surrounded by baskets of dried corn waiting to be ground. The tile floors feel cold on my bare feet, but I do not mind, for I know no one will find me here.

This diary is mine because the **eldest** of the Medina daughters, Miguela, tossed it over her balcony into the courtyard. My fingers quickly rescued it from a watery death in the fountain. Señorita Miguela threw it away in a fit of resentment after it was given to her by an American suitor, Señor Henry Johnston. With flashing black eyes she cried out that a girl has no more use for reading and writing than a snake has for gold earrings. She said the diary was an insult to her beauty and charm, then tossed Señor Johnston out, too.

I feel sorry for Señor Johnston, or for any man who has the misfortune of courting headstrong Miguela, but I am not sorry that I now hold her **discarded** diary in my hands. I must not let anyone see me writing, for I am a servant, a half-Indian orphan, a girl. I am supposed to know nothing but work and **obedience**. How amazed the Medinas would be if they knew I learned to read and write from a kind old padre at Mission Rafael, many miles from here. Maybe someday I will tell them.

October 11

I've been thinking about Padre Ygnacio all day. It was he who found Domingo and me eight years ago beside our dying mother in the rose garden of Mission Rafael near San Francisco Bay. Her body was ravaged with smallpox, and I had placed roses over her face. I think I was about five years old and my brother was about two, but no one knows our ages for sure.

Padre Ygnacio named me María Rosalia – after the Blessed Virgin and because of the roses. He named my brother Domingo because it was a Sunday morning. For a last name he called us Milagros – for it was a miracle indeed that we did not die of the horrible plague that claimed the lives of so many Indians in Alta California. They say that out of forty thousand Suisun people, only two hundred lived. Some smaller tribes lost everyone. How Domingo and I survived is one of the many mysteries of my life.

When Padre Ygnacio found us, we did not speak much Spanish and he did not know our Indian dialect. But of one thing he was sure: Though our mother had the bronze skin of an Indian, our skin was the light brown of *mestizos* – half-Indian and half-Spanish. It was obvious that our father had been a white man. Whether he was a wealthy Spanish landowner, a Spanish soldier from the *presidio* at San Francisco, a Russian fur trapper, or an American merchant sailor, no one knows.

Lupita, the cook, is the closest thing to a mother I have. Her husband, Gregorio, is the head *vaquero* on the ranch. He oversees the men who tend the cattle and horses. It was Gregorio who found me and Domingo at Mission Rafael four years ago and brought us to live at the Medina ranch – Rancho Agua Verde. Lupita and Gregorio have no children of their own but have raised several orphans. I know they care about me, yet my heart feels empty. If I do not know my past, how can I plot my future? I must stop thinking such things and get back to work. If I don't finish grinding this corn, there will be no *tortillas* tomorrow.

Sunday, October 12

I have no place to hide this diary. My room in the servants' quarters is so tiny that I can hardly turn around. I share it with Ramona, the seamstress. We sleep on woven straw pallets on the floor and roll them up each morning. We take turns sitting on the one chair at the one tiny table. Whoever doesn't get the chair sits on an overturned wooden bucket. The adobe walls and ceiling are stained with black soot from the fireplace and tallow candles.

But our quarters are not as bleak as some. Ramona saves scraps of cloth from the sewing projects. Our walls are alive with color – a wool tapestry, one finely embroidered hanging that **depicts** the Holy Virgin, and another hanging that shimmers with flowers. Even our floor has a wool rug made of remnants from the spring sheepshearing. Pegs line the walls for our sparse clothing. Baskets hang from the heavy timber beams for food and miscellaneous items. It is better than the room I shared with four other orphans at Mission Rafael.

October 13

The Medina daughters saw me in the courtyard today carrying the diary. Miguela was amused and said I could keep it. "Perhaps you might use it for fire kindling, Rosa," she said with a toss of her black curls. Miguela is seventeen and has been available for marriage for two years. She is a great beauty but has **ignored** all the men who call on her and has refused several proposals. If I were rich, I would pay a man every *peso* I owned to take her away from this ranch.

Rafaela, the middle daughter, who is aged fifteen, is gentle and sweet but very sickly. She coughs often, and her skin is paler than white lilies. She told Miguela not to be so unkind because I am more like family than a servant. Bless her soul, how I wish her words were true.

Gabriela, who is eleven and like a little sister to me, said to just ignore Miguela. Everyone knows how Miguela is, but her words stung.

October 14

I am in the goat pen seizing a moment to write in my diary. I milked the goats faster than lightning so that I might have a free moment. I carry the diary with me all the time, tied to my waist with a sash and hidden under my skirt. I dare not write at night in my room for Ramona is a light sleeper.

I have no ink, so I am using beet juice. It leaves an uneven pale red color, but it must do until I find real ink. For a pen, I am using a sharpened black feather from the tail of Paladin, Señor Medina's favorite fighting rooster. Domingo stole the feather from the chicken coop and gave it to me. All I think of while doing chores is the moment I will open this diary and write. It is my island of **refuge** in a sea of work.

October 15

Señor Johnston is here again. I like him very much. He speaks to me kindly and does not order me around. He owns a merchant business in the small town of Yerba Buena on San Francisco Bay south of here. Being twenty-eight years of age and settled, he is now looking for a wife. He has decided upon Señorita Miguela (may Heaven help him!) and has visited Rancho Agua Verde many times this year.

Señor Johnston is waiting for his brother and family, who are coming by wagon train from Missouri to join him in California. They will arrive first at Sutter's Fort in the Sacramento Valley, where Johnston will go to meet them. A few years ago there were very few foreigners in Alta California, just some sailors and fur trappers. Now they come in a steady stream – mostly farmers from Missouri. There are hundreds of them, especially in the Sacramento Valley northeast of here.

Lupita does not trust the *norteamericanos.* She says they are supposed to become loyal Mexican citizens, learn to speak Spanish, and become Catholics in exchange for land. But not all of them do as they agreed. She especially dislikes the foreigner Johann Sutter, who encourages other foreigners to come to California illegally without permission from the Mexican government. There are already squatters on Señor Medina's lands. Lupita thinks they will take over Alta California before long.

I do not care what Lupita says. I like Señor Johnston, even if he is an *americano.* He is beside himself with excitement about his brother's arrival. But he is worried. The snows will soon start to fall on top of the Sierra Nevada mountains to the east, causing deep drifts and icy rocks that make the passes treacherous to cross. If the Johnston family does not clear the mountains by the end of this month, they are surely doomed.

October 16

Spent a pleasant morning working in the courtyard that is surrounded by the thick walls of the *casa grande* on four sides. I wonder if the Medina house will ever be completed. Every year, the Indian workers add a bit more. When the main house was first built, it was a simple, one-story structure like nearly all the *ranchos* in northern Alta California. But after Señora Medina and Miguela saw the grand *rancho* that General Vallejo was building at Petaluma a few miles away, they insisted on having a second story with balconies and rambling rose vines. At the moment, only the Medina family has upstairs bedrooms with balconies. Everyone else, servants and guests alike, sleeps downstairs. I do not mind for walking up and down stairs makes my legs ache.

Drew ten buckets of water from the well to tend the herbs, beans, squash, pumpkins, melons, onions, and hot chiles in the garden near the kitchen door. Swept the veranda that is roofed with brown clay tiles. Pruned the rambling Castilian roses that climb up the posts to the upstairs bedroom balconies. Picked late maturing pears from Señor Medina's cherished fruit trees.

I am tired, but am writing during *siesta* while everyone else rests. Writing brings me more joy than sleep! Nothing would make me happier than to write all day and all night.

October 17

¡Madre mía! My secret is uncovered! While I was in the courtyard writing in my diary today, Señor Johnston appeared out of nowhere. I was afraid he would be angry that I had it, but his large blue eyes grew wide like an owl's. He said to me in his best Spanish (which I am sorry to say is not very good): "Rosalia! I cannot believe you are writing! How did you learn such skills?"

I begged Johnston not to tell anyone, for it would only mean trouble for me. I explained how Padre Ygnacio taught the Indian boys at Mission Rafael to read and write. He let me sit quietly at the back of the room and I helped Domingo, who **detested** lessons and being indoors. The California missions were closing down, anyway, and the padre did not care if the rules said girls did not need an education. He said if a girl wanted to read and write, he would not stop her. He was very generous and tolerant when it came to the mission *indios.*

Johnston was so astonished that he dug into his leather saddlebag and handed me a bottle of ink, a very nice brass point, and two turkey quills. Now the ink flows onto the pages almost as fast as I think of words.

About the Author and Illustrator

Sherry Garland grew up in Texas, the youngest of nine children. She started writing in high school and had her first book published in 1982. She loves to do research and enjoys traveling to different places to find information about a topic. It usually takes her about a year to research a new book. Sherry says that she gets "ideas from real events, things that appear in newspapers, on TV, or things that really happened years ago."

Kristina Rodanas enjoys writing and illustrating. She has written and illustrated a number of Native American folktales and likes learning about different cultures. She lives in Orleans, Massachusetts.

Author's Purpose

Why would the author choose to present María Rosalia's story as a series of diary entries?

(t) Clyde Garland; (b) Kristina Rodanas

Respond to the Text

Summarize

Use the most important information from *Valley of the Moon* to summarize the selection. Information from your Theme Chart may help you.

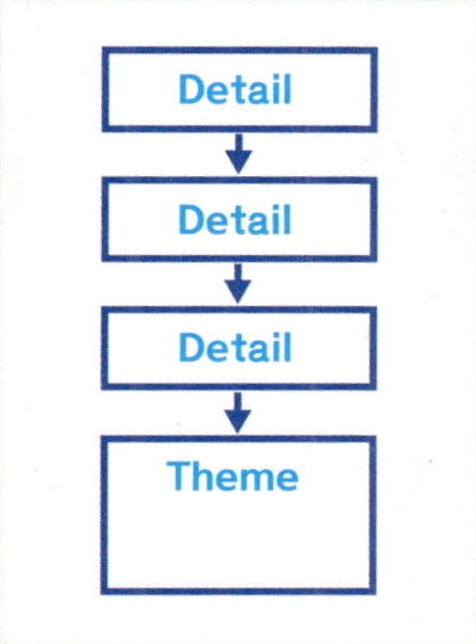

Write

How does the author use María Rosalia's diary entries to help you learn about her character and what's important to her? Use these sentence starters to organize text evidence.

The author uses María Rosalia's diary entries to . . .
She uses words and phrases to help me visualize . . .
This helps me understand . . .

Make Connections

Why does the diary become a refuge for María Rosalia? **ESSENTIAL QUESTION**

Why is keeping a record important to people? **TEXT TO WORLD**

Genre • Expository Text

Compare Texts

Read about the impact of immigration on American culture.

One Nation, Many Cultures

A Land of Immigrants

Have you ever heard that America is a melting pot? How about a salad bowl or an ethnic stew? There are many theories and many debates about our culture in the United States. This is because our country is made up of people from all over the world.

The United States has been a land of immigrants ever since the Spanish explorers came ashore way back in the 16th century. Over time, as our country developed, declared its independence, and gave rise to industry, immigrants came from all over the world. Most came from Europe—mainly Great Britain, Ireland, Germany, Russia, and Italy. For an opportunity to live in our nation, immigrants often spent many **treacherous** weeks at sea battling hunger and illness.

A Land of Opportunity

In the 18th and 19th centuries, the term "melting pot" was a popular metaphor used to describe how immigrants assimilated into our culture—that is, they left behind their homeland's customs to forge a new American identity.

Immigrants viewed moving to our nation as a chance for a better life. Many Europeans endured hardships in their home countries. They dealt with poverty and hunger. They did not have jobs. Many were unable to feed their families. The United States, however, was brimming with opportunities. Unskilled laborers could work in factories. Finally they could earn enough money to provide for their families. Some immigrants longed to move west and own land. Others wanted to work on the railroad.

Immigrants cheer and raise their hats as they approach Ellis Island in the early 1920s.

As more immigrants made the United States their home in the 1920s, the term "salad bowl" seemed more appropriate for describing the nation's cultural identity. In this theory, immigrants do not completely assimilate—instead they hold onto their individual beliefs, languages, and customs. As in a salad, each ingredient is separate, but all of the ingredients together contribute to the overall taste. Diversity defined what it meant to be an American.

Immigration Today

A more recent theory on American culture—the stew pot theory—is a combination of the melting pot and salad bowl theories. It compares immigrants to ingredients that take on other flavors and tastes as new ingredients are added to the pot. In other words, immigrants take on American characteristics to blend in and show **obedience** to national laws, but they also hold onto their cultural backgrounds. This adds to the diversity of the country.

Today, immigrants still arrive from all over the world. The majority of them come from Latin America. These immigrants come here for the same reasons that immigrants came here hundreds of years ago. They come for freedom and for a chance at a better life. They might be escaping poverty or war in their homelands. Some immigrants come to the United States to work and send money back to their families.

Immigration is more than just a part of our past or present. It is the very foundation that this country continues to build upon. Melting pot, mixed salad, or stew pot—these images all suggest how immigrants have given the United States its unique blend of cultures. Because of this variety, our country is unlike any other.

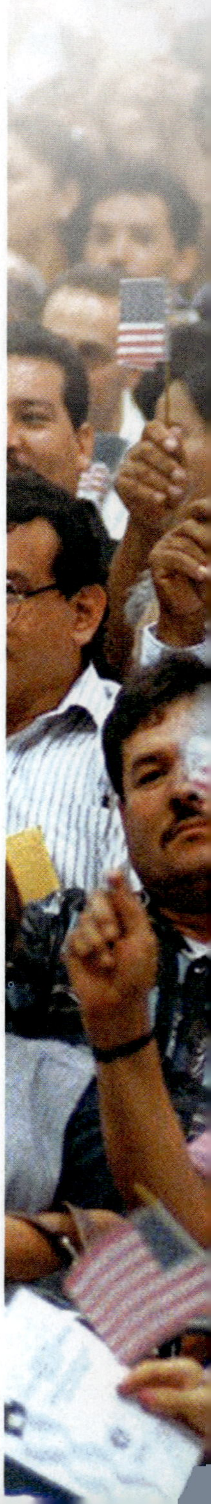

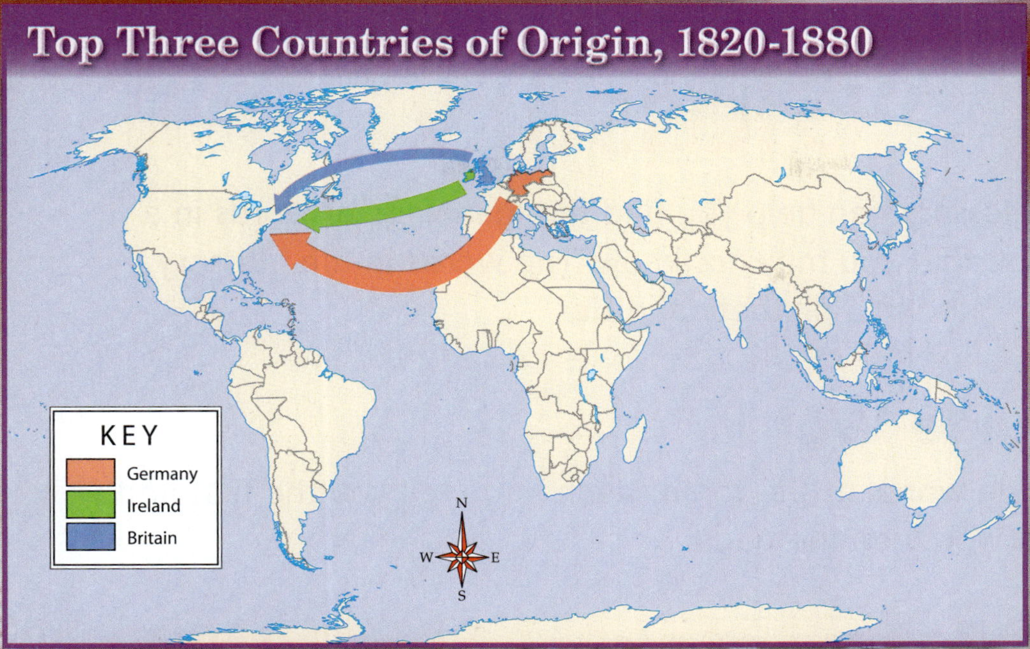

The map above shows the top three countries of origin for immigrants from 1820 to 1880. As the width of the arrows indicates, the largest number of immigrants came from Germany during this period.

The map below shows the recent top three countries of origin. The largest number of immigrants today come from Mexico.

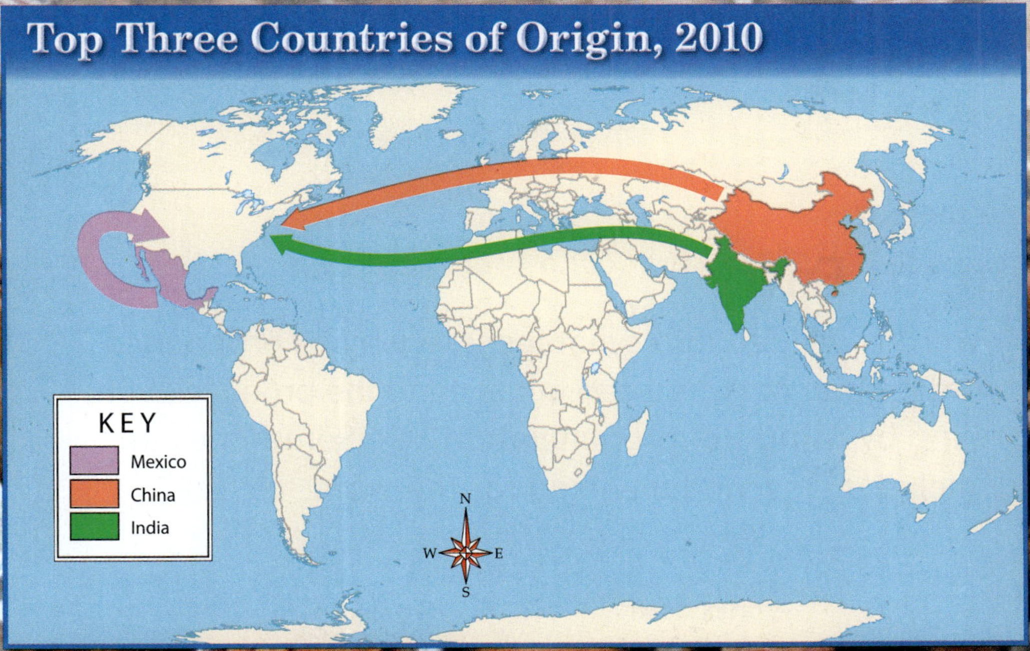

Make Connections

What impact has immigration had on American culture? **ESSENTIAL QUESTION**

Why is history important to people? **TEXT TO TEXT**

Glossary

A glossary can help you find the meanings of words in a book that you may not know. The words in the glossary are listed in alphabetical order.

Guide Words

Guide words at the top of each page tell you the first and last words on the page.

Sample Entry

Each word is divided into syllables. The way to pronounce the word is given next. You can understand the pronunciation respelling by using the pronunciation key. Sometimes an entry includes a second meaning for the word.

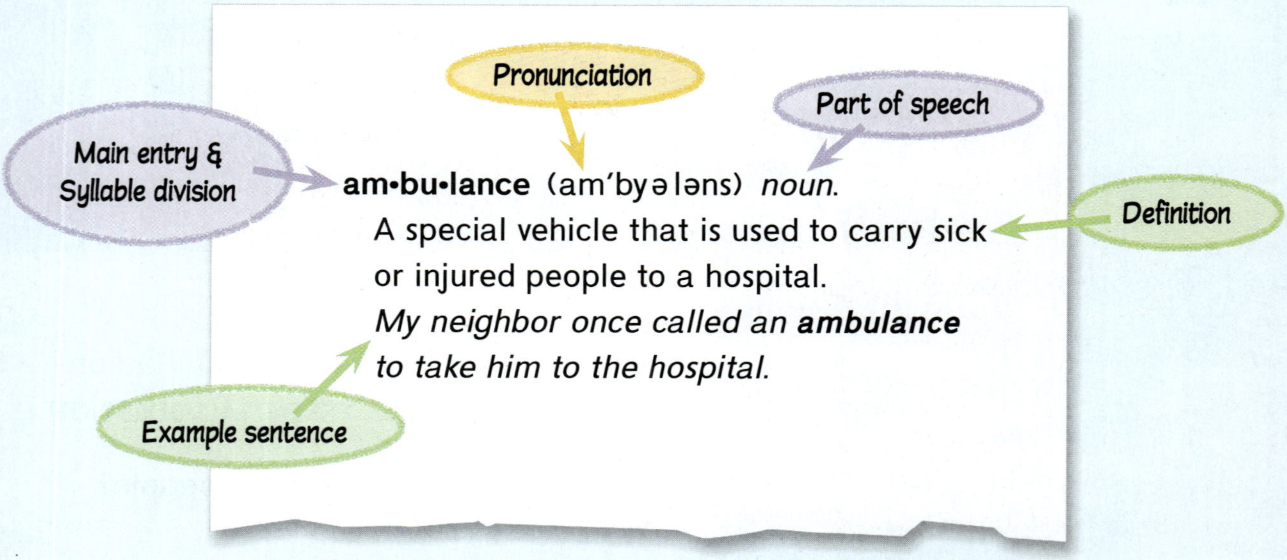

Pronunciation Key

You can understand the pronunciation respelling by using this pronunciation key. A shorter key appears at the bottom of every other page. When a word has more than one syllable, a dark accent mark (**′**) shows which syllable is stressed. In some words, a light accent mark (′) shows which syllable has a less heavy stress.

Phonetic Spelling	Examples	Phonetic Spelling	Examples
a	**a**t, b**a**d, pl**ai**d, l**au**gh	d	**d**ear, so**d**a, ba**d**
ā	**a**pe, p**ai**n, d**ay**, br**ea**k	f	**f**ive, de**f**end, lea**f**, o**ff**, cou**gh**,
ä	f**a**ther, c**a**lm		ele**ph**ant
âr	c**are**, p**air**, b**ear**, th**eir**, wh**ere**	g	**g**ame, a**g**o, fo**g**, e**gg**
e	**e**nd, p**e**t, s**ai**d, h**ea**ven, fr**ie**nd	h	**h**at, a**h**ead
ē	**e**qual, m**e**, f**ee**t, t**ea**m, pi**e**ce, k**ey**	hw	**wh**ite, **wh**ether, **wh**ich
i	**i**t, b**i**g, g**i**ve, h**y**mn	j	**j**oke, en**j**oy, **g**em, pa**g**e, e**dge**
ī	**i**ce, f**i**ne, l**ie**, m**y**	k	**k**ite, ba**k**ery, see**k**, ta**ck**, **c**at
îr	**ear**, d**eer**, h**ere**, p**ier**ce	l	**l**id, sai**l**or, fee**l**, ba**ll**, a**ll**ow
o	**o**dd, h**o**t, w**a**tch	m	**m**an, fa**m**ily, drea**m**
ō	**o**ld, **oa**t, t**oe**, l**ow**	n	**n**ot, fi**n**al, pa**n**, **kn**ife, **gn**aw
ô	c**o**ffee, **a**ll, t**au**ght, l**aw**, f**ou**ght	ng	lo**ng**, si**ng**er
ôr	**or**der, f**or**k, h**or**se, st**or**y, p**our**	p	**p**ail, re**p**air, soa**p**, ha**pp**y
oi	**oi**l, t**oy**	r	**r**ide, pa**r**ent, wea**r**, mo**r**e, ma**rr**y
ou	**ou**t, n**ow**, b**ough**	s	**s**it, a**s**ide, pet**s**, **c**ent, pa**ss**
u	**u**p, m**u**d, l**o**ve, d**ou**ble	sh	**sh**oe, wa**sh**er, fi**sh**, mi**ss**ion, na**ti**on
ū	**u**se, m**u**le, c**ue**, f**eu**d, f**ew**	t	**t**ag, pre**t**end, fa**t**, dress**ed**
ü	r**u**le, tr**ue**, f**oo**d, fr**ui**t	th	**th**in, pan**th**er, bo**th**
u̇	p**u**t, w**oo**d, sh**ou**ld, l**oo**k	<u>th</u>	**th**ese, mo**th**er, smoo**th**
ûr	b**ur**n, h**urr**y, t**er**m, b**ir**d, w**or**d,	v	**v**ery, fa**v**or, wa**v**e
	c**our**age	w	**w**et, **w**eather, re**w**ard
ə	**a**bout, tak**e**n, penc**i**l, lem**o**n, circ**u**s	y	**y**es, on**i**on
b	**b**at, a**b**ove, jo**b**	z	**z**oo, la**z**y, ja**zz**, ro**s**e, dog**s**, hou**s**es
ch	**ch**in, su**ch**, ma**tch**	zh	vi**s**ion, trea**s**ure, sei**z**ure

Aa

ac·cel·er·ate (ak sel′ə rāt′) *verb.* To cause an object to move faster. *In order to **accelerate** the car, you have to step on the gas pedal.*

ac·com·pa·nies (ə kum′pə nēz) *verb.* Goes along with. *My mother always **accompanies** me to the doctor's office.*

ac·count·a·ble (ə koun′tə bəl) *adjective.* Responsible; liable to be called to account. *The person who threw the baseball is **accountable** for the damage to the window.*

ac·quaint·ance (əkwān′təns) *noun.* A person one knows who is not a close friend. *Since she is only an **acquaintance**, she is not coming to my party.*

ad·dress *noun.* 1. (ə′dres) An official speech. *The President's **address** to the nation was detailed and motivating.* 2. (ad′res) The place where someone or something is located. *What is your **address**?*

ad·vance·ments (ad vans′mənts) *plural noun.* Improvements or progress. *Scientific **advancements** have led to new research on the human mind.*

ad·van·tage (ad van′tij) *noun.* Something that is useful or helpful; benefit. *My height was an **advantage** on the basketball court.*

ad·vise (ad vīz′) *verb.* To give an opinion or advice to. *I asked my teacher to **advise** me about which classes to choose.*

ag·ri·cul·ture (ag′ri kul′chə r) *noun.* The business of producing crops and farm animals; farming. ***Agriculture** is the one of the most popular businesses in the country.*

al·ter (ôl′tər) *verb.* To make different; to change. *I needed to **alter** my weekend plans when my best friend got sick.*

a·mend·ments (ə mend′mənts) *plural noun.* Formal changes made to laws or official documents. *There were many **amendments** made to the Constitution.*

an·ces·tors (an′ses tərz) *plural noun.* People from whom one is descended. *My **ancestors** came over on the Mayflower.*

an·noyed (ə noid′) *adjective.* Bothered; irritated. *The **annoyed** woman left the library when the people around her began to talk.*

ar·chae·ol·o·gy (är′kē ol′ə jē) *noun.* The study of the way humans lived in the past. *If you study **archaeology**, you will learn how ancient people lived.*

as·signed (ə sīnd′) *verb.* Gave out as a task. *Each student was **assigned** a different topic for the project.*

as·tron·o·mer (əstron′əmər) *noun.* An expert who studies the sun, moon, stars, and planets. *The **astronomer** provided us with information about the phases of the Moon.*

at·tain (ə tān′) *verb.* To achieve through work or effort. *I am trying to **attain** high honors on my report card.*

at·ti·tude (at′i tüd′) *noun.* A way of thinking or acting. *You have a wonderful* ***attitude*** *towards school.*

at·tract·ed (ə trak′tid) *verb.* Drew the attention of. *The bee was* ***attracted*** *to the beautiful flowers in the garden.*

Bb

bou·quet (bō kā′) *noun.* A gathering of picked flowers. *The bride carried a* ***bouquet*** *of her favorite flowers.*

boy·cott (boi′kot) 1. *verb.* To join others in refusing to do business with a person or organization. *The politician decided to* ***boycott*** *with the community against the raising of rent.* 2. *noun.* A planned joining with others in refusing to do business with a person or organization. *My father joined the* ***boycott*** *against the giant department store chain.*

brain·storm (brān′stôrm′) *verb.* To attempt to solve a problem through a group discussion. *The manager had to* ***brainstorm*** *all afternoon on ways to attract new customers.*

brit·tle (brit′əl) *adjective.* Very easily broken. *While walking through the woods, a* ***brittle*** *twig snapped underneath my foot.*

Cc

cam·ou·flaged (kam′ə fläzhd) *verb.* Hid by blending in to its surroundings. *The chameleon* ***camouflaged*** *itself to look like the tree trunk.*

cam·paign (kam pān′) *noun.* A series of planned steps carried out towards a particular goal. *The presidential candidate had volunteers help with her* ***campaign****.*

ca·pa·bil·i·ties (kā′pə bil′i tēz) *plural noun.* Qualities or abilities. *The young man had many* ***capabilities*** *as an athlete and honor student.*

cau·tious·ly (kô′shəs lē) *adverb.* Carefully, watchfully. *The young child* ***cautiously*** *crossed the street for the first time alone.*

char·ac·ter·is·tics (kar′ik tə ris′tiks) *plural noun.* Qualities or features that help identify a person or thing. *Being generous is one of Maria's many fine* ***characteristics****.*

cling (kling) *verb.* To stick closely, as if glued. *Small children often* ***cling*** *to their mothers.*

co·in·ci·dence (kō in′si dəns) *noun.* A remarkable, unplanned happening of two events at the same time. *It was such a* ***coincidence*** *to bump into my best friend at the concert.*

at; **ā**pe; f**ä**r; c**â**re; **e**nd; m**ē**; **i**t; **ī**ce; p**î**erce; h**o**t; **ō**ld; s**ô**ng; f**ô**rk; **oi**l; **ou**t; **u**p; **ū**se; r**ü**le; p**ů**ll; t**û**rn; **ch**in; s**ing**; **sh**op; **th**in; **th**is; **hw** in **wh**ite; **zh** in trea**s**ure.

The symbol ə stands for the unstressed vowel sound in **a**bout, tak**e**n, penc**i**l, lem**o**n, and circ**u**s.

col·lapse (kə laps′) *verb.* To fall down; cave in. *Stand back, the building might* ***collapse****!*

com·mit·ment (kə′mit mənt) *noun.* Sense of obligation to someone or something. *When two people get married, they make a* ***commitment*** *to one another.*

com·mo·tion (kə mōsh′ən) *noun.* A noisy confusion. *There was a lot of* ***commotion*** *in the class when the bird flew in the window.*

com·pas·sion·ate (kəm pash′ə nit) *adjective.* Showing feeling or sympathy towards others. *My grandmother was one of the most* ***compassionate*** *people I have ever known.*

com·ple·men·ta·ry (kom plə men′tə rē) *adjective.* Making complete or whole. *The umbrella was* ***complementary*** *to my rain gear.*

com·pro·mise (kom′prə mīz′) *verb.* To reach an understanding by agreeing each side will give up some parts of its demands. *We had to* ***compromise*** *on where to go on vacation this year.*

con·cerns (kən sûrns′) *plural noun.* Serious worries or interests. *The parent shared his* ***concerns*** *about the child's poor behavior.*

con·se·quen·ces (kon′si kwəns ez) *plural noun.* The results of an action or event; outcomes. *If you do not do your homework, you will suffer the* ***consequences****.*

con·sume (kən süm′) *verb.* 1. To use up. *The project will* ***consume*** *a lot of my free time.* 2. To eat or drink up. *Did they* ***consume*** *all the snacks already?*

con·vert·ed (kən vûr′tid) *verb.* Changed in condition or usage. *We* ***converted*** *the garage into an apartment.*

crank·y (krang′kē) *adjective.* Irritable; grouchy. *The* ***cranky*** *baby desperately needed a nap.*

cre·a·tive (krē ā′tiv) *adjective.* Having the power to do something in a new or imaginative way. *The* ***creative*** *artist designed a unique sculpture.*

cres·cent (kres′ənt) *noun.* The shape of the Moon when you can only see the thin, curved part. *A moon shaped like a* ***crescent*** *is used as a design on many countries' flags.*

cri·sis (krī′sis) *noun.* A dangerous or difficult situation for a period of time. *People often depend on a strong leader in times of* ***crisis****.*

crum·bled (krum′bəld) *verb.* Broke into small pieces. *I* ***crumbled*** *pieces of stale bread for the birds.*

cur·ren·cy (kûr′ən sē) *noun.* The money that is used in a specific country. *The* ***currency*** *of the United States is different from that of Mexico.*

Dd

dan·gling (dang′gling) *verb.* Hanging loosely. *The kitten was* ***dangling*** *from the tree limb.*

daz·zling (daz′ling) *adjective.* Extremely bright and splendid. *The model had* ***dazzling*** *white teeth.*

dec·ade (dek′ād) *noun.* A time period of ten years. *She has been working at the bank for over a **decade**.*

de·moc·ra·cy (di mok′rə sē) *noun.* A government that is run by the citizens who live within it. *Since the family wanted to live in a **democracy**, they left their home country.*

de·picts (di pikts′) *verb.* Shows in pictures or words. *The story **depicts** life in eighteenth-century England.*

de·scrip·tive (di skrip′tiv) *adjective.* Providing a picture in words. *Mary's **descriptive** essay about her vacation was so detailed that I felt as if I went with her.*

des·per·ate·ly (des′pər it lē) *adverb.* Recklessly because of having no hope. *She **desperately** held on to the lifeboat.*

de·spised (di spīzd′) *verb.* Looked at with hatred or unpleasantness. *It was clear she **despised** liars.*

de·struc·tion (di struk′shən) *noun.* Serious damage or ruin. *The **destruction** from the earthquake was a devastating sight.*

de·test·ed (di tes′tid) *verb.* Disliked very much; hated. *I **detested** shoveling the heavy snow during the snowstorm.*

di·rect·ing (di rekt′ing) *verb.* Giving orders or instructions. *The principal was always **directing** the students where to go.*

dis·a·greed (dis′ə grēd) *verb.* Differed in opinion. *The lawyers **disagreed** about the verdict of the case.*

dis·card·ed (dis′kärd id) *verb.* Threw aside as worthless; rejected. *While sorting through my winter clothes, I **discarded** some worn shirts.*

dis·solves (di zolvs′) *verb.* Mixes a solid thoroughly with a liquid so that eventually it becomes liquid. *The hot cocoa powder **dissolves** in the hot water.*

di·vid·ed (di vī′did) 1. *verb.* Split into parts or pieces. *The two children **divided** the pizza pie in half.* 2. *adjective.* Separated. *The president brought together a **divided** nation.*

diz·zy (diz′ē) *adjective.* Having the feeling of spinning or being about to fall. *The young girl got **dizzy** after spinning around in a circle.*

doc·u·ment (dok′yə mənt) 1. *verb.* To record something with facts and evidence. *The teacher made sure to **document** the student's progress.* 2. *noun.* A written and official piece of information about something. *A birth certificate is an important **document**.*

drib·bles (drib′əls) 1. *verb.* Flows or trickles, usually from mouth. *The teething baby **dribbles** all over his clothes.* 2. Bounces a ball. *The basketball player **dribbles** the ball down the court.*

at; **ā**pe; f**ä**r; c**â**re; **e**nd; m**ē**; **i**t; **ī**ce; p**î**erce; h**o**t; **ō**ld; s**ô**ng; f**ô**rk; **oi**l; **ou**t; **u**p; **ū**se; r**ü**le; p**u̇**ll; t**û**rn; **ch**in; si**ng**; **sh**op; **th**in; **th**is; **hw** in **wh**ite; **zh** in trea**s**ure.

The symbol **ə** stands for the unstressed vowel sound in **a**bout, tak**e**n, penc**i**l, lem**o**n, and circ**u**s.

droughts (drouts) *plural noun.* Long periods of time with little or no rain. *The crops had a hard time surviving because of the **droughts**.*

Ee

ec·o·nom·ics (ek ə nom′iks) *noun.* The study that deals with how money, goods, and services are produced, distributed, and used among people. *Since my college major is business, I am taking classes on **economics**.*

ec·o·sys·tem (ē′kō sis′təm) *noun.* All nonliving and living things in a particular area. *Plants, water, fish and dolphins are just some of the things in an ocean's **ecosystem**.*

ef·fi·cient (i fish′ənt) *adjective.* Able to get the results wanted with little effort or time. *The **efficient** student finished the assignment before it was due.*

eld·est (el′dist) *adjective.* Born first; oldest. *She is the **eldest** of eight children.*

e·mo·tion (i mō′shən) *noun.* A strong feeling, such as love, hate, sorrow, happiness, or fear. *I could not contain my **emotion** of joy when I won the race.*

en·cir·cle (en sûr′kel) *verb.* To form a circle around; to surround. *The cats tried to **encircle** the mouse.*

en·cour·age·ment (en kûr′ij mənt) *noun.* The act of supporting and giving hope or confidence. *Thanks to the **encouragement** of my teacher, I passed the test.*

en·dur·ance (en dủr′əns) *noun.* The power to put up with hardships or difficulties. *Pioneers showed much **endurance** when they traveled west.*

en·gi·neer·ing (en′jə nîr′ing) *noun.* The work that uses scientific knowledge for practical things. *Skyscrapers are an amazing feat of **engineering**.*

en·ter·prise (en′tər prīz) *noun.* A difficult and important project a person plans to do. *The inventor started an **enterprise** with her new creation.*

en·tre·pre·neur (än′trə prə nủr′) *noun.* One who organizes and runs a business. *A young **entrepreneur** opened a new computer business in our neighborhood.*

e·ra (er′ə) *noun.* A time period throughout history marked by events, people, things, or conditions. *Wolfgang Amadeus Mozart was the most important person in that **era** of classical music.*

e·ven·tu·al·ly (i ven′chü ə lē) *adverb.* Finally; in the end. *I **eventually** finished reading the very long book.*

ev·i·dence (ev′i dəns) *noun.* Proof or sign of something. *The detectives looked for **evidence** at the scene of the crime.*

ex·cep·tion·al (ek sep′shə nəl) *adjective.* Not ordinary; extraordinary. *An acrobat has **exceptional** talent.*

ex·pe·di·tion (ek′spi dish′ən) *noun.* A journey made for a specific reason. *The scientist made an **expedition** to the Arctic to study the wildlife.*

ex·per·i·ment (ek sper′ə mənt) *noun.* A test done to discover something of a scientific nature by watching results very carefully. *As part of the science fair, I did an **experiment** about plant life.*

ex·press (ek spres′) 1. *verb.* To say or put into words. *Please stop crying and **express** your feelings with your words.* 2. adjective. Having to do with fast transportation or delivery. *I was lucky to catch the **express** train that brought me straight to the city.*

ex·tinct (ek stingkt′) *adjective.* No longer in existence. *Dinosaurs were animals that lived long ago but are now **extinct**.*

ex·tra·or·di·nar·y (ek strôr′də ner′ē) *adjective.* Very unusual; remarkable. *The class put on an **extraordinary** performance of* Romeo and Juliet.

Ff

fab·ric (fab′rik) *noun.* A cloth material that is knitted or woven. *My grandmother made a beautiful dress from a shiny **fabric**.*

fa·mil·iar (fə mil′yər) *adjective.* Well-known because of having been seen or heard before. *That woman looks very **familiar**.*

flat·tened (flat′ənd) *verb.* Made or became flat. *The chef **flattened** the dough to make a pizza.*

flour·ished (flûr′ishd) *verb.* Grew strongly; thrived. *The tomato plants **flourished** despite the drought.*

for·feit (fôr′fit) *verb.* To lose or have to give up because of a fault, accident, or mistake. *The football team had to **forfeit** the game when their bus broke down.*

frag·ile (fraj′əl) *adjective.* Easily broken; delicate. *The crystal bowl is very **fragile**, so please handle it with care.*

fran·ti·cal·ly (fran′tik lē) *adverb.* With strong emotion because of worries or fear. *She **frantically** searched for her missing beagle in the park.*

fric·tion (frik′shən) *noun.* A force that slows or stops movement between two surfaces. *The **friction** between my rollerblades and the grass slowed me down.*

frus·tra·ted (frus′trā tid) *adjective.* Disappointed in being prevented from doing something. *I became very **frustrated** when I could not solve the math problem.*

ful·fill (ful fil′) *verb.* To finish or carry out. *The generous woman wanted to **fulfill** the needs of the children in the shelter.*

at; āpe; fär; câre; end; mē; it; īce; pîerce; hot; ōld; sông; fôrk; oil; out; up; ūse; rüle; pu̇ll; tûrn; chin; sing; shop; thin; <u>th</u>is; hw in white; zh in treasure.

The symbol ə stands for the unstressed vowel sound in about, taken, pencil, lemon, and circus.

funds (fundz) *plural noun.* Amounts of money set aside for a specific purpose. *Our parents used their **funds** to take us on summer vacation.*

fuss·y (fus'ē) *adjective.* Picky; hard to please. *The **fussy** baby would not eat his food.*

Gg

gen·er·os·i·ty (jen'ər os'i tē) *noun.* The characteristic of being willing to share or give freely. *The millionaire showed his **generosity** by donating money to the charity.*

gen·u·ine (jen'ū in) *adjective.* Being what it seems to be; real. *The boots were made out of **genuine** leather.*

gin·ger·ly (jin'jər lē) *adverb.* Carefully; in a cautious manner. *I **gingerly** walked across the frozen pond.*

gleam·ing (glēm'ing) *verb.* Shining; reflecting bright light. *Her earrings were **gleaming** in the sunlight.*

global (glō'bəl) *adjective.* Relating to the world; worldwide. *With customers all over the world, Jane's business has truly become **global**.*

gob·ble (gob'əl) *verb.* To eat something quickly in large chunks. *The dog could not wait to **gobble** up his treats!*

gov·er·nor (guv'ər nər) *noun.* The person elected to be the head of a state government in the United States. *The **governor** took office last week.*

gra·cious (grā'shəs) *adjective.* Showing kindness and good manners. *The **gracious** guests thanked their host for the invitation.*

grav·i·ty (grav'i tē) *noun.* The force that pulls things to the center of the earth and causes items to fall when they are dropped. *Due to **gravity**, people and objects remain on the surface of the earth.*

greed (grēd) *noun.* A selfish desire to want more than one has. *His **greed** for money became obvious when he overcharged his customers.*

grit·ty (grit'ē) *adjective.* Containing small bits of small sand or stone. *The cement mix looked very **gritty** in the pail.*

Hh

haste (hāst) *noun.* Hurry; quickness in movement. *We left the house in great **haste** so we would not miss our plane.*

haz·ard (haz'ərd) *noun.* Something that can cause danger or harm. *The icy road was a **hazard** to drivers.*

hes·i·tat·ed (hez'i tā'tid) *verb.* Waited or stopped a moment; paused. *The dog **hesitated** before chasing the rabbit through the yard.*

hi·lar·i·ous (hi lâr'ē əs) *adjective.* Very funny. *The **hilarious** comedian made fun of himself.*

honest (on'ist) *adjective.* Truthful. *Please be **honest** with me.*

hon·or (on′ər) *verb.* To show or regard with great respect. *The monument was built to* ***honor*** *our troops.*

hov·er·ing (huv′ər ing) *verb.* Staying in the air over one place. *The eagle is* ***hovering*** *over its prey.*

hu·mid (hu′mid) *adjective.* Containing a lot of water vapor in the air; moist. *On* ***humid*** *days, I usually go for a swim in my pool.*

hu·mil·i·at·ed (hū mil′ē ā′tid) *adjective.* Made someone feel ashamed. *I felt* ***humiliated*** *when my little sister sang in public.*

Ii

i·den·ti·ty (ī den′ti tē) *noun.* Who or what a person or thing is. *The masked man took off his disguise to reveal his* ***identity****.*

ig·nored (ig nôrd′) *verb.* Refused to pay attention to. *The principal* ***ignored*** *my question during the assembly.*

im·bal·ance (im bal′əns) *noun.* Lack of balance; unsteadiness. *The scale showed the* ***imbalance*** *of the two objects.*

in·cred·i·ble (in kred′ə bəl) *adjective.* Impossible or hard to believe. *It is* ***incredible*** *to look at how technology has changed over the last decade.*

in·di·vid·u·al·i·ty (in′də vij ü al′i tē) *noun.* A characteristic that makes one person or thing different from another. *Even though the girls were identical twins, they still showed their* ***individuality*** *through their clothes.*

in·her·it (in her′it) *verb.* 1. To receive property or money after a person has died. *Since the millionaire passed away, his nephew is to* ***inherit*** *his riches.* 2. To get from one's parent or parents. *I was lucky enough to* ***inherit*** *my mother's blue eyes.*

in·jus·tice (in jus′tis) *noun.* Unfairness; something that is not right. *Many people protested against racial* ***injustice*** *during the Civil Rights Movement.*

in·no·va·tive (in′ə vā′tiv) *adjective.* Introducing a new idea. *The* ***innovative*** *idea led to a new business venture.*

in·quir·y (in kwīr′ē) *noun.* A search for knowledge or information. *A scientific* ***inquiry*** *will often lead one to experiment.*

in·spi·ra·tion (in′spə rā′shən) *noun.* A bright, sudden idea. *I got a stroke of* ***inspiration*** *and wrote a poem.*

in·stalled (in stôld′) *verb.* Put in place for service or use. *The contractor* ***installed*** *the new dishwasher.*

in·tend (in tend′) *verb.* To have in mind as a purpose. *I* ***intend*** *to be on time for class.*

at; **ā**pe; f**ä**r; c**â**re; **e**nd; m**ē**; **i**t; **ī**ce; p**î**erce; h**o**t; **ō**ld; s**ô**ng; f**ô**rk; **oi**l; **ou**t; **u**p; **ū**se; r**ü**le; p**u̇**ll; t**û**rn; **ch**in; si**ng**; **sh**op; **th**in; **th**is; **hw** in **wh**ite; **zh** in trea**s**ure.

The symbol **ə** stands for the unstressed vowel sound in **a**bout, tak**e**n, penc**i**l, lem**o**n, and circ**u**s.

in·ten·si·ty (in ten′si tē) *noun.* The state of being strong and extreme. *The **intensity** of the fire kept the firefighters from entering the building.*

in·vest (in vest′) *verb.* To put money towards something that will make more money. *The businesswoman wanted to **invest** her money in the new product.*

ir·ri·tat·ing (ir′i tā ting) *1. verb.* Annoying; pestering. *The eyelash in my eye is **irritating** me. 2. adjective.* Making painful or sensitive. *The insect was making **irritating** noises throughout the night.*

Jj

jum·ble (jum′bəl) 1. *verb.* To mix or throw into a confusion. *My uncle sometimes will jumble two different stories together.* 2. *noun.* A mess. *The dog made a **jumble** out of his toys.*

Ll

leg·is·la·tion (lej′is lā′shən) *noun.* The laws made or passed. *Congress has the power to pass new **legislation**.*

log·i·cal (loj′i kəl) *adjective* 1. Having to do with sensible way of thinking. *The teacher gave a **logical** explanation as to why to behave during a fire drill.* 2. Being as expected. *It is **logical** that if you drop a fragile glass, it will break.*

Mm

mag·ni·fy (mag′nə fī) *verb.* To make something look larger than it actually is. *To **magnify** the insect, put it under the microscope.*

mar·ket·place (mär′kit plās′) *noun.* A place where food and other goods are bought and sold. *Can you stop at the **marketplace** on the way home for some food?*

ma·ture (mə chůr′) *adjective.* Having characteristics of an adult. *The **mature** girl made a speech to the assembly.*

mer·chan·dise (mûr′chəndīs′) *noun.* Things that are bought and sold; goods. *The clerk had to stock the **merchandise** in the store.*

mi·cro·scope (mī′krə skōp′) *noun.* An instrument that uses lenses to enlarge any image seen through it. *The students used the **microscope** to view plant cells.*

min·gle (ming′gəl) *verb.* 1. To come or mix together. *The scientist wanted the chemicals to **mingle** in the test tube.* 2. To associate with others. *I like to **mingle** with other people at parties.*

mis·chief (mis′chif) *noun.* A behavior that may be playful but can cause harm or trouble. *The babysitter tried to prevent my brother from getting into any **mischief**.*

mist (mist) *noun.* A mass or cloud of tiny drops of water in the air. *The mountain had a heavy **mist** over it this morning.*

mis·treat·ed (mis trē′tid) *verb.* Treated badly or in a cruel way. *The child **mistreated** the dog by pulling on its ears.*

mut·tered (mut′ərd) *verb.* Spoke in a low, unclear way. *During the meeting, the disgruntled worker **muttered** complaints under his breath.*

Nn

now·a·days (nou′ə dāz′) *adverb.* In the present day. ***Nowadays** people send more e-mail than letters.*

Oo

o·be·di·ence (ō bē′dē əns) *noun.* The act of obeying or carrying out orders. *The dog showed **obedience** when he listened to me.*

of·fi·cial (ə fish′əl) *adjective.* Approved by authority. *The principal announced the **official** results of the school election.*

op·po·nent (ə pō′nənt) *noun.* A person who competes with another in a fight, discussion, or contest. *Before the race, I shook the hand of my **opponent** to wish him good luck.*

op·posed (ə pōzd′) *verb.* To have been against; resisted. *Many people **opposed** the curfew being enforced on the town.*

or·gan·i·za·tions (ôr′gə nə zā′shənz) *plural noun.* Groups of people who join together for a specific purpose. *I joined several **organizations** to help the community.*

o·rig·i·nal (ə rij′ə nl) *adjective.* New; done for the first time. *The idea for the math project was **original**.*

out·stretched (out′strecht′) *adjective* Stretched out or extended. *I greeted my grandparents with **outstretched** arms.*

o·ver·whelm·ing (ō′vər wel′ming) *adjective.* Making helpless; overpowering completely. *The amount of work I had to finish in a short period of time seemed **overwhelming**.*

Pp

per·ish (per′ish) *verb.* To be destroyed; die. *If the ship sinks, then many people may **perish**.*

per·ma·nent (pûr′mə nənt) *adjective.* Meant to last without change. *After many interviews, I finally landed a **permanent** job.*

phases (fāz′iz) *plural noun.* 1. Stages of growth. *The tadpole goes through several **phases** as it grows.* 2. Shapes of the moon at a particular time. *It is very interesting to study the different **phases** of the Moon.*

at; āpe; fär; câre; end; mē; it; īce; pîerce; hot; ōld; sông; fôrk; oil; out; up; ūse; rüle; pu̇ll; tûrn; chin; sing; shop; thin; <u>th</u>is; hw in white; zh in treasure.

The symbol ə stands for the unstressed vowel sound in about, taken, pencil, lemon, and circus.

plung·ing (plunj′ing) *verb.* Diving or falling suddenly in a downward direction. *Those penguins are **plunging** into the ocean.*

poi·son·ous (poi′zə nəs) *adjective.* Containing a substance that harms or kills by chemical action. *When the **poisonous** snake escaped the tank, people ran in the other direction.*

pol·i·ti·cian (pol′i tish′ən) *noun.* An individual who holds or runs for a government office position. *The **politician** shared her ideas for improving the park.*

por·traits (pôr′trits) *plural noun.* Pictures of someone. *The Mona Lisa is one of the most famous **portraits** in history.*

pounce (pouns) *verb.* To leap suddenly and take hold of. *The kittens love to **pounce** on each other for fun.*

pred·a·tor (pred′ə tər) *noun.* An animal that hunts other animals in order to live. *Foxes, wolves, hawks, and bears are **predators**.*

prev·a·lent (prev′ə lənt) *adjective.* Commonly used or accepted in an area; widespread. *Money is **prevalent** throughout the world.*

prey (prā) *noun.* An animal that is hunted or killed by other animals for food. *Mice and other small rodents are the **prey** of hawks.*

priv·i·lege (priv′ə lij) *noun.* A special right given to a group or person. *We had the **privilege** of going to shows for free because we worked for the theater.*

pro·ce·dure (prə sē′jər) *noun.* An appropriate way of doing something, usually by a definite series of steps. *Our teacher went over the evacuation **procedure**.*

proc·ess (pros′es) *noun.* A series of actions that are done in making or doing something. *What does the **process** of creating a book involve?*

proc·la·ma·tion (prok′lə mā′shen) *noun.* An official public announcement. *Abraham Lincoln made a very famous **proclamation** in 1863.*

pros·pec·tor (pros′pek tər) *noun.* An individual who explores for gold and other minerals. *A **prospector** will often pan through dirt to find gold.*

pro·test (prə test′) *verb.* Complain or express disapproval against something. *The workers are planning to **protest** the closing of the factory.*

Qq

qual·i·fied (kwol′ə fīd) *adjective.* Having the needed abilities for something; meeting the requirements. *Bobby's advertising expertise made him **qualified** for the job.*

Rr

ref·uge (ref′ūj) *noun.* Shelter or protection from harm and danger. *The scared kitten took **refuge** under the porch.*

reg·is·tered (rej′ə stərd) 1. *verb.* Wrote on a list or recorded officially. *My brother has **registered** to vote.* 2. *adjective.* Officially licensed. *The **registered** nurse assisted the doctor in the surgery.*

re·new·able (ri nü′ə bəl) *adjective.* Able to be made new again. *Trees are an example of a **renewable** resource.*

re·quest·ed (ri kwes′tid) *verb.* Asked for. *I **requested** time off from work so I can visit my relatives.*

res·i·dents (rez′i dənts) *plural noun.* People who live in a particular place. *My family and I are **residents** of South Carolina.*

re·sist·ance (ri zis′təns) *noun.* The ability to overcome or resist something. *As a teacher, you need to build up a **resistance** to germs.*

re·treat·ed (ri trē′tid) *verb.* Moved back or withdrew. *The troops **retreated** the grounds under the president's command.*

rip·pled (rip′əld) *verb.* Formed small waves. *The water **rippled** when our dog waded in the pond.*

roots (rüts) *plural noun.* 1. Origins; where something begins. *Our family's **roots** in this country go back to the eighteenth century.* 2. Parts of a plant that grow into the ground. ***Roots** help the plant get water from the soil.*

ro·tates (rō′tāts) *verb.* Turns around. *Our planet Earth **rotates** on its axis as it travels around the Sun.*

rou·tine (rü tēn′) *noun.* A regular way of doing something. *Going to school is part of my weekly **routine**.*

Ss

scat·tered (skat′ərd) *verb.* Threw and spread about in different places. *The toddler **scattered** his toy cars around the house.*

scoffed (skôfd) *verb.* Made fun of; mocked; teased. *He immediately **scoffed** at my idea for the project.*

scorn·ful·ly (skôrn′fəl lē) *adverb.* In a way that shows hatred for someone or something thought of as worthless. *The man looked **scornfully** at the cat eating out of his garbage can.*

scout·ed (skou′tid) *verb.* Searched for in order to bring back information. *We **scouted** the town library for books on animal adaptations.*

scroung·ing (skroun′jing) *verb.* Getting, collecting, gathering, or foraging with great effort or difficulty. *The stray dog was **scrounging** for some food.*

at; **ā**pe; f**ä**r; c**â**re; **e**nd; m**ē**; **i**t; **ī**ce; p**î**erce; h**o**t; **ō**ld; s**ô**ng; f**ô**rk; **oi**l; **ou**t; **u**p; **ū**se; r**ü**le; p**u̇**ll; t**û**rn; **ch**in; si**ng**; **sh**op; **th**in; **th**is; **hw** in **wh**ite; **zh** in trea**s**ure.

The symbol **ə** stands for the unstressed vowel sound in **a**bout, tak**e**n, penc**i**l, lem**o**n, and circ**u**s.

se·lec·tive (si lek′tiv) *adjective.* Able to pick out carefully. *I was very **selective** in buying only healthful food.*

self-esteem (self i stēm′) *noun.* Having confidence and respect in oneself. *I had really high **self-esteem** when I won the spelling bee.*

self·ish (sel′fish) *adjective.* Thinking only of oneself; not thinking of others. *My **selfish** brother ignored me when I told him I needed to use the computer.*

se·ries (sîr′ēz) *noun.* A number of related things coming one after another. *I want to purchase the book **series** from the store.*

set·tle·ment (set′əl mənt) *noun.* A colony or new region where people start living. *The people started building homes in their new **settlement**.*

se·vere (sə vîr′) *adjective.* Dangerous or serious. *The **severe** fire caused much damage to the forest.*

shat·tered (shat′ərd) *verb.* 1. Broke into pieces. *The glass **shattered** after being dropped.* 2. Destroyed or damaged. *My dreams were **shattered** when I lost my job.*

shriv·el (shriv′əl) *verb.* To wrinkle and shrink. *If you leave the grape in the sun, it will slowly **shrivel** into a raisin.*

sliv·er (sliv′ər) *noun.* A slender, thin piece. *Please cut me a **sliver** of cake.*

soared (sôrd) *verb.* Flew high in the air. *The eagle **soared** high into the sky.*

spar·kles (spär′kəlz) *verb.* Shines and gives off light; glitters. *Her necklace **sparkles** in the light.*

spe·cial·ty (spesh′əl tē) *noun.* A particular thing that a person knows a lot about. *My aunt's **specialty** is baking cakes.*

spe·cif·ic (spi sif′ik) *adjective.* Exact; precise. *Our teacher left **specific** instructions on how to do the assignment.*

squirmed (skwûrmd) *verb.* Twisted and turned one's body. *The toddler **squirmed** in his mother's arms.*

stale (stāl) *adjective.* Not fresh. *The cookies were left out and became **stale**.*

sub·stan·tial (səb stan′shəl) *adjective.* Large or considerable in amount. *My aunt made a **substantial** amount of food for the party.*

Tt

tech·nol·o·gy (tek nol′əj ē) *noun.* The use of scientific knowledge for practical purposes. *We are able to accomplish so much these days through the use of **technology**.*

tel·e·scope (tel′ə skōp′) *noun.* A tool that makes distant objects seem closer. *The kids took turns looking at the stars through the **telescope**.*

ten·sion (ten′shən) *noun.* A feeling of pressure caused by too much emotional strain or worry. *Since work was so busy, it started causing **tension** among my coworkers.*

ter·ri·to·ries (ter′i tôr′ēz) *plural noun.* Large areas or regions of land. *The **territories** were populated with people from different countries.*

thrill·ing (thril′ing) *adjective.* Causing a sudden feeling of excitement. *The roller coaster ride was a **thrilling** experience.*

tin·ker·ing (ting′kəring) *verb.* Attempting to fix something in an aimless way. *The mechanic was **tinkering** with his car in the garage.*

tol·er·ate (tol′ə rāt) *verb.* To put up with; stand. *The teacher does not **tolerate** students who are disrespectful.*

top·ple (top′əl) *verb.* To fall or make fall forward. *The waiter tried carefully not to have the dishes **topple** over.*

trans·ac·tion (tran zak′shən) *noun.* A business deal that includes buying and selling of something. *The clerk wrote down our **transaction** on the receipt.*

treach·er·ous (trech′ər əs) *adjective.* Hazardous or dangerous. *We carefully crossed the **treacherous** bridge over the valley.*

tre·men·dous (tri men′dəs) *adjective.* Very large or enormous. *The mansion was **tremendous**.*

tri·umph (trī′umf) *noun.* A great victory or success. *Climbing that mountain was an absolute **triumph** for the hiker.*

trudged (trujd) *verb.* Walked slowly with heavy steps. *The tired construction workers **trudged** up the building steps.*

trust·wor·thy (trust′wûr′thē) *adjective.* Able to be trusted; reliable. *My cousin is **trustworthy** so I told him my secrets.*

typ·i·cal (tip′i kəl) *adjective.* Showing usual characteristics or qualities. *Pizza is a **typical** food item on our school lunch menu.*

Uu

un·com·fort·a·bly (un kum′fər tə blē) *adverb.* Uneasily; not comfortably. *The witness spoke **uncomfortably** about the robbery.*

un·cov·er (un kuv′ər) *verb.* To discover; make known. *There was much to **uncover** about the colony at the historic site.*

un·der·tak·ing (un′dər tāk′ing) *noun.* Something undertaken as a task. *Opening a new restaurant is a huge **undertaking**.*

un·pre·dict·a·ble (un′pri dik′tə bəl) *adjective.* Not behaving in a way that is expected. *The weather is sometimes **unpredictable**.*

at; āpe; fär; câre; end; mē; it; īce; pîerce; hot; ōld; sông; fôrk; oil; out; up; ūse; rüle; pu̇ll; tûrn; chin; sing; shop; thin; th͟is; hw in white; zh in treasure.

The symbol ə stands for the unstressed vowel sound in about, taken, pencil, lemon, and circus.

Vv

ver·sion (vûr′zhən) *noun.* A description given from a specific point of view. *The siblings had their own **version** of the story.*

vi·bra·tions (vībrā′shəns) *plural noun.* Rapid, continuous movements back and forth and up and down. *Many towns felt the **vibrations** from the earthquake from far away.*

Ww

wea·ry (wîr′ē) *adjective.* Really tired. *The **weary** puppy laid down on the floor.*

whirl (wûrl) *verb.* To spin or turn rapidly in a circle. *Little girls love to **whirl** around in a circle with their dresses.*

with·ered (wi*th*′ərd) *verb.* Shriveled or dried up. *The flowers **withered** because I forgot to water them.*